CANCELLED

DAWN FRENCH

The Biography

Also by Alison Bowyer

Noel Edmonds: The Unauthorised Biography
Delia Smith: The Biography

DAWN FRENCH

The Biography

ALISON BOWYER

HEADLINE

The right of Alison Bowyer to be identified as the Author of
this Work has been asserted by her in accordance with the
Copyright, Designs and Patents Act 1988.

First published in 2000
by HEADLINE BOOK PUBLISHING

10 9 8 7 6 5 4 3 2 1

British Library Cataloguing in Publication Data

Bowyer, Alison
    Dawn French : the biography
    1.French, Dawn
    2.Television actors and actresses - Great Britain -
    Biography
    3.Comedians - Great Britain - Biography
    4.Women comedians - Great Britain - Biography
    I.Title
    791.4'5'092

    ISBN 0 7472 7265 4

Typeset by
Letterpart Limited, Reigate, Surrey

Printed and bound in Great Britain by
Mackays of Chatham PLC, Chatham, Kent

HEADLINE BOOK PUBLISHING
A division of Hodder Headline
338 Euston Road
London NW1 3BH

www.headline.co.uk
www.hodderheadline.com

✳ CONTENTS ✳

✳ ACKNOWLEDGEMENTS ✳

When I began researching this book in the summer of 1999, it was my intention that it should be a candid and balanced account of Dawn French's life and career, unhampered by the constraints of 'authorisation' by the star herself. *Dawn French: The Biography* is therefore an unauthorised account of her life, and includes numerous interviews with people who have known and worked with her over the years.

I would like to thank my husband Paul Scott for his counsel and resourcefulness; my agent Judith Chilcote; Andy for sending me his old French and Saunders book; fellow journalist and former *Sun* colleague Karen Hockney; Tim Ewbank and Stafford Hildred; the Comedy Store's Don Ward; comedian Malcolm Hardee; Peter Rosengard, who kindly gave me permission to quote from *Didn't You Kill My Mother-in-Law?*, his book about the history of alternative comedy, co-written with Roger Wilmut; Arnold Brown; Marie-Louise Cook; Andy Harries; Charles Lawrence and his daughter Susan; Christine Abbott; Dr David Lewis; Sue Rollinson; and Christopher Malcolm.

Finally, a big thank you to Chester – my constant companion and muse.

CHAPTER ONE

Queen of Comedy

Shortly before the new millennium, a poll voted Dawn French the twentieth century's funniest British woman, confirming her status as Queen of Comedy.

Being chosen as one of the most influential comedians of the century cemented her position at the top of Britain's show-business elite, and was significant for Dawn on several counts. First, she was the only woman to appear in the top ten, no mean feat in such a male-dominated profession, and she was in fine company, appearing alongside recognised all-time greats such as Charlie Chaplin, Tommy Cooper and John Cleese.

Second, she came only three places behind her own comic hero Eric Morecambe, who polled 26 per cent of the vote to win the title of the twentieth century's funniest Briton. To be so closely linked to the one person who had inspired her above everyone else was a fantastic achievement for Dawn. But third, and perhaps most significantly, the poll, commissioned by a top Internet bank, chose Dawn French as an individual, not Dawn French as one half of French and Saunders.

Dawn's fans would say that this was only fair; she is, after all, a star in her own right, arguably more famous as a solo artist than she ever was as one half of a double act. Strong roles such as Geraldine Granger, the chocolate-loving reverend in television's popular *Vicar of Dibley*, and the myriad characters she creates in her series *Murder Most Horrid* have won her a whole new army of fans. She is the acknowledged doyenne of British comedy. Her unique blend of talent and charisma appeals to people from all backgrounds, and to both men and women equally. She frequently tops magazine reader polls on subjects as diverse as who they would most like to live next door to, to naming the sexiest women in the world.

Her appeal lies in the fact that, while her wit has bite, it is never savage. She has an eye for the ridiculous and the silly that strikes a chord with people of all ages. She is fêted as the undisputed queen of the 'alternative set' but although she made her name as an alternative comedian, in reality she owes more to the variety tradition set by Morecambe and Wise. Critics have even dubbed her and Jennifer Saunders 'Morecambe and Wise on oestrogen'.

She has undoubtedly been influenced by people like Joyce Grenfell and Victoria Wood, but in many ways her comic roots go back further still, to the early twentieth century and the slapstick of Charlie Chaplin and Laurel and Hardy. Clowning antics such as when she cavorted as a roly-poly ballerina with the Royal Ballet's Darcey Bussell, for example, are pure farce and are only funny because of Dawn's size. There is nothing new or alternative about people laughing at fatties. Fat is a staple diet of comedy: we have all laughed at Oliver Hardy, Les Dawson, Bernard Manning, Jo Brand and Roseanne Barr. Dawn claims to be annoyed at the erroneous equation 'fat equals jolly', but at the same time relies heavily on her size to get laughs. Who, after all, could forget her portrayal of Hollywood sex siren Jane Russell, or the infamous *French and Saunders Baywatch* sketch?

In a world seemingly populated by slim blonde actresses and television newsreaders, Dawn has shown that you don't have to be skinny to be successful. She has, in effect, become a professional large woman, launching her own range of outsize clothing and becoming an outspoken advocate of 'fat lib'. But although she is Britain's most famous ambassador for the concept of big is beautiful, there is no denying that she has capitalised on people's natural inclination to snigger at the circumferentially challenged.

'There's nothing particularly jolly in being fat,' she insists. 'Look, I'm not the fat one that gets the custard pie in the face, I'm the one that ducks 'em. Dawn on top – that's me.' But she has always appeared happy to send up her appearance, whether it's by donning a red leotard and long blonde wig to be Pamela Anderson, or hamming it up as a less than svelte dancer. In fact, some might say that her weight has been a major determining factor in her career. Comedians are often created rather than born, developing the ability to make people laugh in order to deflect mockery or criticism. They make themselves the butt of jokes before anyone else can, and a lot of Dawn's jokes are at her own expense. The *Sunday Mirror* summed it up: 'She can stand alone on your television screen, attempt to hold her stomach in and by the slightest gesture make ten million people laugh,' it said. 'Dawn French is to fat girls what *Blackadder*'s Baldrick is to dimwits!'

In many ways Dawn couldn't lose weight even if she wanted to. Like celebrity chef Gary Rhodes's spiky hair, it is her trademark. In the words of Nana in television's *Royle Family*, to many people she *is* 'that big funny girl who dresses up as a vicar'.

Her comedy has won her numerous plaudits and awards but Dawn can also play it straight, winning critical acclaim for a series of drama roles, both on television and on the West End stage. She is highly prized by the BBC, and Alan Yentob, when he was controller of BBC1, described her as a 'particularly rare breed of entertainment'. Faced with big-name desertions like Des Lynam, Barry Norman, Clive James and Frank Skinner to commercial television, the BBC is determined not to lose any more of its main stars, and

Dawn is handsomely rewarded for her talent.

A six-year 'golden handcuffs' deal, signed in the autumn of 1999, will keep her at the BBC until at least 2005. She firmly believes that it is still the best place for her, as the BBC has for some time given her far more flexibility than other stars enjoy. Although she has been offered a lot of money by other channels, she fears that switching sides will cramp her creativity and style.

Her decision to stay was rewarded when she was chosen to spearhead the all-important 1999 Christmas schedule. Faced with a crucial ratings battle with ITV, the BBC wanted to ensure the best possible chance of winning on the day. The theme of the festive season, they agreed, would be decidedly French in flavour.

The BBC appeared to be pinning all its hopes on Dawn. Viewers tuning in over the holiday were served a five-course treat of Dawn French. She made one of her occasional forays into straight acting with a role in the BBC's lavish production of *David Copperfield*, playing David's drunken landlady, Mrs Crupp. She teamed up with Jennifer for a fifty-minute *French and Saunders* Christmas special. But the icing on the Christmas cake was three episodes of her most popular show, *The Vicar of Dibley*.

The sitcom, one of the Beeb's flagship shows, was trumpeted as *the* highlight of the BBC's Christmas. It was a huge responsibility for Dawn to shoulder. Well aware of the high-calibre precedent set by previous Christmas Day BBC success stories such as *Only Fools and Horses*, she knew she would look like a prize turkey if no one tuned in.

The programmes were shown on Christmas Eve, Christmas Day and the Boxing Day Holiday Monday. More than twelve million people watched the Christmas Day show, making it the most-watched programme after *Coronation Street*. It may have been down on the twenty million viewers who tuned in to the last ever *Only Fools and Horses*, as one critic pointed out, but at a time when the BBC is increasingly competing with digital, cable and satellite stations, to pull in twelve million viewers was a huge achievement.

The trust that the BBC invested in her on its most important day of the year was a personal triumph for Dawn. It is still men who are deemed to 'sell' programmes, and accordingly it is generally men who are chosen to carry the majority of prime-time TV shows. Most of the biggest names in British television today – those who are considered guaranteed audience-pullers – are men. Bankable stars like David Jason, John Thaw and Robson Green are inundated with offers from TV companies who know their very name alone guarantees a ratings winner.

Dawn is one of only a select few actresses credited with having the same pulling power. The fact that she is judged capable of carrying a show as a woman is a great feather in her cap. But making it as a woman in a predominantly male domain has taken guts and courage, and it is perhaps inevitable that she has come to be known within the industry as a somewhat formidable character. 'There's no doubt about it, I am a very confident person,' she admits. 'Having control over everything really excites me. I'm not as tolerant as I used to be. I don't like it if mistakes that go on screen stem from other people's wrong decisions or dubious judgements.'

In her current position as one of the most sought-after television actresses of her age, she enjoys all the trappings of success. Two decades in show-business have made her a rich woman, and she has an outwardly enviable lifestyle. She and husband Lenny Henry are reported to be worth in excess of £4 million, thanks to a string of TV successes and lucrative advertising contracts. Home is a beautiful £1 million Queen Anne farmhouse surrounded by open fields in an affluent Berkshire village, and they drive his and hers matching Jaguar sports cars.

It is a far cry from her early days in showbiz, when she earned seven pounds a night doing stand-up at the legendary Comedy Store in Soho. A complete novice who spent her days teaching schoolgirls in the genteel surroundings of Highgate, north London,

Dawn lived an extraordinary double life. When school had ended for the day and she had finished marking the girls' homework, she would head into the heart of London's seedy red-light district and take her chances with the Comedy Store's notoriously boisterous late-night audience.

Managing to remain on stage for anything more than a couple of minutes without being booed off was a continual challenge, and one that she didn't always meet, frequently getting 'gonged off' by the Comedy Store's crazy compère Alexei Sayle. Sometimes she would appear on stage to find that she was performing in front of only five people. But despite the humiliations and the distinct lack of frills, the Comedy Store proved an invaluable training ground for the young comedienne. It was a baptism of fire, but it gave her much-needed experience in the tough world of stand-up. She also worked at The Comic Strip, a club situated in a building occupied by the Raymond Revue Bar, where she struggled to hone her rudimentary act while the dirty-mac brigade leered at semi-naked women in the bar next door.

Her time at the clubs made her realise that stand-up was not for her. Dawn's trick of making people laugh comes not so much from the one-liners, but because she has an eye for the mannerisms and nuances that are part of everyday life. 'One thing I can't do is say funny lines,' she confesses. 'But I'm probably quite funny in that I can latch on to the amusing side of people's natures quite easily.'

She will for ever be associated with the right-on, trendy, alternative comedy that sprang up in the early eighties, but while it has a large following, not everyone is a fan. To some it just isn't funny. Alternative comedy has been described as comedy without laughs, or – as Dame Edna Everage put it – 'being funny every other day'. Others have been disappointed by the safe path that Dawn and her contemporaries now appear to have chosen. Part of the criticism levelled at them is that they have somehow 'sold out' by becoming mainstream. This is a pertinent point, as the majority of the so-called alternative set now earn their living exclusively from the decidedly staid world of the BBC sitcom. It is an accusation that annoys Dawn. 'I've never been interested in this alternative comedy thing,' she insists. 'We never invented the phrase. We were given it and then told we weren't it. So I don't know how you win, really. When it comes down to it you're either funny or you're not.'

And Dawn *is* funny. She is no stranger to controversy, and at times during her twenty-year career her irreverence and schoolgirl sense of humour have landed her in hot water. But somehow she always manages to get away with it because people can't help but laugh. When radio disc jockey Steve Wright refused to believe her claim that her bosoms were the same size as his head, she pulled off her bra and had him try it on – on air. She caused a row when she made lewd remarks about the Queen during a French and Saunders Christmas special, and she got into trouble for apparently calling newsreader Michael Buerk 'a fucking ninny' during the BBC's Comic Relief marathon. She caused more furore by launching a tirade about willies on breakfast television, and *The Vicar of Dibley* has been the subject of several complaints to TV watchdogs.

Never backward in coming forward, Dawn has also posed nude for the men's magazine *Esquire*, and was offered £30,000 to be a *Penthouse* 'Pet of the Month'.

Success has brought her fame and fortune, but life hasn't always been easy for Dawn French. The bad times, when she has had them, have been of a magnitude that would have probably destroyed some people. She has known pain on a scale that only a few are unfortunate enough to experience, and has struggled to overcome a string of devastating blows in her private life. She projects an aura of confidence and achievement, yet just eight years ago she considered giving it all up to return to her first job as a drama teacher as her self-esteem hit an all-time low. Even the one thing she thought was rock-solid – her marriage to Lenny Henry – was recently tested when lurid allegations about her husband made front-page news.

But throughout the highs and lows of her life, many of which she has kept secret from her fans, Dawn has managed somehow to hold everything together. Behind the jolly smile and clown-like image is a strong, determined woman who has survived life's knocks.

Her Christmas success ensured that she entered the new millennium at the pinnacle of her career and the zenith of her popularity. Today she is in the rare position of being a star in her own right, with the ratings to match, while still remaining committed to the double-act formula that made her name.

CHAPTER TWO

New Dawn

Dawn Roma French made her debut in the world on 11 October 1957 in Holyhead, Anglesey. It was the home town of comedian Sir Harry Secombe, and she always jokes that she was given his legs.

Her parents, Denys and Felicity French, were both Devonians born and bred, but Denys's job in the Royal Air Force had temporarily taken the family to Wales. Dawn, the couple's second child, was born in the Gors Maternity Hospital. Leaving hospital with her mother a few days later, she was taken home to the family's services accommodation house at nearby RAF Valley, the main jet training school for the air force.

The village where the camp was situated was originally called Llanfihangel yn Nhowyn, which means The Church of St Michael Among the Dunes, but from 1941 onwards it was completely swallowed up by the RAF development. By the time Dawn and her family were living there, the old village had effectively ceased to exist and had become part of Caergeiliog, the next-door village situated on the main trunk road to Holyhead.

Her first home was at number 84 Mintfordd Road, a modest

semi-detached house in the middle of the camp. It was a typical services camp, with blocks of uniform red-brick houses placed either side of the road, similar in style and layout to a council estate. The only clue to what the area might have been like before the RAF moved in was provided by the small centuries-old parish church situated close to the French family's house.

Denys and Felicity – who is known by her middle name, Roma – had been childhood sweethearts, meeting in their home town of Plymouth in the early fifties. Denys was born in the Devonport district of the city in August 1932, the eldest son of milkman Leslie French and his wife Marjorie. Roma was born in January 1935, to John O'Brien, an able seaman in the Royal Navy, and his wife Lilian.

The couple married young, when Denys had just turned twenty-one and Roma was eighteen, at the parish church of St Budeaux, Plymouth on 8 August 1953. Denys was a corporal in the RAF at the time, and Roma was a shop assistant. Their first child, Gary, was born in February 1955, and two and a half years later the family was completed when Dawn arrived.

The house at Mintfordd Road was to be the first of many homes for the young Dawn. As a corporal technician, and later a sergeant in the air force, Denys's job would take the family far and wide. The family never settled in one place for long. On average they moved every eighteen months, each time to a house that looked exactly like the last, containing virtually the same furniture, wallpaper, curtains and carpets. To begin with, Dawn and Gary accompanied their parents from place to place, but later on their parents would reluctantly make the decision to pack them off to boarding school, to give them some much-needed stability in their lives.

When Dawn was seven, her father was posted to Cyprus and the family went with him. They stayed for three years but managed to come home every bit as British as when they'd left. It was perhaps not so surprising, for in many ways it was just like being in Britain. As part of a large contingent of British services families who were living on the island, most of their contact was with other Brits. Dawn and her brother attended an English-speaking school and much of their lives revolved around the RAF camp and the other services staff. The only difference was the sunshine.

Even the food they ate was the same as they'd always eaten at home. Unwilling, as the majority of British people were in the early sixties, to try foreign food, the family stuck rigidly to the type of fare they knew they liked. Dawn's parents never cooked or ate anything foreign. Even though they did two tours of Cyprus, it was sausage and mash, not moussaka, that the family sat down to at teatime. Roma French specialised in traditional English fare, proudly feeding up her son and daughter on staples like egg and chips and meat and two veg. Such was their determination to stick to home cooking, they even arranged for food parcels to be specially shipped over from Plymouth, including supplies of their favourite Dewdneys pasties, which were made with swede.

And the portions Roma served up were huge. Right from when she was a little girl, Dawn was actively encouraged to eat heartily and was praised for clearing her plate of food. 'I was lucky, my family are all Devonshire dumplings like me,' she recalls warmly. 'In my family there was no suggestion that I should eat less. I suppose we did eat a lot. My mother used to give us stew in huge serving basins, because ordinary plates weren't big enough.'

Given the family's fondness for food and a genetic tendency to be small and plump, it was probably inevitable that Dawn would not be a slim youngster. 'I was a very chubby child,' she admits. 'But my mother managed to find clothes for me and luckily my auntie May was a seamstress and she made my dressing-up clothes.' At that point in her young life, the fact that she was larger than the other children on the camp did not bother her unduly. Although later on as a teenager she would suffer great angst as her weight made her stand out from the other girls, as a ten-year-old Dawn was far more concerned about her name.

'I loathe being called Dawn,' she once told *Woman's Own*. 'I just don't feel like a Dawn. I'd much rather be called Gorgeous French or maybe Sexy French. When my father was stationed in Cyprus, our Greek landlady used to call me Dawnie-mu. Evidently the "mu" bit is a Greek endearment. When we returned to England the name stuck, and eventually got shortened to "mu". Even on my school register I was down as Mu French. Unfortunately, Alf Garnett was calling his wife a silly moo at the time, so everybody assumed it was because I was a complete cow.'

After the spell in Cyprus the family returned to England, and Denys took up a posting in Bury St Edmunds, Suffolk. Not long afterwards, when talk of yet another move was being mooted, Dawn's parents realised that they couldn't keep uprooting the children. Every time they became settled in a new school and began to make friends and gain headway in their studies, Denys's job would take them to an entirely different part of the country and they would have to start all over again. While they had been very young it had not proved too much of a problem, and Denys and Roma calculated that the experience the youngsters gained from living in different countries probably outweighed the negative aspects. But as they approached their secondary education and the crucial O-level years, they reluctantly accepted that they needed some consistency in their lives.

Boarding school was the obvious answer. It is the way many services families choose to educate their children, but for a small, close-knit family like Dawn's it was a tough decision for her parents to make. None of them relished the idea of being separated for long periods of time, but in the end a compromise was reached. It was decided that Dawn and her brother would be sent to boarding school, but to lessen the blow they would go to schools in Plymouth where they had relatives, and they would only be weekly boarders. Weekends would be spent with Granny and Grandpa, Denys's parents Leslie and Marjorie, at their newsagent's shop in the town.

It was duly arranged. Gary was sent to the prestigious Plymouth College for boys, and in September 1970 Dawn started at St Dunstan's Abbey. Both were private schools to which only the most affluent families in the area could afford to send their children. But because Gary and Dawn were services children, the RAF paid their school fees. When Dawn arrived at the all-girls school, one month away from her thirteenth birthday, she didn't feel as nervous as other new girls might have felt. As a seasoned RAF daughter, well used to travelling around and making fresh starts, enrolling at yet another strange school held no fear for Dawn. She knew all about being the new girl and the problems of making friends, and was aware that it wouldn't last for long. But what she hadn't bargained for was the terrible sadness she felt at being separated from her parents.

That first night she wept into her pillow as she contemplated the prospect of getting through the coming months without seeing her mum and dad. It was an unhappiness that didn't fade. Lying in her dormitory at night with fifteen other girls tucked up in their beds around her, she would think about her parents and would frequently cry herself to sleep. Her sobs became a familiar sound to the other girls in the dormitory, and her misery is well remembered by fellow pupil Susan Lawrence. Like Dawn, Susan was also a services child, only her father was in the Royal Navy. She was a year older than Dawn but shared a dormitory with her. 'I remember her being very homesick when she first started at St Dunstan's,' Susan recalls. 'She missed her family, and although she was just a weekly boarder, her parents were often abroad so she didn't see them for months on end.'

Homesickness is not uncommon among boarding-school pupils, but it doesn't generally last much beyond the first week of a new term. As children get into the swing of being back at school, memories of their life at home get pushed to one side and school life takes over. Dawn's unhappiness, however, seemed to go on and on. 'It took her quite a long time to come to terms with her homesickness,' says Susan. 'In fact she got on our nerves a bit, crying at night even when the youngsters had got over it. There was some sympathy to start with, but the kids soon got fed up of her because it went on for so long. From my own point of view you tended to look down on the younger ones and say, "Pull yourself together".'

Dawn would often wake up in the morning puffy-eyed from crying herself to sleep. It was an anguish which her mother and father shared. 'My mother couldn't even take us to school on the first day of term because she would be weeping,' says Dawn. 'So my father had to take us, and he would put on a very strict face and try hard not to cry himself. It was heartbreaking for my parents, but they were travelling all over the place and they would never have been able to afford the kind of education we had if the RAF hadn't helped with our fees. I understood that. Especially as there were other kids at our school who *were* there because their parents didn't want to deal with them.'

Her natural sense of loss at being separated from the people she loved most was compounded by the fact that, for the first time in her life, she was having trouble settling in at her new school. Other schools she'd attended had been either ordinary state schools or, when she was abroad, RAF schools full of other rolling stones like herself. She had never had any difficulty adapting to change, but this time it was different. St Dunstan's Abbey was a private school, and the majority of the girls who attended it were from well-off West Country families. Within minutes of entering the wooden gates of St Dunstan's on the first day of the autumn term, Dawn felt as much like a fish out of water as it is possible to feel.

Watching the other young girls spill out of their parents' Range Rovers and Jaguars, and clocking their expensively dressed mothers and fathers, Dawn felt awkward for the first time in her life. Hearing the girls' cut-glass accents as they excitedly greeted their friends after the holidays, she was struck by how posh they all seemed. In time, Dawn would grow to love the school, but she never stopped hating the fact that almost everybody except her was middle-class and rich.

'It was friendly and caring, but it was also posh, and I was aware that I didn't belong with all those rich kids, that I didn't live the way they did,' she admits. 'I was only there because the RAF paid the fees. I'm pretty gregarious and really enjoyed being in a huge dormitory and having loads of chatting and midnight feasts, but I came from quite a poor family and I wasn't from the same class of people as most of the girls. I felt completely separate, and it was obvious because I didn't have a fabulous home and a mother who dressed in Jaeger outfits.'

This feeling of being less privileged than the other girls had quite an effect on the teenage Dawn. So acutely did she feel the contrast between the kind of lifestyle her school chums enjoyed and her own more humble home life, that she became for a while quite embittered. It brought out a less than pleasant side to her character, and her feelings of inferiority manifested themselves in resentment towards her parents for not being rich. It was a stage in her life that she would later have cause to regret bitterly.

'I went through a terrible period of blaming my parents for not having money or chintz or beige things, like the others did,' she admits. 'I did begrudge the fact that my parents obviously didn't have the money the other girls' parents did. When I went to their homes I was amazed – I'd never seen beige furniture or cream carpets before. The girls used to go to places like Gstaad for holidays, and when I stayed for the weekend, they used to have salad. *Salad.* I mean, where was the meat and two veg? And I was terribly impressed if they had sinks in their bedrooms. I thought that was the height of luxury.'

Like Dawn, fellow pupil Janet Bryant was crushingly aware of the differences between her and the other girls. 'The majority of the girls came from well-off backgrounds, myself and Dawn perhaps not necessarily,' she says. 'There were a lot of services people who were on bursaries. You had to grit your teeth and get on with it. You had to accept the fact that there were those who were more fortunate than yourself.'

Dawn, it seems, had trouble trying to accept this harsh fact of life. When she first joined St Dunstan's, she strove to emulate the middle-class girls that she so wanted to be like. She was desperate to become one of them, even if it meant alienating her family in the process. She had been raised to have sound, working-class values and to know where she came from. According to all who knew him, Denys French was an exceptionally kind and good-natured man, and somebody who had a strong sense of right and wrong. Dawn's mother Roma is known to be a remarkably strong woman, who nowadays runs a drug rehabilitation centre for women with children. Both Denys's and Roma's backgrounds were solidly working-class, and the family traditionally voted Labour. But once she had spent a few weekends with her better-off school friends in their big houses or farms, and glimpsed how the other half lived, Dawn didn't hesitate to turn her back on the socialist values her parents had taught her.

She couldn't see anything attractive about being working-class if it meant that she was denied the luxuries that her contemporaries had. She became completely enthralled by the glamorous lifestyles she imagined her school chums enjoyed, and these feelings of envy and yearning would stay with her for years to come. Later, when television success brought Dawn her own share of riches, she remembered how she'd marvelled at the thought of bedrooms with washbasins, and promptly installed one in her own room.

Looking back at her behaviour now, Dawn believes that she was like a lot of services children who find it hard to see where they fit into the grand scheme of things. She told the *Observer* in 1991 that a number of RAF children, ashamed of their own roots but unsure of how to acquire any others, became 'extremely screwed-up'. This, for a while at least, threatened to happen to her. She became so full of airs and graces as she tried to copy the middle-class girls at school that the old Dawn was in danger of disappearing. Many of her school friends had their own horses, and attended gymkhanas and pony clubs. Dawn persuaded her parents to buy her a pony so she could be like them. She stabled the animal, which she called Shula, near her grandparents' shop, and eagerly looked forward to joining the horsy set.

The change in Dawn did not go unnoticed by her family, who were not altogether happy about what they saw and heard. Whether consciously or unconsciously, Dawn had learned to behave a certain way at school in order to fit in with the other girls. She began to talk in an affected manner, and adopted pretentious mannerisms. Perhaps without even realising it, she had taken on the attitudes and conservative values of her school fellows. She didn't have the guile to be able to hide her new hoity-toity attitude, and when she went to visit her grandparents at weekends, they could see the unwelcome change in her.

They didn't like the influence that being with such well-off girls appeared to be having on her. To put it bluntly, they thought their granddaughter was in danger of becoming a snob and, in the absence of her parents, her grandparents took charge of the situation. Whatever they said to her was radical enough to bring her to her senses. 'My family has always been Labour, but at school I was among all the little Cons,' she explains. 'My grandparents took me in hand because I think they felt I was turning into an insufferable little snob. I'm glad they did.' She's now a Labour voter 'and proud of it'.

Dawn was not the only girl from a humble background at St Dunstan's. 'It was one of the few private schools in Plymouth, and most of the girls did come from moneyed backgrounds,' says ex-pupil Sarah Rawle. 'But having said that, there were a lot of parents like mine who struggled to pay for us to be there. Dawn wasn't the only one who wasn't from an affluent background, by any means. In my class I had several hospital consultants' daughters and the university chancellor's daughter, but there was quite a big mixture. A lot of the girls were from farming families, and there were obviously some like Dawn whose parents sent them there because they were away a lot. It was that kind of a small, caring school. Dawn would have done well wherever she went because she had a technique with drama, but there were those of us who were only mediocre students who needed to be brought out and encouraged to do better.'

As Dawn settled into school life and her homesickness finally abated, she found that she began to enjoy St Dunstan's enormously. 'Obviously I got homesick,' she says. 'But I was lucky to go to the jolliest boarding school in the world.' With her parents abroad for much of the time, school became the focal point of her life, and her memories of her time there remain fond to this day. 'I enjoyed boarding school very much because my parents made it clear that I was there because of all the moving about they had to do, not because they didn't love me,' she says.

Boarding-school life was a lot like Mallory Towers or St Clare's, the fictional jolly-hockey-sticks schools created by Enid Blyton. 'We would have midnight feasts, and I suppose it was a bit like the Blyton books,' recalls Susan Lawrence. But surprisingly, given her self-professed love of food, Dawn wasn't one of the ringleaders. 'She wasn't really instrumental in this,' says Susan. 'Dawn was quite quiet. I don't remember her being a particularly outgoing girl, nor was she one of the most popular. But then I was older, and we didn't take much notice of the younger girls.' Just as in Blyton's books, however, the girls weren't above getting their own back on beastly members of staff. Dawn tells how she and her classmates extracted revenge on a matron nicknamed Hitler because she was so strict. 'We collected our guinea-pig droppings at the weekend, the entire dormitory, which was a dozen girls and a lot of guinea pigs, and put them in her room,' she says. 'She was aware that we were trying to get rid of her and she went. We were so happy.'

As its name suggests, St Dunstan's was a former abbey, built of brick and flint and situated in North Road West, overlooking Victoria Park, Plymouth. In the early part of the nineteenth century it had been occupied by nuns, who ran it as a shelter for the 'dishonest' women of Plymouth until it became a Church of England school in 1850. Today the school has moved to a new site, and the abbey building lies empty and neglected, but for six years it was the only permanent home Dawn knew. Comparatively small in Dawn's day, the school had only 300 girls, aged between five and eighteen. Classes were small – only eighteen or twenty girls to a class – and the majority of the pupils were day-girls. Consequently boarders like Dawn often shared dormitories with girls who were several years older or younger than herself.

St Dunstan's was ruled with a rod of iron by the headmistress, Hazel Abley. An ex-naval officer, she had exceptionally high standards that she expected 'her girls' to live up to. Impeccably turned out, she required the girls to present themselves well and to behave properly at all times. And woe betide anyone who stepped out of line. 'Miss Abley was very efficient – we were all quite scared of her,' reveals former pupil Marie-Louise Cook. 'She was scary but she was a good headmistress, and I think at the end of the day that won out. We all looked up to her because the standards she laid down she kept herself. She was ex-military, and was very much like a man who had been in the services. She liked a certain uniformity, not just in the way you looked, but in how she expected the girls to be, which was at times frustrating. She walked tall and always looked very smart. You'd hear her clipping along in her high heels, and she wore a black cloak over her clothes. She was a bit stuffy, but that's probably just the side she showed us. I'm sure there was a different side to her.'

Dawn's former classmate Janet Bryant also recalls how rigid the school was at that time. 'It was very strict. Lots of things would get you into trouble: running, talking, just general things. You respected your elders, you respected everyone around you. I think Dawn managed quite well. If you're living in those circumstances, you toe the line.'

Despite the often uncompromising rules that her formidable headmistress laid down, Dawn got along well with Hazel Abley and the two remain friends to this day. 'Dawn was quite an individual,' explains Marie-Louise. 'But she wasn't a rebel by any means, she was someone Miss Abley liked. Dawn was bossy and had a slight disciplinarian side to her, and I think Miss Abley could see that. She was very much one of the favourites, a little bit of a teacher's pet really. We used to say, "Oh, there's Dawn again, up in assembly".'

Marie-Louise, who is four years younger than Dawn, recalls how Dawn stood out even then. 'We all remember her because she was quite a character within the school,' she says. 'She was very much as she is now; she wasn't as big, but her personality and her brightness were the same. She was always slightly larger than life. She was very good at drama and sometimes took assembly. She was often on the stage because she won various drama awards and was very much into amateur dramatics.'

The importance the school placed on subjects such as drama was part of the reason that Dawn was so happy at St Dunstan's. She struck up a close relationship with her drama teacher, Christine Abbott, and excelled in the subject. Miss Abbott recognised Dawn's obvious talent for drama and made Dawn her protégée. In turn, the adolescent Dawn hero-worshipped the older woman and vowed to follow in her footsteps and become a teacher herself. 'I always wanted to teach in order to be like my drama teacher at school, Christine Abbott, who was wonderful, spoke beautifully and had been to the Central School of Speech and Drama,' she says. 'I idolised her so much I wanted to do the same. I wanted to be her.'

Miss Abbott, who is now retired, says: 'Dawn always used to say, as a bit of a giggle, that I was the person who inspired her. I've no idea what it was about my teaching that inspired her, but I must have done something right. She was fond of performance and I think it showed. She did a drama class with the rest of the girls, and then asked if she could come along for extra work in speech and drama. She was definitely enthusiastic and was prepared to give up her spare time, after school or in the lunch hour.' Dawn's old teacher is effusive in her praise of her star pupil. 'She was very imaginative and creative, right from the start, and very lively,' she says warmly. 'She was always full of energy. She had lots of confidence – I think services children often do – and got on very well with everyone. She had a mass of friends. She was perfectly lovely. She was always a bubbly girl, right the way through.'

Dawn was fortunate in that while St Dunstan's was a traditional school that attached a great deal of importance to academic achievement, it was at the same time quite forward-thinking regarding the girls' overall schooling. 'The approach we had to a girl's upbringing was that she should be allowed to develop in whatever direction seemed to show the most promise,' explains Miss Abbott. 'We liked to encourage the girls in whatever way they seemed to find their talents. It was pretty strict. It was a very highly disciplined school, there's no question of that. But within those parameters a girl could develop her talents because there was scope for that too.'

It was obvious to the other girls that Dawn had a special bond with her drama teacher, and under Christine Abbott's careful tutelage she easily outshone her classmates in the subject. 'Miss Abbott certainly felt that Dawn had that spark,' says Sarah Rawle. 'She was always a very flamboyant character, and there was a definite rapport between them.' Janet Bryant also recalls how Dawn willingly put in the effort and took drama seriously. 'Dawn paid attention and the rest of us didn't,' she laughs. 'Miss Abbott was very charismatic. She made her classes interesting, whereas most of the classes were very formal.' Even the younger girls were aware of Dawn's passion for drama. 'She was always very good at diction and drama and ran away with all the points and prizes,' recalls Sandra Harvey, who is three years her junior. 'Everybody at school knew of Dawn French because she was always winning prizes. She was a bit of a star even then.'

Christine Abbott eschewed traditional drama favourites such as Shakespeare in favour of more unusual exercises. 'The English department used to look after the classical things; I like to think that we were more creative,' she says. 'Dawn always participated in whatever was going on. I think performing might have been at the back of her mind all along, although she never said it was. I never had any inkling that she would be famous; we just encouraged the girls as much as we could in whatever direction seemed the most appropriate. I certainly didn't think, "That girl will go far". I hoped she would do well: we hoped everybody would do well, and if someone was going to put themselves out and give up things in order that they could achieve some sort of fame, that's good. But it wasn't encouraged to that extent; we weren't a breeding ground for the stars.'

As a favourite of both Miss Abbott and Miss Abley, Dawn had a special status within the school, and when she entered the sixth form no one was surprised when she was made a prefect. And when it came to important occasions such as the prestigious sixth-formers v. teachers tennis match, Dawn was naturally one of those chosen to play. 'Other sixth-formers came and went and you wouldn't have remembered them, but we all knew Dawn,' explains Marie-Louise. 'She was much more high-profile than the other sixth-formers. Because she was so good at drama she was a bit of a showpiece within the school. Even then she was obviously someone with a talent. Miss Abley and Miss Abbott were very proud of her. She was quite treasured at the school. Miss Abbott thought she was the bee's knees, and looked upon her as her protégée, someone she had brought up and felt very proud of.

'Dawn was great fun, but she was quite bossy. She had a warmth about her, but if she was cross with you, you'd be told. She was kind of scary and bossy at the same time. We were a bit in awe of her because much of our contact with her would be her telling us off. She used to stand outside the dinner hall and inspect our fingernails before we were allowed into lunch. If a girl's nails were anything less than scrupulously clean, Dawn would send them away to scrub them.'

Dawn took to her prefect duty with great gusto, and recalls one of her less savoury techniques for enforcing her views on her peers: a beetle- and spider-infested broom which she could bang with impunity as she was impervious to creepy-crawlies. 'I should have gone into the Gestapo,' she laughs.

Another, less welcome reason why Dawn stood out from the other girls at St Dunstan's was that she was, even then, quite plump. Barely five foot tall and a size 16 by the time she was fourteen, the St Dunstan's school-issue clothes were unforgiving and unbecoming on Dawn. She was not alone in her humiliation. Classmate Janet Bryant still cringes when she remembers their school clothes. 'The uniform was horrendous, quite revolting,' she shudders. 'It was very traditional: a blue knee-length kilt, which a lot of the girls, including Dawn, would hitch up a few inches, and a blue and yellow striped blazer. In the summer we would wear straw boaters, and bowler hats and heavy navy-blue coats in winter. The summer uniform was a blue nylon dress, which didn't do much for your figure.

'Dawn was well built, and I was quite large at the time as well. I think I might have been the largest one in the class — I was twelve stone when I was twelve — and they used to put me in goal, basically because I filled most of it! Being an all-girls school there wasn't teasing like there would have been if boys were around. Dawn never discussed being overweight with me – I think I was more conscious of it myself.'

Marie-Louise also recalls the less than flattering ensemble that Dawn and her friends selected for their last year at school. 'The sixth-formers could choose their own uniform,' she explains. 'They all had to wear the same, but the privilege was that they could choose it. I have memories of Dawn wearing an awful black skirt with white spots on. It was virtually a miniskirt, and for girls who were bigger, that sort of Seventies look was probably not the most flattering.'

The midnight feasts and visits to Lavinia, the St Dunstan's Abbey cook, who was generous with bread and butter to girls who helped her clean up the kitchen, hadn't helped matters. Neither had arriving back at school on Sunday evening with a tuck box filled up with sweets from her family's newsagent's. As a young teenager, Dawn was faced with the fact that she simply couldn't wear the kind of clothes that her friends did. Weekend forays into Plymouth to look around the shops and search out the latest fashions ended in frustration and misery for the teenage Dawn. It was 1971; hot pants and micro-skirts were all the rage, but it seemed that none of the garments had been made big enough to fit her.

When her friends popped into Dorothy Perkins, Dawn knew that for her there was no point. 'You want to spend two hours trying on everything and looking at each other,' she explains. 'But I couldn't do that at all.' It is a familiar scenario that anyone who has ever been overweight can identify and sympathise with. While her girlfriends went home happily clutching bulging shopping bags full of trendy things to wear, Dawn often returned empty-handed. It made her sad, but it also made her cross. 'Throughout my teenage years I felt oppressed because I could never find clothes to fit me,' she says. 'I remember at about fourteen getting angry when I went out with my friends to buy clothes on Saturdays and there was nothing to spend money on because you were maybe a size 16, and they didn't exist. I'd feel grateful if something fitted over my head. If it went over my head, I'd buy it. I'd wear atrocious things just because I could get them on.'

Like many large children, Dawn attempted to laugh off her discomfiture by cracking jokes at her own expense. She tells journalists that as a girl she wanted to be an air hostess 'cos people don't eat all their meals on planes, and I could scoff everything left behind the secret curtains'. And she makes out that one of the reasons she liked it at St Dunstan's was because the food was so plentiful. 'The food was good and the older you were, the higher you moved up the table, the more you ate,' she says. 'There'd be raids on the kitchen, and as only margarine and marmalade were not under lock and key, we ate that.' But, as is often the case, the wisecracks hid more complex feelings. While Dawn had been brought up to value herself and not worry about her weight, it was, for a while at least, nonetheless a source of angst for her. Quite early on she realised that it was a bar to her doing certain things, including her dream of becoming an air hostess.

Although she jokes about it now, Dawn really did want to be an air stewardess. But by the time she was fourteen she realised that she was never going to be petite enough to meet the airlines' strict recruitment requirements. It was a bitter disappointment, and one that she hugely resented. Fortunately for Dawn, she found another avenue for her talents and threw herself wholeheartedly into drama. Her time at St Dunstan's proved useful in many ways, not least in that it provided her with a rich source of material for her television sketches. Marie-Louise has followed her career, and easily spots the oblique references to their old school. 'I think a lot of her sketches come from having been at an all-girls school,' she says. 'There are certain references she makes, to certain characters or things, that are very much from St Dunstan's.

'Those years are hugely formative years in your life, and by the way she refers to it so often, and in so many of her sketches, I think it must be something she looks back on and finds quite amusing. I remember when *French and Saunders* first appeared on television there were a lot of sketches about girls sitting in a classroom, and they brought up the names of some of our old teachers. There is something about all girls together, the silly conversations and the bitchiness that, for women particularly, is why Dawn makes you laugh. She's very much got that female thing, that really giggly silliness that girls have and men think, "That's not funny". But it is for us.'

CHAPTER THREE

Love

Dawn discovered the attractions of the opposite sex at a young age. She claims to have been desperate to kiss a boy in her primary-school class, by the name of Michael Le Pellier, simply because she fancied his exotic-sounding name. While the other young girls played with their dolls and busied themselves with finger-painting, Dawn sat and daydreamed about what young Michael's lips would taste like. Sadly she was never to find out. She had to wait a few more years, until she entered her teens, before she had her first proper kiss.

But she thought about it a lot in the meantime. Attending an all-girls school did nothing to dampen her interest in boys; if anything, their exclusion made them appear all the more exciting and forbidden. St Dunstan's Abbey overlooked Victoria Park, and from the vantage point of her dormitory window, Dawn could ogle the boys from Devonport High as they walked through the park on their way to school. Like many young girls, she spent a lot of time dreaming about lads and wondering what it would feel like to be in love.

Having an older brother was an advantage because it meant she got to meet his friends, and the first boy she fell in love with was her brother's best friend, David Eccles. At fifteen, he was two years older than Dawn, and although they indulged in teenage necking it was more a case of infatuation than real love. 'I kissed him a lot but he wasn't really interested in me,' she admits ruefully.

Not long after she had started at boarding school, Dawn's father came out of the RAF and took over the running of 'Frenchies'', his parents' newsagent's shop in the Ernesettle district of the town. Leslie and Marjorie French had owned the shop for almost forty years but when his father died, his mother decided to retire. Denys and Roma became the new proprietors, and moved into a house in nearby Saltash, just across the River Tamar into Cornwall. Dawn was overjoyed that the family could be together again, but her parents decided that she and Gary should continue as weekly boarders as they would be working long hours in the shop. They started work at four-thirty a.m. to mark up the morning papers, and frequently didn't close until teatime.

So in the event, things remained much the same for Dawn. All that changed was that instead of spending the weekends with her grandparents, she would be at home with her parents. The new set-up was not without its advantages, the most obvious being that Dawn and Gary often found themselves at home alone. Arriving in Saltash on a Friday afternoon, the youngsters frequently found the house empty, giving them plenty of opportunity to do what teenagers do. Making the most of the time before their parents returned from work, she and Gary would settle down with David Eccles and a friend of Dawn's for what she describes as 'four hours of solid snogging'. The kissing sessions would go on until either their parents returned from work, or, as Dawn puts it, 'we all had huge fat lips that were sore and painful'.

It was a freedom they took full advantage of. 'We were kind of latchkey kids because both my parents worked and I had an hour and a half after school before they came back,' she recalls. 'I spent it kissing David Eccles. Nothing else, just perfectly innocent lip movement. He was a dead good snogger.'

Such behaviour, although touching in its naivety, felt thrillingly sinful to the young Dawn. Being cooped up under the watchful eyes of her teachers all week lent an added frisson of excitement to her innocent kissing sessions. Had she not been a pupil at an all-girls boarding school, she might arguably not have been quite so obsessed with the opposite sex. 'Of course boarding school made being let loose at the weekends even more fun,' she acknowledges. 'I was very interested in boys and desperately wanted to get snogged. I always hoped to have very bruised lips by Monday morning.'

Back at St Dunstan's, Dawn's raging hormones often got her into bother with the authorities. 'I was very randy at an early age, and at school I got into trouble for flirting with boys,' she says. 'I had loads of energy and did lots of snogging. I got tits before anybody else and I wanted boys touching them right from the minute they grew. At school we ended up inviting boys in off the street. Once, when they came out of the pub opposite, we started flirting with them out of the window. You can imagine all these girls at the window in their nighties, and they took us seriously, broke in and came up and sat on our beds. The police were called and wanted us to identify them, but we refused because we thought it wasn't fair as we'd encouraged them. It was very disgraceful. Our parents were informed, we were very shamefaced. Then we did it all over again the following week!'

It is extremely doubtful, however, whether Hazel Abley would have tolerated such goings-on under her roof, and the story has no doubt benefited from a bit of topspin on Dawn's part. The truth is probably far less racy. Despite the advantage of having an older brother and the potential to date his friends, Dawn found her early teenage years to be quite frustrating on the romance front. She quickly realised that the fifteen-year-old David Eccles wasn't really interested in dating a thirteen-year-old, and while Gary's mates all liked Dawn and considered her to be a 'good laugh', they didn't necessarily see her as girlfriend material.

'Unfortunately I spent my teenage years being the joky girl who didn't get the boy,' she admits. 'I used to be very jealous of pretty girls, and would wonder why I didn't get to go home and snog when I'd been the centre of attention in the pub. It was slightly sad when I used to be the funny girl at weekends in the cars with the lads, but never the girl they wanted to take home. Everyone would have a good laugh, but you weren't the one getting snogged at the end of the evening.'

It was a crushing experience, and combined with the insecurities that had been brought on by her disappointing clothes-shopping trips, these doubts about her sex appeal added up to something of a crisis of confidence for Dawn. Young girls who are naive in the ways of the world, especially those who feel that they aren't as pretty or attractive as their friends, are in peril of gratefully accepting the advances of the first boy who comes along. Dawn wouldn't have been the first teenager to succumb to 'the wrong type', and the fact that she didn't is down to one special man.

Denys French intuitively guessed that his daughter might have difficulty valuing herself as highly as she should. He had seen her face when she arrived home from her shopping expeditions disappointed and empty-handed, and sensed her envy when her slimmer, prettier friends got asked out on dates and she didn't. Some fathers might baulk at the idea of attempting to talk to an adolescent girl about such delicate matters and choose to simply hope for the best, but Dawn's father decided on direct action.

He knew how loved and adored Dawn was, and how special, and decided that it was time she knew it too. Five minutes prior to her very first trip to a discotheque, at age fourteen, he sat her down for a talk. She would never forget what he said to her that day. 'He knew I was going out with a lot of thin girlfriends, and there was the potential there for cruelty,' she explains. 'He knew he had to make sure my self-esteem was buoyed up, and that he had to protect me from those who might decide to reduce my confidence. I was ready to get into a huff because I thought I was going to hear the usual litany about not drinking too much and what time I had to be in, and not getting too involved with boys, but instead I was the recipient of the most extraordinary emotional eulogy.

'He told me that I was uncommonly beautiful, that I was the most precious thing in his life, that he prized me above all else, that he was proud to be my father and that if any randy geek, biker, shithead, ever laid a finger on me, he would hurt them badly in their Brut-sprinkled soft places. He went into this great overture of praise for me. He told me that I should be proud of myself physically, and that I was going to be desirable to all the boys I would meet that night. In fact, I was probably going to be the most desirable girl out of all my friends, and any boy who managed to get a bit of a snog with me was very lucky. Well, my chest just got bigger and bigger the more he spoke. He succeeded in making me so proud of myself, and making my self-esteem so high, that I wasn't going to let any boy kiss me at all that night – I was just too good.'

What Denys French did for Dawn on that auspicious day is perhaps the most important thing any father can do for a daughter. His words had such a profound effect on her that she was never again to doubt herself in that way. Instead of approaching her adolescence as the short, fat girl who couldn't get a boyfriend, Dawn was secure in the knowledge that she was loved for who she was, not what she looked like. She believed her father when he told her that she was something special, and that knowledge gave her an inner confidence that made her positively shine. 'It was my father who taught me to value myself,' she says. 'How wise of my father to say those words to me. It affected my whole life. How could you not come out of it well equipped to deal with life, when you felt so loved and supported?'

Boys didn't immediately start beating a path to her door over-night, but she now realised that it didn't mean there was anything wrong with the way she looked. 'I remember sometimes not getting a boyfriend and wondering if it was because I was fat,' she says. 'Then I realised it was because I was too funny. I would be the one who'd make everyone laugh. It was the wimpy girls who didn't stand up for themselves who'd get the boys – because they'd let the boys into their knickers. At that stage I just wasn't like that.'

She was understandably distressed, therefore, when an innocent date with another of her brother's friends threatened to sully her good name. The boy, whom she had initially thought of as 'a knight in shining white armour', completed an enjoyable date with a chaste peck on the cheek, only to boast in double chemistry the following day that he and 'Frenchie' had done it 'this way, that way, every way'. The cad forgot that her brother was in his class until Gary's fist sent him flying for tarnishing his sister's name.

Her father's words were to remain uppermost in Dawn's mind throughout her life. Any doubts she had about her size went out of the window, and she developed a noticeable self-assurance. Others might have adopted the shrinking-violet posture that many over-weight people develop, but Dawn walked proudly. 'Dawn always had great confidence,' recalls Marie-Louise Cook. 'A lot of sixteen-year-olds who were a bit overweight and fat would have tried to cover it up or been a bit round-shouldered, but she had an air about her; you could feel she felt good about herself. That's what I remember most about Dawn.'

Confidence is an attractive quality in itself, and as she entered her late teens Dawn found that she no longer had difficulty getting boyfriends. Stripped of the negative niggling doubts about the way she looked, she became more relaxed and easygoing, and her natural beauty shone through. The young men she came into contact with saw a bright and amusing girl with a pretty face and a beautiful smile, and found her self-confidence alluring.

It was exactly these qualities that a young naval officer saw when he first laid eyes on her. David Smith, a nineteen-year-old Irishman who had come to Britain to join the Royal Navy, was destined to be the first serious love of her life and the man whom she very nearly married. They met at a party in Looe, a picturesque Cornish fishing village, when Dawn was seventeen and it was love at first sight. 'We met at the end of 1974 or the beginning of 1975,' David recalls. 'She must have been about seventeen as she was in her last year of school. I'd been in England about a year and I was staying with a naval friend in Looe, and Dawn came to a party that he had at his house. I suppose there was an instant attraction. She was a very attractive girl. She was vivacious, good fun, highly independent, highly intelligent – everything you see in her now, really.'

Dawn, in turn, found herself strongly attracted to the good-looking, blond-haired young officer with the engaging Irish accent. They spent the entire evening with each other, scarcely noticing the people around them, and she was over the moon when he asked to see her again. During the following weeks she could think of nothing but David, and impatiently counted the hours and minutes until she could see him again. As their relationship grew more serious, she found that she missed him dreadfully when they were not together. It was a situation that she would have to learn to live with, however, as David was often away at sea. During his absences, Dawn would lie on her school bunk and write him long, passionate love letters. The enforced separations did nothing to dampen her ardour, and only served to make the relationship seem even more romantic. The minute his ship docked in Plymouth harbour Dawn would run down to the quayside to greet him, and each time they were reunited it was like falling in love all over again.

She would often accompany her beau to formal dinners at his naval barracks. Dawn's initial reaction the first time David invited her was excitement, but her exhilaration quickly evaporated when she remembered the perennial problem: she had nothing to wear.

Military dinners are extremely showy affairs with men wearing full dress uniforms and ladies in long dresses, and from past experience Dawn knew it would be hopeless looking for anything in the shops. In later years she would be able to call on top designers like Betty Jackson and Jasper Conran to run her up something special, but as it was she resigned herself to the fact that she wouldn't be able to go. However, she had reckoned without her very own fairy godmother, Auntie May the seamstress. Like Cinderella, she would go to the ball. A quick visit to Auntie May saw her kitted out in a ritzy chiffon number that had the added advantage of being an original one-off creation that no other girl would be wearing.

Dawn introduced David to her family and he got on well with her parents and brother. Before long they were a recognised item, and it was with David that Dawn chose to lose her virginity. With her father's words forever in mind, she had vowed to remain a virgin until someone special came along. In her dormitory at school it seemed that lovemaking was all she and her friends ever talked about, but while she outwardly professed to know what it was all about, inwardly she was far more hesitant. 'It's probably true that I was a drama queen when I was a kid, embellishing the little things you don't know,' she admits. 'If you don't quite know how sex happens, you make the rest up. I was a bit more of a blabbermouth and less of a doer. All mouth and no trousers. I didn't do it until I was quite grown-up.'

In the event, Dawn didn't experience sex until the relatively late age of eighteen. She and David went on a camping holiday and she lost her virginity in a tent. Dawn has admitted that she had often worried about 'her first time'. 'I was dead scared of sex, especially as I had been making up the stories,' she confessed. 'You lie yourself into a corner eventually.' But after she had made love with David she had no regrets. She loved him and believed he would be the man whom she would eventually marry. David felt the same. 'It was a serious love affair in every sense of the word,' he explains.

Although the subject wasn't actually mentioned by either of them, Dawn began to think about the day when she and David would be married, and took it for granted that she would one day become Mrs David Smith.

Dawn had reached another important stage in her life too: it was time to say goodbye to St Dunstan's. She had done well in her exams and the school was keen for her to go on to Oxbridge, but she had other ideas. She decided to follow in the footsteps of her mentor Christine Abbott and train as a drama teacher, and looked into the idea of doing a drama course at Exeter University. But before she had time to do anything about it, fate stepped in and took her along a completely different path.

Each year St Dunstan's Abbey entered a public-speaking contest run by the English Speaking Union. Many schools took part, the majority of which were far bigger and grander than St Dunstan's, but that year it was won by Dawn. The prize was a year's scholarship at a school in New York, and the whole school celebrated her win. 'I remember when she won the debating scholarship,' recalls Marie-Louise. 'She was up on stage with Miss Abbott and Miss Abley, and there was a big announcement. It was a big thing for the school, bearing in mind that it was just a local little school in Plymouth, and to have won it was very prestigious. I remember that if anyone got into Oxbridge, and it only happened twice, the whole school had a day off. Because it was a small all-girls school big things didn't often happen, so when something did happen, or someone won a special award, a lot was made of it.'

Dawn left school in the summer of 1976, when Britain was in the grip of a heatwave that caused the worst drought in 250 years. While her friends prepared for university or their first job, Dawn lay in the sun and thought excitedly about her forthcoming trip to America. For someone like her, whose parents were far from well off, it represented a fantastic, once in a lifetime opportunity. Nowadays people can cross the Atlantic by aeroplane for little more

than a hundred pounds, but in 1976 a trip to the States was still out
of reach for the majority of people. Winning the scholarship
presented Dawn with a unique chance to experience a completely
different way of life.

She was thrilled to have won the award, but was in two minds as
to whether she should actually go. 'She was torn between going and
staying,' recalls David Smith. 'She didn't want us to be apart, but I
was in the Navy and we were used to separations so we weren't going
to make an issue of it. It was an opportunity which she didn't want to
miss, and something I thought she shouldn't miss out on either.
Leaving me wasn't too much of a problem; I think it was probably
more of a decision on her part for her to leave her parents.'

Dawn knew that if she went to New York she would not see her
mother and father for the best part of a year. Even when Denys was
in the RAF she had never gone that long without seeing her parents,
and she had serious reservations about leaving them. In the end
they managed to persuade her to go by promising to write frequently and insisting that the time would 'fly by'. Somewhat
reluctantly, Dawn set aside her worries and packed her bags.

She arrived in New York in September 1976, two months before
Jimmy Carter was elected President of the United States. Everything had been arranged for her by the English Speaking Union:
she would be attending the sixth-form college at Spence School in
New York City and would be staying with a host family. It was her
first trip abroad on her own, and her excitement at arriving in such
a vibrant city was tinged with fear. Alone in a completely alien
environment and thousands of miles from home, she was desperately miserable. She missed David and her family, and felt exactly as
she had as a twelve-year-old girl arriving at boarding school for the
first time. History began to repeat itself as once again she struggled
to settle in at a new school, and she sobbed herself to sleep at night.
'I went to New York and cried for two months,' she says. 'Then I
loved it. Still do. But I could never live there.'

While she was at Spence, Dawn wrote a thesis on American education but, asked by an interviewer what she had learned in New York, she replied, 'Mostly pizzas'. 'All I did was eat lots of biscuits, learn to say "tacky", "gross" and "peachy", and come back wearing baseball caps,' she says. Living in a country where a huge percentage of the population is obese did nothing for Dawn's figure. Every kind of food was on offer, particularly junk food. It was cheap and the portions were huge, which appealed no end to a self-confessed foodie like Dawn. 'I got really fat,' she admits. 'There was just so much choice and it didn't cost much. I stayed with families whose children had gone to England, who fed me very well.'

To Dawn, who had been born and raised in the West Country, New York initially appeared to be an intimidating and noisy place. But once she settled in and found her feet she began to enjoy herself. She also realised that she was within striking distance of some spectacularly beautiful countryside, providing her with a much-needed antidote to city life. During her time in the US she lodged with several American families, one of which had a weekend home in Connecticut. It was while she was staying with them, quite early on in her trip, that she was almost killed in a horrific car accident. Her hosts, who had a daughter the same age as Dawn, had invited her to Connecticut for the weekend, but as they set off for the journey back to New York on the Monday morning they were involved in a terrifying crash with a lorry.

Dawn was horribly injured in the accident, and was lucky to escape with her life. But it left her badly shaken up and to this day she is haunted by recurring nightmares about the crash. She can still remember every little detail of how it happened, certain moments appearing almost in slow motion. 'Snow had fallen steadily throughout the previous night, and everything was quiet and still as our car climbed a hill,' she recalls. 'I was in the back, behind the bench seat in front. I remember watching as a truck went into a graceful skid and slowly veered on to our side of the road and into our oncoming path. It was like being in a dream. It seemed to take forever, certainly long enough for my friend's father to tell us to hang on, to brace ourselves.'

While the occupants of the car watched helplessly, the lorry began heading straight for them. 'I can see the truck now, drifting towards us,' says Dawn. 'I can hear the crunch. I can see the other driver as he crashed through, first his windscreen and then ours. He lost most of his teeth and his face was terribly cut. My friend's mother hit the dashboard. Her father was thrown on to the steering wheel and broke his jaw. My friend hit her head. And me? No cuts, nothing as far as I could see.'

Totally oblivious to the fact that she too was seriously injured, Dawn's first instinct was to help the people around her. The shock of what had happened served to numb the pain that she should have been feeling, and she genuinely had no idea that she was hurt. 'The bench seat in front of me had collapsed and I can remember thinking I couldn't get my foot free,' she explains. 'So I lifted the bench seat, got out of the car, checked that everyone was alive and ran to the nearest house for help.' Deathly pale and leaving a trail of blood in the snow behind her, she presented quite a shocking sight to the owner of the house she went to. 'The man who answered the door said, "My God, what's happened to your foot?" ' recalls Dawn. 'I looked down and it was just sort of hanging off the bottom of my leg. That's when I passed out.'

She ended up in hospital, where doctors fought to save her shattered foot. 'Eventually I was put into a plaster cast stretching to my thigh, and hobbled around on crutches for weeks,' she says. 'I remember all the cab drivers in New York, every time I told one of them what had happened, saying, "Gee, are you going to sue? You'd get millions for that". But it was my friend's father. I just couldn't, and anyway, it wasn't his fault.'

Her narrow escape from death was one of two major things that happened to her in New York. The second was equally momentous, though a great deal more pleasant: she became engaged. To his delight, David discovered that his ship was going to be docking in the Caribbean for a few days, and, on the spur of the moment, he decided to go and see Dawn. 'I extended a weekend's leave and flew up and we met in New York,' he reveals. 'I just wanted to see her.'

The lovers hadn't seen each other for several months, and discovering that David was coming to New York to see her was the best surprise Dawn had ever had. It was an extremely romantic gesture – something that was not lost on either of them. Being young and in love in one of the most exciting cities in the world, it was almost inevitable that David would ask her to marry him. Caught up in the passion of the moment, he proposed and Dawn joyfully accepted. 'I hadn't planned to ask her to marry me, it was fairly spontaneous,' he admits. 'Seeing her again and being in New York, I suddenly decided to propose. I suppose it does sound romantic. I don't think of myself as a smoothie, although maybe twenty years ago I was!'

Dawn didn't have to be asked twice. 'She didn't need persuading,' says David. 'She said yes straight away.' It was a gloriously happy weekend. They walked hand in hand through Central Park and saw all the sights, and telephoned Dawn's parents in England to tell them the happy news. When David's leave was over and he had to return to the Caribbean, it was all she could bear to say goodbye to him. She counted the days until she could return to England to be with her fiancé.

Her homecoming, however, was destined to be far from joyous. Dawn arrived back in Plymouth to a scene of utter tragedy, and her whole world was about to fall apart.

CHAPTER FOUR

Heartbreak

Part of the reason why Dawn hadn't wanted to go to New York was that everything was far from well at home. For some time her father had been seriously ill with depression, and she was desperately worried about him.

Denys French had found it hard adjusting to life outside the RAF, and in the years following his return to Civvy Street things hadn't got any easier for him. He missed the air force and the order and sense of belonging that being part of a huge organisation had brought to his life. As a civilian he felt no sense of purpose, and began to experience increasingly prolonged bouts of depression. On top of his complex emotional problems he had money worries, and these had combined to sink him into deep despair. Nothing and no one could get through to him, and Dawn was beside herself with worry about what he might do.

It is a burden that she has kept to herself for more than twenty years, shared only with the people who are closest to her. The nature of her father's illness and the effect it had had on her family life was a terrible weight for a teenage girl to carry. Seeing the person she loved so ill had a debilitating effect on her, which is why her family and teachers had encouraged her to go to America. Her year in the States had provided some respite from the stress, but now her sabbatical was over.

As soon as she arrived home it became clear that not only was Dawn's father no better, he was actually far worse. While she had been gone his state of mind had deteriorated alarmingly, and by the time she returned he was in the grip of a mental breakdown. In fact, things had got so bad for Denys French that he had even tried to take his own life.

Unbeknown to Dawn, this was not the worst of it. The situation was about to reach crisis point and full-scale tragedy was waiting around the corner. Her safe world was about to be savagely torn apart and her life to change inexorably. Exactly one month before her twentieth birthday she would be robbed of the father she loved so dearly, in the very cruellest way possible.

On the morning of 11 September 1977 Dawn's worst fears were realised when her father committed suicide. He left the family's home in Saltash and drove five miles along winding country lanes to the tiny Cornish hamlet of Pillaton. He had set up a rabbit-breeding business on some land outside the village, and it was there that he chose to kill himself.

Denys French had planned his death with precise calculation. As it was a Sunday, he knew he was unlikely to be disturbed by farm workers, and there were no houses close enough to raise the alarm. He was confident that he would be able to carry out his plan without anybody stopping him. He parked alone on the remote piece of land by the rabbit hutches and contemplated death. He had with him a garden hosepipe, which he connected to the exhaust of his car. Although he rarely touched alcohol, he had taken some sherry from the house to help numb his pain, and he drank this before feeding the other end of the hosepipe into the vehicle. He then locked himself inside the car and started the engine. This final, pitiful act was the last thing Denys French did on this earth. For him, as he sat in the car and prepared to die, his actions would bring a welcome escape from his torment. But for Dawn, it would herald the beginning of the darkest period of her life. As the toxic exhaust fumes flooded the inside of the car, Denys quickly slipped into unconsciousness, and by the time he was found he was dead from carbon-monoxide poisoning. He was forty-five.

When his body was discovered later that day, the police were called to the scene. It was apparent by the manner of his death that he had intended to kill himself, and foul play was immediately ruled out. Neighbours in Old Ferry Road, where the French family was living, watched as a police car pulled up outside the house and wondered what had happened to bring them out on a Sunday. Hearing the news that her father was dead was the most terrible moment of Dawn's life. Her grief hit her like a hammer blow and sent her reeling in shock. She couldn't believe it was true. Her father loved her, he'd told her so himself, and he knew that she loved him. He would surely walk back through the door any minute, and explain that it had all been a silly misunderstanding.

And yet it was true. The police explained to the shell-shocked family that the coroner would be informed and there would have to be an inquest. There would also be a post-mortem to establish the cause of death. The cogs of officialdom duly whirred into action and the following weeks passed in a blur for Dawn and her family. Roma French had the unpleasant task of making a statement to the police about her husband's frame of mind. This proved to be an ordeal in itself as she relived the history of Denys's illness and the distressing effect it had had on them all. An intensely private woman, it was not easy for her to tell total strangers such deeply personal things about her married life. Over the years she had tried hard to keep Denys's depression, and the resultant problems, a secret from all but his very close family. Now, she realised, everyone would know their business.

The day after Denys's death, the *Western Morning News* carried a report of the tragedy. Two sombre paragraphs on page five under the heading 'Body in Vehicle' described how the body of a Saltash man in his early forties had been found in a car at Kernock Lodge, Pillaton, and identified the dead man as Denys French. Over the following days more than a dozen obituaries appeared in Plymouth's local paper, the *Evening Herald*, as Denys's loved ones paid tribute to him. Many of the notices were placed by his family; others were from some of his many friends. Most of them fondly referred to him by his nickname, 'Den', and they all spoke of how much they loved and missed him.

From Dawn and her brother were the moving words: 'Goodbye to a perfect dad. We'll miss you more as each sun sets.' Roma wrote lovingly of a 'wonderful husband taken suddenly. I'll remember all our years.' She included a passage from Kipling which read, 'Father in heaven who lovest all, O help thy children when they call, that they may help build from age to age, an undefiled heritage.' They had been married for twenty-four years. The message from his own family said simply: 'The road was too long.' His friends thanked him for a 'loving relationship and talks that ended with sunrise', and from Dawn's fiancé David was the poignant message, 'I only wish we had known each other longer.'

It was clear from the sheer number of notices that Denys French had been enormously loved by all those who knew him. He was a family man, devoted to his wife and children, and would never have knowingly hurt them. Everyone was at a loss to understand what had made him do such a terrible thing. The depth of his depression was known to only a handful of people, and consequently his death came as an enormous shock. Although Plymouth is a city with many thousands of inhabitants, in many ways it is like a small town. Having lived there for generations, and running a local newsagent's shop, the French family is well known in the area. Everyone was shocked and appalled by what had happened, and struggled to make sense of it.

At the inquest in Liskeard, Cornwall, four weeks later, the full extent of Denys's suffering was revealed. The court heard that he had tried to kill himself twice before: once involving a similar method, and on the other occasion with a gun. Whether these previous attempts had gone wrong or had simply been cries for help was not disclosed. The pathologist reported that he had alcohol in his system, and Roma French told the police in her statement that some sherry was missing from a bottle. The coroner for north and east Cornwall, George Northey, said that Mr French did not normally drink very much and 'could have become fuddled'.

Denys's brother-in-law Frederick Martin, who lived at Kernock Lodge, the house at the bottom of the lane where Denys died, told the inquest that Denys had been worried about money. He said he had been in the rabbit-breeding business for two years but had financial problems and 'was not a good businessman'. The coroner recorded a verdict of suicide and blamed Denys's death on the fact that he couldn't adjust to life outside the air force. 'Mr French became worried, whether for good reason or not, and took his life,' he said. 'It is particularly sad that a man who had spent so many years in the RAF, and had such a successful career there, should find it so difficult to adjust to civilian life.' On the death certificate, under cause of death, the coroner wrote: 'Carbon-monoxide (motor-car exhaust gas) poisoning. Deceased killed himself.' In those few stark words a line was drawn under Denys French's life.

The inquest was reported in the *Western Morning News*, the *Western Evening Herald* and the *Cornish Times*. For the majority of people who knew Denys, the coroner's explanation for his death was the only one they would get. For after the funeral, Dawn and Gary and Roma retreated into their own private grief and were not seen in the town for several months. Sue Rollinson knew the family well and had worked for Dawn's parents since she was an eleven-year-old schoolgirl. She had delivered newspapers for them and when Roma later set up a dog-grooming business when Sue was fifteen, she became her apprentice. She remembers how stunned everyone was by Denys's death. 'It came as such a shock and I haven't got a clue why it happened,' she says. 'We were so sad because Mr French really was the most amazing, wonderful man. He was friendly and considerate, a real gentleman.'

Although Roma had a business to run, she was not seen at the poodle parlour for a long time. 'We didn't see Mrs French for nearly six months,' Sue recalls. 'A lady ran the pet shop, and myself and another young girl looked after the parlour. We never saw sight nor sound of her. We never knew what was going on, we just didn't see her for many months. We didn't see any of them.'

For Dawn it was a time of total devastation. It seemed to her that one moment she had been travelling home from America, looking forward to seeing her father and telling him all her news, and the next he had disappeared from her life. He had been the one person above all others whom she had looked up to and turned to for help and advice. He was the man who had made her have faith in herself, and the person those closest to her believe may even be responsible for her fame and success. She had taken it for granted that he would always be there to love and encourage her. She'd assumed that it would be Denys who would give her away on her wedding day. But now he was gone.

Her grief was immense, and mixed up with the feelings of sadness and loss was anger at her father for abandoning her. That he was dead was bad enough, but if he had died of a disease or in an accident she would at least have known why he'd died. The fact that he had chosen to take his own life, the fact that he *wanted* to die and leave them all, made it a million times worse. How much he must have been suffering in order to have committed such a terrible act was too dreadful for Dawn to contemplate.

Psychologists agree that there are few things more stressful than the death of a loved one. Suicide is probably the hardest bereavement of all to come to terms with because of the implicit rejection involved. It can have a devastating effect on those who are left behind, particularly if they blame themselves. 'When a person commits suicide the effect on their loved ones can be absolutely shattering,' says psychologist Dr David Lewis. 'After a bereavement, one goes through a fairly well-established series of emotional stages which usually starts with denial. If you break bad news to somebody, often the first stage is to deny it and say, "No, that can't be true, that can't be right". When they realise that it *is* true, there is anger expressed at the person who has died: "How dare they do this to me, how could they put me through this misery?" '

Anyone in that position would surely have asked themselves the same questions: how could their father have done this to them? What had they done to deserve it? Were they in some way to blame?

'There is often guilt,' says Dr Lewis. 'Every unkind word you've ever said, every selfish act you've ever done, comes back to haunt you. For a child in a family where a father or mother has killed themselves, there is often a crushing burden of guilt. A teenager might think, "If only I hadn't been so horrid to Dad last week", or, if the parent had financial worries, they would regret pestering for new clothes.'

It wasn't only the anguish of the death itself that was hard for Dawn to bear. Years of worrying about her father's unhappiness had taken its toll on her. She had hoped desperately that he would once again become the happy father whom she loved so much, but over the months his illness only got worse. It was an extremely stressful situation for Dawn and her family, and placed an enormous amount of pressure on them all over a long period of time. 'You've got to bear in mind what it is like living with the situation before it ever comes to a suicide attempt,' points out Dr Lewis. 'Living with a depressed person is enormously traumatic, and dealing with depressed people is very difficult.

'Suicide is often symptomatic of things going wrong in a relation-ship, events which might well lead to a feeling of despair but are not of themselves likely to prove to be the trigger. Sometimes a suicide attempt is a gesture, where the person is saying, "Now look what you've made me do, you have driven me to this". It can be a cry for help, but it is very difficult to tell. If someone says they are going to kill themselves you can never assume that they are just trying to show off, or are attention-seeking. Any claim that people are going to kill themselves should always be taken seriously.'

Gary French takes after his father and is quieter, shyer and less outgoing than Dawn. She more resembles her mother. Both women are short and plump, and Dawn has inherited her mother's for-midable strength of character. It was this trait that was to see her through the bleakest time in her life. Her former fiancé David Smith recalls the heartache she suffered after Denys died. 'It was certainly a difficult time for Dawn when her father died, but she's a strong character,' he says. As her boyfriend, David was keen to support Dawn as much as he could, but even he could not help. He could comfort her when she cried and he could listen to her when she wanted to talk, but he could not bring him back for her, and he could not really understand what she was going through. No one could. Only someone who has lost a loved one to suicide could ever understand the complex series of emotions that she felt.

Roma French understood, and so did Gary. With her father gone, Dawn turned automatically to them for support. The three who were left behind looked to each other to get by. Already a close family, the trauma of Denys's death served to strengthen further their bond with one another. 'They were a strong family,' says David. 'Her mother is a very strong woman and her elder brother is a fairly strong chap as well.'

When the family finally reappeared it was as though nothing had ever happened. 'When they came back they were just themselves again,' says Sue Rollinson. Denys's death was never mentioned. 'To be honest, I don't think people really knew what had gone on, so nothing was ever said.' Sue and the other people who had known and worked with Denys had no idea what had caused him to take his own life. His wife did not enlighten them. 'We never discovered what had happened,' says Sue. 'Mrs French was not the sort of person you would have dared ask. She is very private. But we weren't aware of any problem. She and Mr French seemed perfect together.'

However, things had not been as perfect as people thought. The truth about her father's death and the distressing events that led up to it have been kept a closely guarded secret by Dawn for more than twenty years. Despite the fact that she has been famous for a long time and has given many hundreds of interviews, she has deliberately chosen to conceal the fact that her father killed himself. In an interview with *Woman's Own*, the interviewer appeared to be under the impression that her father died from a heart attack. She paints an idyllic picture of her upbringing. 'I had a wonderful childhood,' she says. 'My parents were loving and encouraging. It came as a surprise to meet people who didn't have such a great start – I thought every family was like ours.'

Her stories of happy mealtimes spent devouring steaming plates piled high with home-made food belie the complex problems that dominated her family life. Instead of revealing the truth about those traumatic years, she chooses to gloss over them with innocuous anecdotes about her schooldays, giving no hint of the difficulties she suffered.

For the truth was far from rosy. For a while when she was in her mid-teens, her parents were living apart, and Dawn and her brother were sent to lodge with the parents of one of Dawn's school friends, Janet Pearse. For several years during the mid-seventies, Dawn and Gary frequently stayed with Allan and Sheilagh Pearse at their home in Whiteford Road, Saltash, when they were not at boarding school. Roma was still in Plymouth, and Dawn would sometimes go

into her mother's dog-grooming salon after school to see her. But
the children saw less of their father, who at one point was
twenty-five miles away near Launceston, Cornwall.

It was hardly an orthodox arrangement, and goes a long way
towards explaining why Dawn and Gary remained at boarding
school even when their father had left the RAF. During what must
have been an emotionally confusing time for Dawn as she moved
between homes, sometimes living with her mother, at other times
staying with the Pearses, St Dunstan's was to provide her with the
only real stability in her life. The fact that she was apparently able
to cope so well with such inconstancy and upheaval in her family
life is down to the fact that, as a boarder, she learned to stand on
her own two feet from an early age. Boarding school made her
strong and enabled her to adapt to her far from normal upbringing.

'Dawn lived in Whiteford Road for a couple of years,' says a
former neighbour. 'She lived across the road to me from when she
was about fourteen until she was sixteen. She and Gary were living
there without their parents, lodging with the family of Dawn's
friend, Janet. They stayed there because there was some problem
with the parents; if not a marriage break-up, then certainly a
problem. I know Dawn's mother was in Plymouth because she
owned a poodle parlour, but Dawn wasn't living with her. Her
father was living in a village close to Launceston, running a shop.
We never talked about what her parents were doing; as teenagers
we didn't spend much time talking about our parents. When she
was living there she had a Messerschmitt three-wheeler, so she must
have been at least sixteen to drive that. She and Gary lived with the
Pearses for a long time, and I think in the end Mr and Mrs Pearse
became almost like surrogate parents to them.'

Allan Pearse confirms that Dawn and Gary stayed with him and
his then wife Sheilagh. 'Gary stayed with us while he was growing
up, and Dawn has stayed here,' he says. 'Dawn and my daughter
Janet were friends, and Gary and Dawn stayed with us for a while.

Her parents hadn't separated but it was something like that. They used to live out in the country, and it was a long way to come to school.' Over the years Dawn established a close bond with the Pearse family, and Janet and her mother were guests at her wedding to Lenny Henry.

By the time of Denys's death the family was living together again in the modest semi-detached house in Old Ferry Road, Saltash. 'I knew Dawn quite well because I used to give her a lift to school,' says retired Royal Navy Lieutenant Charles Lawrence, who lived opposite. 'My daughter Susan was also a weekly boarder at St Dunstan's Abbey, and I used to take her and Dawn to school on Monday mornings and collect them again on Friday afternoons. Her family came to live here at the end house, and although I knew Dawn's mother very well because she used to play bridge, I never really saw anything of her father. They hadn't been living here long when he committed suicide.'

Mr Lawrence remembers being struck by how well Dawn and her mother appeared to be coping with Denys's death. 'Dawn was here at the time that her father died, and when I saw her afterwards she seemed all right,' he says. 'She was just the same really. Her mother seemed all right too. Her mother was a very attractive woman and had a good social life after her husband died, or at least lots of partners for bridge.'

Being neighbours as well as fellow boarders, Susan Lawrence spent a lot of time with Dawn and remembers her terrible home-sickness when she first started at St Dunstan's. But she says Dawn never let on to her or anyone else about the problems with her father. 'I was aware that there was trouble at home,' says Susan. 'I had heard things; just that things weren't quite right. But I didn't hear it from Dawn. She didn't appear to confide in anybody.' Dawn's self-reliance, inherited from her mother and strengthened by boarding school, helped her through the period when her parents were apart. And she drew on it again in the bleak months following her father's suicide. She had her mother and brother to comfort her, and her fiancé David. She needed no one else.

The truth about the way Denys met his death is something that Dawn has never felt able to speak about publicly. She has, however, spoken movingly of her loss. 'He died when I was nineteen and that was the saddest thing in my life,' she says. 'I was just beginning to know him as a person, not just as a dad. My mum, brother and I all supported each other, but it was so sad. Like anyone that age, it had a major effect on me. I wish he was here to see what I do and witness any great thing that happens to me. I think he would have been proud of me.'

And the words that her father said to her on the day of her first disco helped to sustain her in the dark days following his death. They have remained uppermost in her mind ever since. 'What he said has always stayed with me, because I believe he was right and I still believe he's right,' she says poignantly. 'He gave me an awful lot of confidence.'

Dr Lewis believes that it is almost impossible for a person to recover fully after a loved one has taken their own life. 'You might never come to terms with it,' he says. 'You would probably need professional help to do so; to be able to talk through and resolve some of your feelings. But I think a lot of it is going to remain unresolved. This can result in a whole series of negative feelings: loss of self-esteem, overwhelming guilt, a feeling that you are a wicked person, unworthy of anybody's love or esteem. It leaves lasting scars; scars which become harder and harder to remove and deal with the further away one comes from the event.

'I think it is probably very difficult to get over it fully. In most cases people have a real struggle, particularly if they blame them-selves for what's happened, however rightly or wrongly, or were blamed maybe, perhaps by other relatives or by someone else. Anger at the deceased is often projected on to another person. You might get a scenario where someone says, "You drove him to that, you made him do that with your constant demands". The person is actually projecting their own feelings of guilt on to the first person they see; that's not at all uncommon.'

One person who can perhaps identify with what Dawn went through more than most is the television presenter Juliet Morris. Her youngest brother, Ed, committed suicide when he was in his early twenties. 'The hardest thing about suicide is that question of why – and that it will never, ever be explained to you,' she says. 'If he had been run over by a bus, although it would have been equally painful, at least I would know the reason.'

For Dawn, it was especially hard because her father had been a person she idolised and admired. 'Losing a father is particularly traumatic for a girl because men are supposed to be strong and unbending emotionally,' says Dr Lewis. 'It would be an enormously shattering experience, and would probably make it quite hard to trust people after something like that.'

CHAPTER FIVE

French, Meet Saunders

Within only a few weeks of her father's death, Dawn had to leave Plymouth once again, this time to go to London.

She still had her heart set on becoming a teacher, and was determined to follow her mentor Christine Abbott to the famous Central School of Speech and Drama in north London. She had applied to do a three-year degree course in drama education, and had been fortunate enough to be accepted. But the timing couldn't have been worse.

The college term started in the first week of October, barely three weeks after Denys French's death. It must have been an enormous wrench for Dawn to contemplate leaving her family at such a time, and she may have considered whether she should be going at all. She and her mother and brother had supported each other as much as they could in the hellish weeks that followed her father's suicide, and the thought of being separated from each other for weeks on end was something that they probably found quite daunting.

But she was determined to forge a career for herself as a drama teacher, and she must have known that winning a place at a top school like Central was too good an opportunity to pass up. She was also sensible enough to recognise that she desperately needed something to take her mind off her grief. Life had to go on, and Dawn presumably hoped that if she threw herself into a new challenge it might stop her thinking about her dad all the time. Once again, her loved ones advised her to go, believing that it would be the best thing for her. So, in October 1977, having just turned twenty, Dawn French arrived in London.

Deciding to go ahead with the drama course would prove to be a fortuitous decision for Dawn. For also arriving at Central that term was one Jennifer Saunders. But the two, who would go on to form one of the most successful double acts in British comedy history, could have had no inkling of what fate held for them as they enrolled at the Central School in Hampstead. Dawn arrived several weeks late and it was a while before the two students even became aware of each other's existence. And when they did, it was hardly portentous. In fact, each detested the other on sight. Although they would later be shocked to discover how very much they had in common, at first glance they appeared to be poles apart. Jennifer Saunders had upper-middle-class stamped through her like a stick of rock, and was only at Central because she had nothing better to do. Dawn, on the other hand, had inherited her parents' Protestant work ethic and was achingly keen to fulfil her ambition of becoming a teacher. Where Dawn was enthusiastic, Jennifer was indifferent, and where Dawn was outgoing and friendly, Jennifer appeared coolly aloof.

Recalling the first time she met Dawn, Jennifer Saunders says: 'I think we were both wearing leotards because we were doing a dance class. When I first met her I didn't think, "This is going to be an important person in my life". It was more like, "I hope I don't ever have much to do with her".' Neither could see anything about the other that would indicate that they could be friends. To a down-to-earth West Country girl like Dawn, Jennifer seemed to be

◀ An early photo of the young comedienne.

▼ St Dunstan's Abbey, Plymouth: the boarding school attended by Dawn French.

▼ The house in Old Ferry Road, Saltash, Cornwall, where Dawn's family lived.

◀ ▾ Dawn French and
Jennifer Saunders at the
Comedy Store in 1983.

▶ Young love:
Dawn and Lenny
soon after they
first met.

◀ Dawn and
Lenny's wedding
day, 20 October
1984.

▲ Out on the town
with husband Lenny,
co-star Jennifer
Saunders and her
husband Adrian
Edmondson.

◀ 'Now look here,
I'm the funny one!'

▲ Dawn French *au naturel...*

▲ ...And dolled up to the nines for a *French and Saunders* sketch.

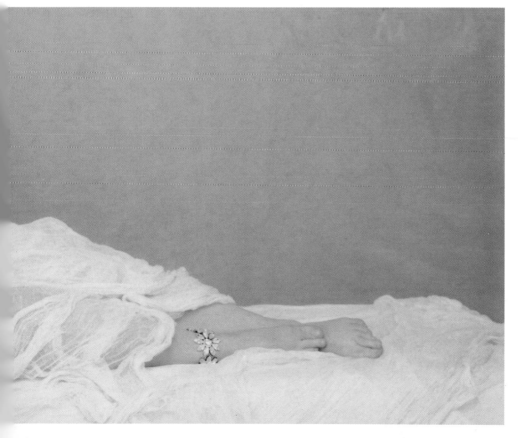

▲ Making a point.

a snobby Sloane Ranger, and in turn Jennifer found Dawn's recently acquired Americanisms quite revolting. 'When we first met we disliked each other intensely,' admits Dawn. 'I was horribly loud-mouthed and she was sort of snooty.' The feeling was mutual. 'I remember not particularly liking Dawn,' recalls Jennifer. 'I was such a snob then. She'd come straight from a year in America and she said cookie instead of biscuit. I thought that was just about the end. She wore a baseball cap at a jaunty angle and she wanted to be a teacher, which was the thing I couldn't come to terms with. She actually *wanted* to be a teacher!'

As first impressions go, they were not exactly promising. But despite their apparent differences, their lives had run along strangely parallel paths. Both had fathers who were in the RAF, both had moved around a lot and been to boarding school, and, somewhat spookily, they had even shared the same best friend. Another similarity they shared was that they both arrived at drama school after taking a year off. While Dawn had been studying in America, Jennifer had been working as an au pair in Italy. But whereas Dawn's background was solidly working-class, Jennifer's was far more privileged. The daughter of an RAF Group Captain, she had had a genteel upbringing. Home was a large house in one of the most affluent parts of the North-West, and her social life revolved around the Cheshire pony-club set.

Although nine months younger than Dawn, Jennifer Saunders had the confidence and self-assurance that comes so easily to girls of her class. To the less sophisticated Dawn, she appeared distant and rather daunting. As she observed Jennifer with a mixture of fascination and apprehension, Dawn felt rather as she had when she first arrived at St Dunstan's Abbey. Once again she found herself to be among people who were from more affluent backgrounds than her, and the realisation that Jennifer was a class apart made her uncomfortable. Jennifer, she realised, was a girl who undoubtedly had a washbasin in her bedroom. 'My first impression of Jennifer wasn't incorrect, but it was only a very small part of what she is,' Dawn explains. 'She was a different class to me. I saw that immediately, and it frightened me. I never thought I would be comfortable with people like her. Jennifer was in with a sort of Chelsea crowd and seemed very confident and loud, and I was frightened of that, although I was just as loud, actually. But now that I know her, I know it was all bravado.'

But it would take Dawn a long time to realise this about her friend. Nor was she the first person to mistake Saunders's shyness for arrogance. It is something that has led to an often uneasy relationship between Saunders and the press. 'If Dawn's image sells largesse, then hers gives out hauteur, and this can lend her an alarming resemblance to Princess Anne in one of her less mirthful moods,' a *Times* journalist once wrote of Jennifer.

The fact that both their fathers had been in the air force did not mean that they had the same kind of upbringing. 'Both our dads were in the RAF, but hers was a pilot,' Dawn points out. 'My dad wasn't an officer, and when you're in the RAF that rank thing matters. Officers live in a different part of the camp, they have detached houses, they have staff, they even have basins in the bedrooms. Jennifer was actually posher than she is now. She was the result of a lot of gymkhanas; she comes from that sort of set up in Cheshire. At college she wore a lot of scarves and had friends with cars. She lived in Chelsea, for God's sake.'

While Dawn had her sights firmly set on a career in teaching, Jennifer had no idea what she wanted to do and had landed up at Central by default. She had been turned down by a number of universities and, with no particular ambitions, was just drifting along. As a last resort, her despairing mother had got the application forms from Central and laid them out on the kitchen table for her when she came back from Italy. As it meant going to the capital, she decided to give it a go. 'I was at Central just as an excuse to be in London,' Jennifer admits. 'It was just something that happened to be vacant at the time. I thought, "I'll go to London, that's good".'

When she first met Dawn, Jennifer had no idea what an important part she would come to have in her life. She recalls her as 'a stout, bossy person, horribly keen on being a drama teacher'. 'She was incredibly bossy, and she wore the most horrible fawn corduroy skirt,' Jennifer says. 'I think she was the only person on the course who wanted to be a teacher. She was about forty-five years old when she arrived and was already a committed teacher. Something had convinced her that it was the profession she was destined for. After all, she had all the right qualities. There was her friendly, easygoing nature with the merest hint of bossiness; she had the kind of, "Hey, we can be friends, but remember I'm the teacher" way with kids, as well as that winning smile for headmistresses and parents; and, of course, there was the fawn corduroy skirt.'

Saunders also remembers ribbing Dawn, who was still full of her trip to the States, about her phoney American accent. 'My first memory of Dawn was, "Hiya, Yankee, cookie jar", she jokes. 'Dawn arrived at college wearing a baseball cap and a UCLA sweatshirt and said, in an American accent, "I just can't get a cookie jar in this country" '. Dawn denies this, of course, but admits that in essence it was true. 'I'd picked up all these horrible Americanisms,' she says. 'But I stopped them when snotty people like Jennifer made fun of me.'

Surprisingly, given the bond that the two would later come to share, Dawn and Jennifer had very little to do with each other for the first couple of years they were at Central. They had very different agendas, and seemed destined to be ships that pass in the night. While Jennifer drifted along with no particular aim, Dawn worked hard at her studies and spent much of her free time back home in Plymouth. Roma had stayed on at the house in Old Ferry Road after Denys died, and Dawn would head back there whenever her studies allowed. As she grappled to come to terms with her father's death, the manner in which he died preyed heavily on her mind. But, while for many people who had suffered what

Dawn had the mere mention of the word suicide would have been more than they could bear, she developed a macabre fascination with the subject.

She became captivated by stories of suicide and read avidly the work of the American poet, Sylvia Plath, who killed herself at the age of thirty. On her death in 1963, Plath, the wife of former Poet Laureate Ted Hughes, became a feminist icon. Like Dawn's father, she had attempted to take her own life once before, and words such as 'Dying / Is an art, like everything else / I do it exceptionally well', which she wrote in her most famous poem, *Lady Lazarus*, struck a chord with Dawn. She read Plath's work compulsively and developed a strange passion for plays about suicide.

The other reason she made such frequent trips home was that David was based in Plymouth. Their love had grown stronger during the three years they had been together, and Dawn was certain that he would be the man whom she would marry. He had helped her cope with the tragedy of her father's death and, with Denys gone, Dawn needed a man in her life more than ever. Most weekends Dawn would either visit him in Plymouth or he would go up to London to see her. In London, David introduced Dawn to a whole new world of different experiences. Being in the Navy, he had travelled a great deal and sampled many different foods and cuisines. He was keen to share his experiences with Dawn. The product of parents who religiously stuck to egg and chips when they had travelled abroad, Dawn knew virtually nothing about foreign food. David, on the other hand, had a keen interest in other countries and their different lifestyles, and set about educating Dawn. She was a willing pupil, and it was with him that she first discovered the pleasures of Indian food. It is a cuisine for which she retains much affection today. 'There was no experience quite like it,' she says fondly. 'Especially at The Standard where they make a butter chicken you would die for.'

Dawn looked forward to David's visits to London and missed him

dreadfully when his job took him away from her. She was overjoyed, therefore, when he told her that he had decided to leave the
Navy. The prospect of no more lengthy trips away was a pleasant
one, but her joy was to be short-lived. He wanted to go into the tea
business as a specialist taster, he explained, and this would inevitably involve long trips abroad to places as far away as India and the
Far East. After her initial disappointment, Dawn was pragmatic.
They had become used to separations throughout their relationship, and could do so again. They had survived David's numerous
stints away with the Navy, and even Dawn's year in America. There
was no reason why anything should change. She was busy with her
studies at Central, in any case, and they would see each other as
often as they could. She was confident of his feelings for her, and
believed that absence would only make the heart grow fonder.
They were both in the relationship for the long haul, and had the
rest of their lives to be together.

So David left the Navy and became a tea taster for Liptons. In
1978, the company sent him to Calcutta on a secondment. Left
behind in London, Dawn consoled herself with the thought that if
he was still in India by the time term ended, she might be able to
visit him there. It was something to look forward to, and helped her
to cope with her sadness at missing him. With her fiancé away, she
threw herself wholeheartedly into her studies. It was something she
took extremely seriously. Although ironically she was to end up as
an actress, and Central is one of the most famous breeding grounds
for young actors, this did not interest Dawn in the slightest. She has
been at great pains to point out that just because she went to drama
school it doesn't mean she was at all 'actressy'. 'We didn't do
hugging and stuff,' she says. 'I was training to be a teacher, which
means you don't learn about putting on plays but about problem-
solving and using children's imaginations.'

In fact she somewhat looked down her nose at the acting
students. 'All these people who had been the biggest show-offs at

school now showed off in front of other show-offs,' she says dismissively. 'There used to be this end-of-year show for special showing off – a bit of poetry or performance art with an interesting piece of Sellotape . . . one of the most pretentious things I've ever seen.' She and Jennifer would later take great pleasure in sending up the earnestness of the drama students at the end-of-term revue, but it wasn't until they were in their final year at Central that they became friends. They ended up sharing a flat in Chalk Farm, north London, with five other girls; a time that would subsequently prove to be the inspiration for their first television show, *Girls On Top*.

'We were both looking for somewhere to live, and a mutual friend had a flat to share but she needed seven people – so we signed up, but not together,' says Dawn. 'Jennifer very quickly became in charge of the flat – and I was her right-hand person who gave all the orders to everybody else.' Having been such a zealous prefect at St Dunstan's Abbey, Dawn was perfectly placed to be Jennifer Saunders's henchman. Naturally bossy, she ensured that whatever Jennifer said, went. 'We had a lot of systems and rotas,' she admits. 'But Jen was more into them than me. I was quite lazy. In those days she was queen of the dirty-knickers department. She used to be very untidy. One day we were burgled and the police came round to check on the damage. The burglars had ransacked the whole house, and when the police went into Jen's room they said, "This is the worst damage we've seen". And that was the only room the burglars hadn't been in!

As they swapped information about their lives thus far, Dawn and Jennifer were amazed by how similar they were. From initially assuming that they would have nothing in common, they ended up realising that in fact they shared an awful lot. 'Jennifer and I have had very similar experiences,' says Dawn. 'She had the same experience of living on RAF camps and moving around a lot. We both love chocolate and Italy, and by coincidence we even had the same best friend. When I was eleven my best friend was a girl called

Camilla Leng, who was an army daughter and very good fun. She left and I was heartbroken. But Jennifer and I discovered that she went to another camp and then was Jennifer's best friend.'

Having virtually ignored each other for two years, the pair quickly became firm friends. 'Once we'd discovered what we were really like, it was great,' says Dawn. 'We're such opposites, that's our secret – and our strength. Jennifer's much more reserved than I am. She thinks before she speaks, and I don't. My gob really gets me into trouble sometimes.' As she became closer to Jennifer, Dawn re-evaluated her initial opinion of her. 'When I got to know her I realised that it wasn't snootiness but nerves,' she says. In time Dawn became used to the difference in their backgrounds, but Jennifer maintains it was something she had never noticed in the first place. 'I wasn't aware of the class difference at all,' she says. 'It just didn't enter my head.'

The one thing that didn't change, however, was Jennifer's incredulity that Dawn actually wanted to be a teacher. Dawn, for her part, was equally shocked that Jennifer had no intention of ever becoming one. 'I loved it, Jennifer hated it,' she says of their time at Central. 'I was dedicated to becoming a teacher and Jennifer certainly wasn't – she didn't know why she was there. She'd got into college by mistake. She had no intention of working with children, and was a bit horrified when she found out that's what it entailed. She thought that going to drama school meant that you got free tickets for the theatre. I was the only person there who seriously wanted to be a teacher.' Saunders admits this to be true. 'I actually had to pretend that I'd seen plays, whereas all I'd ever seen was *Charlie's Aunt* in Worthing when I was about seven,' she says sheepishly.

As well as a lifetime of similar experiences, French and Saunders also realised that they shared a sense of humour. 'It was the situation where you say something and the other person doesn't just laugh, they say something back that makes *you* laugh,' explains Jennifer.

'That's what Dawn does, she hits the right nerve, which energises you in some way. And that's when we found we were a double act.' Together they would make up routines to amuse their household, and their fellow flatmates were the first people to hear French and Saunders in full swing. 'We used to make up characters and do little scenes on our own, late at night,' says Dawn. 'Like most women who are good friends, we had our own little jokes and invented little characters of our own. Lots of girls do that sort of thing. It's not peculiar to people who turn out to be awfully talented ac-tors (sic). We never wrote anything down for a long time, we used to improvise stuff and just remember the best bits.'

The late seventies, when Dawn and Jennifer were at drama school, saw the height of the punk movement and at student parties they would dance to bands like The Sex Pistols and The Clash and go in for the full punk look. 'We were outrageous and dressed up as punks, wearing chamber pots and plastic macs,' says Dawn. 'At one party we called ourselves The Menopause Sisters and sang about the host's gerbil!' Jennifer also recalls their wild get-up. 'We used to dress in long macs with tampons hanging on our ears and safety pins stuck in various places. It was a perfect time to have no money. You could go to the Swiss Cottage market, pick up great clothes and just wear them.' But looking through some photographs of herself taken at that time Dawn was later to admit, 'I was the most hideous-looking student. Although I thought at the time that I was the most stylish and bohemian.'

When they first started writing sketches for each other, neither dreamed in a million years that it would lead to a proper career. 'It was never for anything,' Jennifer stresses. 'We started doing it as a joke in the flat, then we did it at the end-of-term cabaret.' As they approached the end of their time at Central, Jennifer still had no idea what she planned to do, other than acknowledging that she would quite like to stay in London. Dawn, on the other hand, looked forward enthusiastically to beginning her career as a teacher.

She too wanted to remain in London, and wrote off to several schools in the city. She was offered a job teaching drama at an all-girls school in Highgate, north London, and couldn't wait to take up her new position.

But in the meantime she had something very special to look forward to. David had left India, and by the end of 1979 was working in Sri Lanka. He was enjoying his new career in the tea business, and was keen for Dawn to visit him and see for herself how beautiful the country was. It had been a long-standing plan that Dawn would fly out there to visit him as soon as she could afford the time off college, and at last she had booked her flight. She had excitedly told Jennifer all about her relationship with David, and confided that they were about to be married. She and David had not yet set a date for the wedding, but it had always been the plan that they would marry as soon as she finished college. That time was now only a few months away, and she spent a lot of time thinking about the wonderful day when she would become Mrs David Smith. She wondered whether they would settle in Sri Lanka as David seemed to like it there so much, or whether he would come back to live in Britain. She was looking forward to seeing her fiancé, and pictured the two of them sitting in the sun and making plans for their wedding.

Dawn impatiently ticked off the days until she could leave, and when the day finally arrived she could barely contain her excitement. She hadn't seen David for months, and realised with a thrill of pleasure that in a few hours' time she would be with him. Even the thought of the gruelling eleven-hour flight couldn't dampen her enthusiasm. Settling back in her aeroplane seat, she told herself that when the plane touched down she would see David.

It would be a trip to remember, but not for the reason Dawn had hoped. For while Dawn had spent virtually every waking moment thinking about David, he had been thinking of another. And whereas she was anxiously looking forward to arriving in Sri Lanka,

David was anxious for an altogether different reason. David had fallen in love with someone else, and Dawn was flying halfway around the world to find out that it was all over between them. Their reunion in Colombo would not be full of kisses and hugs as she had imagined, but full of heartbreak and tears. And instead of spending a romantic sunshine holiday with the man she loved, she would fly home broken-hearted.

Dawn had no idea of the kind of emotional minefield she was stumbling into by going to Sri Lanka. David had fallen in love with an English girl called Jane who was also in the tea business, and the two were having a relationship behind his trusting fiancée's back. During his time in Sri Lanka he had realised that his future lay not with Dawn, his girlfriend of five years, but with his new love. But he had no idea how he was going to break the news to Dawn. He had given her no hint in his letters that anything was wrong between them, and was at a loss to work out how he could tell her it was over between them. In truth, he was dreading her visit. He had promised Jane that he would end it with Dawn, but he baulked at having to confess what had been going on. It was a mess, and Dawn stepped right into the middle of it.

'I was there when he dumped her and it was awful,' says one of David's close friends. 'It was a terrible way for an affair to end. Dawn didn't exactly walk in on David and Jane in bed, but it was almost as bad and it was quite painful for her. David had talked about Dawn, as bachelors do, and it was clear that it was a serious relationship and they were to be married. But then he went abroad and met up with somebody else, and that was it. He went down to Colombo for Liptons, and met Jane.'

Dawn was completely devastated when she discovered what had been going on. In the space of a few short minutes her dreams were smashed to smithereens. She had trusted David implicitly, and truly believed they would spend the rest of their lives together. They had shared so much. When her father died, David had seen the grief and unhappiness that no one else had been allowed to see. He was the love of her life, but now he had broken her heart. She was all at sea as she realised that the life she had mapped out for herself was now never to be.

Making one's fiancée travel thousands of miles only to ditch them is not exactly chivalrous behaviour, and it is not a chapter of his life that David Smith feels proud of. 'It wasn't an ideal circumstance,' he admits. 'But on the other hand I think it was better addressed face to face rather than over the telephone. Obviously I regretted any pain I'd caused her, certainly, but on the other hand it was something that had to be done.' Looking back on their relationship now, more than two decades after they split up, David believes that it was probably doomed from the moment he left England. 'We didn't set a date for the wedding, but it was something that obviously would have happened at some point when she'd finished college or whatever,' he says. 'But I guess we just went our separate ways because I had a career which was taking me overseas and Dawn had gone off to the Central School of Speech and Drama. And clearly our existences weren't going to be altogether compatible. It was possibly going to end anyway, although I suppose the sequence of events may have precipitated it all.'

David never returned to live in the UK. He subsequently married Jane and now lives with her and their children in Mombasa, where he is the sales and marketing manager for Brooke Bond, Kenya.

Dawn has never spoken about her relationship with David. The only thing she has ever let slip was when she told Clement Freud in an interview for the *Radio Times* that she had once had an affair with an Irish tea taster. When the relationship ended six weeks before the end of her drama course, she admitted she 'went a bit crazy'.

CHAPTER SIX

Gong!

Dawn returned to England with a broken heart and a badly bruised ego. Her friends were desperate to know how the trip had gone and when the big day was going to be. Instead she was forced to admit that there would be no wedding and that she and David were no longer an item. The realisation that he would no longer be a part of her life left an aching void. She was utterly distraught by the break-up, and could not believe that the man she loved could have betrayed her so badly. The plans they had made together lay in pieces, and she was completely bereft. The news had come totally out of the blue, and David's infidelity had hurt her deeply.

But once the initial shock of what had happened started to wear off, anger began to take over. David Smith admits that Dawn was so hurt and angry by his betrayal of her that she never forgave him. 'We are not in touch,' he says. 'I haven't spoken to Dawn in more than twenty years. We met up about six or eight months later and basically agreed that it was probably best if we just went our separate ways. It wasn't going to be easy for us to remain friends. It would always be a problem, particularly as we'd had such a close relationship. I never heard from her again.' Dawn had devoted five years of her life to David, and, like many people arriving at the end of a long-term relationship, she decided to make up for lost time. Having been discarded for another woman, she was keen to prove to herself that she was still attractive and desirable. David might not want her, but there were plenty of men out there who would. On the rebound, and with something to prove, she launched herself into the singles lifestyle with a vengeance. Before long she had a whole string of boyfriends, including a saxophonist. Jennifer Saunders remembers how popular her flatmate was with men at that time. 'Dawn always had more boyfriends than I did,' she admits. Dawn also claims that she had an enormous crush on Rowan Atkinson, who lived near their flat. 'Jennifer bet me sixty quid I wouldn't ask him for a date – but I couldn't go through with it,' she laughs.

On graduating from Central, Dawn excitedly took up her teaching post at the Parliament Hill School for Girls, in Highgate. The day she arrived at the school was an important one for Dawn. She had dreamed of becoming a teacher ever since she was a thirteen-year-old girl in Miss Abbott's class at St Dunstan's Abbey, and now the dream had become a reality. She had no idea that teaching was not in fact where her future lay, and she threw herself into her new job. She was determined to be like her former drama teacher and inspire the girls by giving them unusual material to work with. But having experienced a strict education at first hand, she was keen for her pupils to enjoy themselves and not be intimidated by her.

'Miss French' breezed into Parliament Hill School like a breath of fresh air, and was an immediate hit with the girls there. 'Everyone looked forward to her lessons,' recalls former pupil Karen Hockney. 'She was a bit unconventional because she didn't fit the mould of the stereotypical teacher. It was a very good school at the time, and there were a lot of grammar-school teachers who had been there for twenty or thirty years, so it was quite traditional. The headmistress was very old-fashioned and there were a lot of very prim teachers who were year heads. Dawn was very relaxed, a little bit of a fish out of water in that a lot of the teachers there were old school – strict, and into keeping their distance from pupils. She definitely wasn't like that; she was very approachable. We called her Miss French but we all knew her first name, and you didn't generally know the first names of the teachers. I don't know what the other teachers thought of her, but all the pupils thought she was quite right-on and fun.'

Not only did Dawn not behave like the other teachers at Parliament Hill School in 1980, she didn't look like them either. 'She used to wear quite colourful clothes,' Karen recalls. 'I remember her being quite sort of Camden market-ish: lots of trainers and things. She was the same sort of size that she is now; she didn't look that different, only younger. She was quite generously propor-tioned, but I think the girls had too much respect for her to tease her, because she was fun and people liked her for the fact that she was a bit different.'

But Dawn's relaxed approach to the teacher–pupil relationship didn't go down very well among her peers. 'I wasn't a typical teacher,' she admits. 'I didn't like them calling me "Miss" so I told them to call me Dawn, which got me into trouble. I wasn't being anarchic, I just wanted the whole experience to be a bit more friendly. You have to earn their respect, otherwise they'll just tell you to fuck off. That was something you'd never have said to the teachers at my school because they went in for teaching by inflicting shame on you rather than by truly trying to earn your respect.'

Within a few weeks of her arrival, word had got around that the new teacher's class was the best one going. 'Girls who had other drama teachers were always insanely jealous of people who had Miss French because she was known to be a really good laugh,' says Karen. 'There was a lot of improvisation in her class and it was the most fun class. It wasn't your usual "Read a passage from Shake-speare". Her lessons were really off the wall and unpredictable, and everyone used to look forward to them. Even if you weren't into drama – and I never was – you still looked forward to her lessons because you'd wonder what she'd have you doing next. She used to get people doing all sorts of odd things.

'We were a group of self-conscious fourteen-year-old girls and Dawn would say things like, "I want you to pretend you are walking into a chemist to ask for a packet of Tampax". Everyone would start blushing and giggling but it was almost like, "You've got to do this". That was her way of teaching us how to be dramatic, I suppose. My sister-in-law Lisa was in the same class as me at school, and she remembers having to pretend to be a dead body and being dragged around the drama studio by the other students. Dawn had a bit of an offbeat sense of humour even then.'

She even made the first-year pupils worship her for a joke. 'I told them there was a tradition to kneel and say, "We beg you for a lesson",' Dawn laughs. But it wasn't all fun and games. The school prefect in her was never far from the surface, and the girls soon discovered how far they could push her. 'I was destined to be a bossy teacher,' says Dawn. 'You have to be bossy to teach, but I had no problem with that. They were tough girls, certainly tougher than me, but I liked them.' Karen Hockney agrees that Dawn was no pushover. 'I don't think she was above telling people off if they mucked around,' she says. 'But she just struck the right note with people. She was very easy to talk to and relate to in a very relaxed teacher–pupil way. You can only be so relaxed when you've got rules to stick to, but when I think of all the other teachers we had, she stands out as the one who was the most fun to be around. She would talk to you like a human being, not like a teacher would usually talk to a pupil. She wasn't patronising – it was much more of an equal thing with her. She struck me as the sort of person you could go to with a problem.'

While Dawn spent her days teaching in Highgate, Jennifer took to her bed in Chelsea. She did half-heartedly try her hand at teaching, working at a convent in Wimbledon and a secondary school in Fulham, but she left after only twelve weeks. 'I couldn't cut it,' she admits. 'It was hell. I was popular but no good.' Instead of working, she spent her time 'hanging out' with a friend in a run-down house in Chelsea. 'It's such a vague time of my life,' she says. 'We just used to scrounge about, living on mattresses on a horrid floor, doing the crossword and occasionally getting up to collect the dole.' Her friend's laziness, and how little it appeared to trouble her, was something that Dawn found extraordinary. 'I could never understand how Jennifer could afford to have champagne, and when we left college she didn't work,' she says incredulously.

'I thought if I didn't work I couldn't live, whereas Jen just used to cash her dole cheque and buy champagne, and spend all day in bed doing the crossword. Great *style*, you know. She was never worried, but I think that's an innate thing about people who come from a moneyed background; they never worry about where the money's coming from. I, meanwhile, have a great fear of not having work; it's the Protestant working-class ethic. I think when we say we want different things, it comes out of that background. Lenny and I live in a big house and we've got a swimming pool and stuff, but it's all new to us. It's not what we grew up with. We sort of believe that someone will take it away at any moment, which is why we are always working. But Jennifer grew up in a house like that. Absolutely expected to live in one and own a couple of them. Doesn't have any guilt about it.'

However, Jennifer insists that her time at Central wasn't completely wasted. 'They did teach me something because you have to stand up in front of people, and you have to speak a poem, which was completely hideous as far as I was concerned – so it gave me a little bit of confidence,' she says. This would stand her in good stead when she and Dawn made their first faltering steps on to the

London comedy circuit. And despite her apparent torpor, it would be Jennifer who would initiate this change in their lives. Lounging around one afternoon with her umpteenth cup of coffee by her side, Jennifer's eye was caught by an advert in *The Stage* magazine, calling for young comedians to try out for a new comedy club. 'I thought, "I'll get Dawn, we're a double act",' says Jennifer. 'So we auditioned and got in.'

The new club was the now legendary Comedy Store in Soho. It was the brainchild of two men: comic impresario Don Ward and Peter Rosengard, who – rather bizarrely – was a life assurance salesman. 'It came about on the back of an idea that I had when I went to America in 1978,' Don Ward explains. 'I went to the Comedy Store in Los Angeles where they had this kind of sausage factory of comics with no host and a voice-off. There was a whole series of comics coming on doing five or ten minutes. Some were doing political stuff, some were doing observational stuff, some were gay, some were black, Jewish, and what have you. There was a wonderful mix of young guys and gals trying out. They were only doing short sets, and it was quite amusing really. Television people went there for their autumn castings to see who was going to be good for sitcoms and I thought, "Christ, if it can work here, how about back home in London town".'

Ward had a great deal of experience in the comedy world. He had been in stand-up for ten years and had worked with Cliff Richard, Marty Wilde, Billy Fury and Russ Conway as the compère linkman on their roadshows. In 1972, he bought The Gargoyle Club in Dean Street, Soho, where he put on people like Larry Grayson and Kenny Goodwin. Not long after his return from America, he fortuitously met up with Peter Rosengard, who by coincidence had also been to the Comedy Store in LA and had thoughts of starting a similar thing in London. 'We met at a garden party and got talking,' says Don. 'We banged ideas at each other, and that's basically how it started.'

Ward told Rosengard that they could use his club on Saturday nights because its members only used it midweek. 'It was perfect,' says Rosengard. 'We shook hands on the spot. I would find the comedians and promote and put on the shows, and Don would supply the premises, drinks and staff.' Rosengard fell in love with The Gargoyle Club. It had opened as The Blue Room in 1926 and was one of London's oldest nightclubs. 'There was a mural by Matisse, who had also designed the beautiful staircase which led down into the club,' he says. 'The room itself was L-shaped and intimate, with a stage at one end and two raised tiers with tables and little gilt chairs around a tiny dance floor. Walking into it for the first time was like stepping back into the thirties, slightly faded but unchanged.'

Unlike most nightclubs, which are usually in basements, The Gargoyle was three floors up and could only be entered by taking a tiny lift into which two people could be wedged face to face. And there lay a potential problem: to get to the Comedy Store you had to take the lift to the fourth floor, which housed the Nell Gwyn strip club, and walk through their topless-waitress bar to The Gargoyle. 'As a self-proclaimed promoter of non-sexist comedy, I was to have a bit of trouble explaining away the topless barmaids to some of the aspiring comedians when they started coming to audition,' Rosengard explained in *Didn't You Kill My Mother-in-Law?*, his book about alternative comedy. 'I said, "They definitely won't be there when we open. They are nothing to do with me, really, they belong to the strip club, and it's closed when we're open".'

'After several heated discussions, during which I attempted to point out to Don Ward that the tits in question could seriously get in the way of any credibility we might stand a chance of having as pioneers of a new kind of comedy, he finally agreed that the contentious boobs could disappear into the new Comedy Store T-shirts I'd had made up, but only after midnight, when we opened. A lot of people thought I was crazy to open there. "Who wants to go to Soho at midnight on a Saturday to a sleazy strip joint to watch a bunch of amateur comics?" they'd say. In 1979 Soho wasn't the hip area it became five years later. When the Comedy Store opened, it was still full of porno cinema clubs, rip-off bars and girlie-magazine shops.'

As well as *The Stage*, where Jennifer Saunders would see it, adverts were placed in publications such as the *Grocer's Gazette*, the *Jewish Chronicle* and the *Irish Times*. Ward explains: 'They said things like, "Are you a very funny man or a funny woman, the next greatest comedy star waiting to happen but you're doing the wrong job selling life insurance or writing books or selling broken biscuits in Woolworths? Well, don't miss your opportunity to become a star, bring yourself and your talent to us and we will invite the heads of media and let's see if we can make you a star". That was how we set the Comedy Store up. We expected twenty to thirty answers but we got a hundred and fifty. We couldn't audition them all, so we did them in batches of twenty each Saturday night until we'd waded through them. Then we started to put them together into a show. It was very hit and miss.'

The Comedy Store opened its doors for the first time on 19 May 1979. Alexei Sayle, a little-known Liverpudlian comedian with an off-the-wall sense of humour, was hired to be the club's compère. He was their first successful signing, handling rowdy audiences and egotistical comics with equal contempt. One of the major problems they had was persuading the really bad acts to leave the stage. 'The more experienced acts understood the system and would do about five or seven minutes and come off,' explains Don Ward. 'But the rookies, who were only down to do four to five minutes, would get star-struck and we had trouble getting them off. We'd try putting the lights and sound off but when we put them back on they'd still be standing there, rabbiting on. Alexei and I used to spend quite a lot of time working out how we could get these acts off. I said, "We could always get a shepherd's crook", and we had lots of laughs about that because at times we'd have liked to break their necks!

'Then I remembered that bit at the beginning of Rank films when the weight-lifter guy hits the gong, and I said to Alexei, "We'll use that. Everyone must obey you and the gong. When you hit the gong, their time's up and they must come off". That worked quite well until one day the audience woke up to the fact that they could control the gong. A comedian would say, "Good evening, I was walking down the street . . ." and somebody would shout "Gong!" and then they would all join in. Strangely enough, a female voice would invariably lead the shout for the gong and everybody else rushed in pretty quickly: 'Gong, gong, gong, gong!' Even the really good acts started to get the gong because people thought it was smart to shout it out. Instead of having inane heckling they would just shout "Gong!" So eventually we had to get rid of it.'

Ninety-nine per cent of the people appearing at the Comedy Store were unknowns. 'To begin with, nobody got paid except Alexei who got fifteen quid,' says Don Ward. 'Later we started to pay the regulars.' Peter Rosengard tried to get well-known comedians to come to try out their new material but was met with an unenthusiastic response. 'Jasper Carrott and Billy Connolly never came down,' he says. 'Rowan Atkinson promised to, but got lost and went into a massage parlour by accident, asked if it was the Comedy Store, got punched in the stomach, was sick and went home. Les Dawson was an exception. He performed a couple of times and was very well received, even though his act was very different from the type of comedy the young audience was expecting. But he was a very funny man. Lenny Bennett came once, was heckled and sneered, "Listen, luv, when I drive home in my Rolls-Royce, you'll be standing in the rain waiting for the bus". Alexei gonged him off.'

Before long the club was packed out every weekend, a phenomenon due almost entirely to the power of word of mouth as people started talking about 'the place with the gong'. The audience was young, early twenties to early thirties, and from all walks of life. Everybody had to queue, even celebrities who thought they should just walk in. 'There was always an electric atmosphere in the club before the midnight show,' says Rosengard. 'People were crammed in everywhere, almost hanging from the ceiling. The first tables were set up only six inches from the front of the stage. The audience never knew who was going to show up to perform, and I was never sure either. One night Robin Williams walked in and did an hour of incredible comedy. I felt that we were doing for comedy what The Sex Pistols had done for rock 'n' roll.'

Early in 1980 two new double acts joined the Comedy Store: Twentieth Century Coyote, comprising Adrian Edmondson and Rik Mayall, and The Outer Limits, made up of Peter Richardson and Nigel Planer. They were followed soon afterwards by French and Saunders, the club's first female double act. Having launched themselves as an act, Dawn and Jennifer had to give themselves a name. French and Saunders may not be the most wittily inventive name in the history of comedy, but it is a huge improvement on what they initially chose. 'We were going to call ourselves Kitsch 'n' Tiles because the Comedy Store advert was next to one for kitchen tiles,' explains Dawn sheepishly. 'That's how funny we were. Alexei Sayle said it was stupid and introduced us as French and Saunders. But even that, he said, sounded like mustard.'

Their act comprised characters in conversation: mother and daughter, lecturer and student, two psychologists discussing sex, Country and Western singers and teenage girls at a disco. Much of it was about girls' adolescence, a theme they were particularly fond of, 'probably because it's what we remember', admits Dawn. Comedy Store regular Arnold Brown was there the evening they auditioned. 'I thought they were very original and it was refreshing to see a female duo,' he recalls. 'They didn't appear at all nervous, they were up front and confident. The thing I noticed about Dawn particularly was her likeability. For comedians to register with the audience there's got to be a warmth, and Dawn can say something quite sarcastic and sardonic but because she's so likeable it is acceptable. She never gets into the kind of Jo Brand vitriol.

'I don't think Jennifer really regarded herself as a comedienne; she thought of herself as an actress, whereas Dawn had a wonderful comedic spirit and theatricality about her. She's like a clown, and that contrasted wonderfully with Jennifer's slightly laid-back, serene aloofness. It was the perfect double act. Their comedy was very accessible; sociological rather than political, which was a good strength because the Comedy Store was full of people like Alexei and myself.'

Material was hastily cobbled together and was often dismally unfunny. Jennifer remembers it as a time of 'such blind, blind panic'. 'We decided to have a go and just used to make anything up; silly stuff that made us laugh,' she says. 'We sometimes outnumbered the audience. I used to look through the crack in the door, praying nobody would be there.' They shared a dressing room next to Rik Mayall and Adrian Edmondson. 'Theirs stank,' says Dawn. 'They'd sweat and sweat and never wash their costumes. Rather than use the sink to wash their armpits, they filled it up with ice and lager.'

Both Dawn and Jennifer say that they weren't much good in those early days. 'We didn't know anything about it really,' explains Jennifer. 'We thought you had to change your costumes and your material every night, so by Saturday it got pretty bad. The boys would never tell us what to do but just by looking at them, we picked up an idea of what we might be aiming towards.' Dawn agrees that that was where they went wrong: 'It was ages before we found out that you didn't have to do a new show every night. Every evening we would write one and then go on with a new and truly terrible sketch. It took us a long time to realise that the boys were doing the same act every night, because of course it's the audience that changes.'

Some of their creations were more successful than others. Dawn's particular favourites were the two uptight New York women who were afraid of everything – coffee, cancer, sex. 'They saw us through a year of material,' she says. 'Another time we did a sketch where we impersonated Thunderbirds puppets. It's an old joke, but we could never get it right. We came on and Jennifer was looking at me as if to say, "Why are we doing this?" It was very, very bad.' On their worst nights they would be gonged off by an impatient audience and would drown their sorrows in wine. 'If it was awful, we had each other and we'd buy a bottle of Blue Nun and go home,' recalls Jennifer.

Comedian Andy de la Tour remembers it differently. 'It's a good line,' he says. 'But it's just not true. They were one of the few that started off funny and got funnier.' Fellow comedian Malcolm Hardee backs this up. 'Getting gonged off could happen to anyone if the audience was really drunk,' he says. 'But because French and Saunders's material was quite strong they didn't get a lot of heckling. Their stuff was more theatrical, and if you go to see a play you don't heckle, do you? The audience was quite well behaved with them, but they weren't with everyone. It was a rough audience.'

Dawn found the Comedy Store a bizarre and strange other world. 'I'd never heard of anything like this,' she recalls. 'I thought these people were a slightly smelly group of boys – there was no idea then of how fashionable it would become. Once we did an entire twenty-minute set in three and a half minutes because it was so full of horrible men. They'd fallen out of the strip clubs and they couldn't understand why we were on stage and still had our clothes on. We did another night there to the Thames Valley River Police who were out on a stag night and they were shouting, "Get 'em off, show us your tits".' Jennifer recalls that Dawn stood up to them rather well by shouting, 'Why don't you show us your knob, sir?' Arnold Brown sympathised. 'Most of the comedy at the

Comedy Store was male-centred, and when French and Saunders first came along they had a hard time with the yob element,' he explains. Their particular style of working made it hard for them to cope with hecklers. 'Their stuff was more theatrical, and if you are a double act you can't break off your character and reply when you are heckled,' he explains. 'It was very hard to do a double act at the Comedy Store unless you were lucky, and it was doubly difficult for them.'

Don Ward remembers how at times French and Saunders would go down like a lead balloon, but on other occasions would be a roaring success. 'They would regularly be booed off,' he says. 'They were experimenting and finding their rhythm and discovering exactly what their role was. But of course what it did employ was pauses, and pauses at comedy clubs can be a dangerous thing. Inevitably someone would shout out, "Oh, it's boring. Gong!"and the girls would be gonged off. And quite often they would be gonged off pretty quickly. At other times there would be a bit of heckling and other people in the audience would say, "Shut up because we want to listen". There would then be an argument among the audience and the two girls would just do their 'tennis-match looks' from one side of the room to the other, which was quite amusing and filled out a bit more time. They never tried improvisation; everything was always sketched out. They knew exactly what they were going to say from the moment they stepped on stage until the moment they stepped off.

'They didn't bother to handle heckling. If they got heckled they just trooped off. Their attitude was rather like a teacher addressing unruly pupils: "If you load of bloody rabble don't want to listen to this quality stuff, goodnight". They said they didn't mind being booed off because they'd got their seven quid each and could bugger off home, or go down the pub. But you had to be tough to get on that stage and survive, and they were both quite strong-willed young ladies. They had to go on with the attitude, "Right,

I'm going to deliver", because it was a tough little world. It was a bit of a lion's den, created by yours truly, of course. It was still very much a boy's business, but I tried to encourage female comedians. There's such a dearth of women in this business that one tries that little bit harder to help them. It adds balance to a bill and funny is funny, whether you're male or female.

'Sometimes they would be good but I could see that the audience wasn't having it and it was going to be a short one. Then another week would go by and it would go well for them and they'd be out there for twelve minutes. Once they got going and found that they had an audience that appreciated them there was some really good stuff. And they enjoyed themselves; that's an old secret of this game.'

Compared to the majority of the acts appearing at the Comedy Store in the early eighties, French and Saunders were distinctly tame. 'They never really set themselves up as radical young socialists,' Ward points out. 'Maggie Thatcher had come into power, so there was very good material for the likes of Andy de la Tour, Tony Allen, Alexei Sayle and Ben Elton to have a field day with. But not French and Saunders. They were quite content to do their middle-class sketchy stuff, which to a certain degree was a bit safe. They'd talk about bodily functions, but they could switch on these twee faces and Cheltenham voices. Their pattern has never changed. What you see now is what you always got: the "straight one putting on the other one" act, which is so similar to Morecambe and Wise. The thing I found most extraordinary about them was that neither appeared to be more talented than the other. I found them quite fascinating because sometimes you'd look at Jennifer and say, "Yes, Jennifer's better than Dawn". Then Dawn would suddenly come back and you'd think, "Oh bloody hell, they're both good".'

However, French and Saunders's involvement with the Comedy Store was not destined to be a long one. A year after the club opened, something of a comedic *coup d'état* occurred, which effectively split the club's performers into two separate camps. The uprising was led by Peter Richardson, who decided to form his own company called The Comic Strip. He recruited his Outer Limits partner Nigel Planer, along with Adrian Edmondson and Rik Mayall, and asked French and Saunders to join his troupe. 'It was Mad Pete who wanted to do it,' recalls Rik Mayall. 'He sat us round a table and we signed some sort of a thing on a menu saying that we would try to start a club together.' But not everyone was welcome, and the breakaway group stirred up a certain amount of ill feeling among their peers. 'When they went on to The Comic Strip we weren't invited, even though we were just as popular down the Comedy Store as they were,' says Malcolm Hardee. 'It was a class thing; they were all middle-class. Some of them try to make out they are working-class, but if they meet a real one they don't like it. They were cliquey and quite aloof. At the Comedy Store they would just run through their stuff and then go; they didn't socialise.'

The group asked Don Ward if they could use his club. 'I said we could come to some arrangement, thinking that they were going to ask me for Wednesdays and Thursdays, but Peter Richardson said they wanted Friday and Saturday,' he says. 'I said, "Hold on, I'm already doing it on Friday and Saturday, don't come to me with my own idea, let's talk about other nights". But he wouldn't have it.' Turned down by Ward, Richardson struck a deal with porn king Paul Raymond to rent the Boulevard Theatre. A small theatre situated adjacent to Raymond's strip club and next to a doorway advertising pole-dancing, the Boulevard became home to The Comic Strip. Problematically, it shared a bar with the Raymond Revue Bar at intervals. 'It was a very strange place,' admits Nigel Planer. 'They eventually had to stagger the intervals because you'd have the non-racist, non-sexist audience walking into the festival of erotica, where there were soft-porn videos playing and all the way up the stairs there would be pictures from the Raymond Revue Bar.'

'I advised Peter against it,' says Don Ward. 'I said, "It's not sour grapes, but you shouldn't go there". I knew he wouldn't get on with Raymond, especially with customers having to rub shoulders with the dirty-mac brigade in the interval for getting drinks. The two lots of punters would not mix. But he wanted to be in Soho, near to where the Store was, because he could see that people came into Soho for the comedy. So he took the place and the girls went off with him, along with Rik and Ade. I didn't exactly lose them to The Comic Strip because they were still coming back and doing things with me, but not as often as I would have hoped because they became quite embroiled with it.'

The Comic Strip opened in October 1980, and was poles apart from the rough-and-ready atmosphere of the Comedy Store. 'The Comic Strip was a better environment for French and Saunders because it was very protected,' explains Arnold Brown. 'It was in a small theatre of about two hundred seats, so there was little or no heckling. At the Store there could be a very disheartening "show us your tits" aspect, particularly late on a Saturday night. Everyone, male and female, had a hard time – except Alexei who had the gong. It used to get quite hectic at weekends when there was a kind of yob element who didn't know much about anything. But the theatrical aspect of The Comic Strip gave them an environment they could work in.'

'The Comic Strip was better,' agrees Dawn. 'Peter wanted to put people in a place where they could do their comedy instead of being gonged off by a lot of hecklers.' But she maintains that she and Jennifer were only asked to go along because they were women. 'We were tripe, but they took us because they needed bosoms on stage for their credibility,' she says self-deprecatingly. 'If there had been another female double act we wouldn't have got in. We'd invented some characters for a lark; we'd speak in silly voices for our own amusement, and the next thing we knew we were performing them – terrible stuff, true crud – on stage. We wouldn't have got the jobs if we were men, but they desperately needed women to make it PC. We were just the first creatures with boobs to walk in the door.'

For a year Dawn moonlighted, teaching by day and appearing at The Comic Strip or the Comedy Store by night. She and Jennifer would sometimes write their sketches in a classroom at Dawn's school. Her transformation from teacher to comedienne did not happen overnight. 'Dawn has a very strong sense of loyalty and commitment to everything she does, and she continued to teach for a full year even when we were performing regularly at The Comic Strip club in the evenings,' says Saunders. 'Imagine my relief when she finally hung up for good the now heavily coffee-stained, knee-length fawn corduroy skirt.' Dawn decided to hand in her notice when The Comic Strip was invited to appear at the 1982 Adelaide Festival.

It was a decision that was greeted with much excitement by her pupils at Parliament Hill School. 'She said she was going to leave to try her luck at a career in comedy and we were all really impressed,' recalls Karen Hockney. 'We thought, "Wow, a street-cred teacher who wasn't just staying to be a teacher". It was terribly glamorous and impressive to a gaggle of thirteen- and fourteen- year-olds that she was mixing in those circles. But she didn't name-drop or try to impress, and in a way that's why she was popular. She wasn't trying to say, "Hey, look at me" all the time, she just seemed very normal and down-to-earth.'

During her year at Parliament Hill, Dawn managed to convince many of the girls in her class that drama could be fun. 'She was a good drama teacher,' says Karen. 'She certainly inspired a few people. One of the girls, Jacey Falles, went on to be an actress and worked with Dawn on *Murder Most Horrid*. Jacey's done well, and I think you could safely say that it was under Dawn's early tuition. Another ex-pupil is a drama therapist, so it's quite a good track record from a London comprehensive. She definitely made an impact, but in a way I think she was a bit too much of a wild card for a teaching career. She was good fun, and in drama you want to inspire people — and she did — but she was quite non-conformist. She was relaxed and fun and a bit wacky and off the wall, so she stood out. Maybe the fact that she only did it for a short time meant that she put more into it.'

When she gave up teaching, Dawn found it strange no longer to be a part of the girls' lives. 'I miss the honesty of the kids I taught; they were always straight with you,' she said in the early days of her fame. 'I often see former pupils when I'm in the area. They call me Miss French.' But her time as a teacher was destined to live on in *French and Saunders* sketches, as Karen Hockney was later amused to discover. 'When she started working with Jennifer Saunders, they did schoolgirl sketches where they were really mouthy and loud and smoking and wearing short grey skirts with bare legs,' she says. 'Our uniform was grey skirts and purple blouses, and it was a real take-off of her days at Parliament Hill.'

The girls followed her career avidly. 'A couple of years after she left, my friend went to see her at Hampstead Theatre with a group of girls we were at school with, and afterwards they hung around to say hello to her,' recalls Karen. 'She remembered a few of the faces and was really friendly and chatty.' Karen, who went on to become a journalist, has since found herself in the slightly strange position of interviewing her former teacher. 'I've interviewed her a couple of times, once when she was on *The South Bank Show* and prior to that when she was promoting *Murder Most Horrid*,' she says. 'I told her that I had been in her class at school, but she didn't remember me because I wasn't a particularly good drama student and hadn't taken drama as an O level. But she half recognised my name and asked what I'd been up to. I was working at the *Sun* at the time, which wasn't a paper that she particularly liked or wanted to be a part of, and she said, "Oh, why are you working at the *Sun*? Go and work at another paper and then I'll give you a proper interview". But she was very friendly and really very sweet.'

Like the Comedy Store, The Comic Strip became the 'in' place to go and as a result, Dawn's life changed dramatically. Instead of being an ordinary teacher at a London comprehensive, she suddenly found herself part of a major new comedy movement. The comedians who found fame in the early eighties – people like Rik Mayall, Adrian Edmondson, Nigel Planer, Peter Richardson, Robbie Coltrane, Ben Elton and French and Saunders – became known as 'alternative comedians'. But what the term actually meant was open to debate. Whether it meant being funny every other day, as Dame Edna had suggested, or involved something altogether more cerebral was a matter for conjecture. The comedians themselves were none the wiser. 'I never understood what it meant,' Dawn admits. 'If it implied that we were anti-sexist and anti-racist, then that's fine. But so were Eric and Ernie and the Pythons. I don't think we understood it. We just thought it was wonderful to have a job where, in six months, you earned as much as for a year's teaching by dressing up and showing off and being with your mates and getting drunk a lot.'

What the new breed of comedians did provide was an alternative to the type of sexist humour symbolised by people like Jim Davidson and Benny Hill, and the racism of Bernard Manning. Though widely different in style, the new comics shared a rejection of most of what had gone before; not only the sexist and racist element, but also the intellectual middle-class approach of the university wits. 'Revue was a dirty word and so was Oxbridge,' explains Rik Mayall. 'We had a down on the Pythons – although we secretly all thought they were great.' The irreverent style and off-the-wall material of the alternative set represented a completely new approach to comedy, and struck a chord with the emerging youth culture.

As a part of this movement, Dawn led an exciting life. 'The Comic Strip became the fashionable place to be in London,' she says. 'It was the time when the New Romantics were around, and you'd look out on a sea of frilly shirts. It was full of minor London celebs and hip people who'd come to be seen there. It was crummy then – but because it had some kind of prestige it meant some people would come to see you when you did the little pub gigs.' But inevitably there were complaints. 'The problem with the place was that it became trendy,' she moans. 'I remember there was one night when Jack Nicholson, Bianca Jagger, those sort of people – jet-setty people – were in. People would treat it like, "That might be going on on stage, but I'm going to chat to my friends". It got so that everybody there was looking at everybody else. Suddenly we had people from Monty Python in the audience. I couldn't believe it. It was suddenly hip, but we weren't hip at all. We were so straight and frightened.'

Dawn's emergence on to the comedy scene happened just as the windows of opportunity were being flung open for the first time. The way that she and her contemporaries almost immediately embarked on hugely successful careers in television was something that had not happened before. 'There was no market when French and Saunders started,' explains Don Ward. 'People didn't come to the Comedy Store hoping to get on TV, they just wanted to improve what they were doing. I used to get people from the BBC and London Weekend Television along, but they were not interested. There was no agenda to go on to; you did what you did and came back the following week hoping to improve upon it. Everybody felt that there was a goal at the end of it all but they didn't know what it was. But they thought the Holy Grail was out there somewhere because the Lenny Bennetts and Jimmy Tarbucks were really running out of time.'

Embarking on a tour of Britain with the rest of the Comic Strip team in July 1981, Dawn found that she rather enjoyed the feeling of being on the road in their own bus. But Jennifer found it less than glamorous. 'Some of it was in horrible places,' she shuddered. 'We did a late-night show after a film in a porn cinema, and a guy came out with insecticide and was spraying all the seats before the audience came in.' The Comic Strip club closed the same month, having existed for only nine months. But it had served its purpose, and Peter Richardson had created a team of performers who were set to become some of the biggest names in British television comedy.

CHAPTER SEVEN

The Bogeyman Cometh

O ne evening towards the end of 1981 when French and Saunders were performing on stage at the Comedy Store, a ripple of excitement went through the club that signified a famous person was in the building.

The celebrity was Lenny Henry, twenty-three-year-old star of television shows *OTT* and *Tiswas*. He was at the Store with his friend and *OTT* co-star Chris Tarrant to scout for writers for their show. To Dawn's amazement he approached her and asked her to write for them. To his equal astonishment she turned him down. 'I said, "We'd like to have you write some material because I think it's important to have women writers on the show and there aren't any",' he recalls. 'But she was really cool and offhand and said she didn't have the time. She said, "It takes a long time to come up with our material, at least six months a sketch, and I just don't think it's possible".'

Rebuffed, Henry retreated to the bar. The way he'd phrased his request should have pressed all the right buttons with an ardent feminist like Dawn, but the reason she gave him the cold shoulder was because she was so overawed by him. 'He walked into the

Comedy Store and I kept thinking, "God, there's a famous person",' she confessed on *The South Bank Show* some years later. 'I tried to keep very cool about the whole thing. He spoke to me about doing some writing and I said I didn't think I was suitable. Then I ran into the dressing room, looked at Jennifer and screamed.'

It was the thrill of being asked to write for a famous celebrity, rather than the fact that she fancied Lenny, that made Dawn so excited. For she admits that when she first met him she thought he was quite dreadful. Just as had happened when she met Jennifer Saunders, with whom she has what she refers to as her 'other marriage', her first impression of her future husband was not favourable. 'I thought he was loud and revolting,' she says. 'He was starring in the telly show *Tiswas*, and specialised in eating condensed-milk sandwiches and wearing a four-foot-high Rasta hat. He was quite successful, and I thought he was a real showbizzy person, on an ego trip and doing the celebrity bit.'

Lenny Henry was already a big star by the time he met Dawn, having found fame on the television talent show *New Faces* when he was just seventeen. He was offered a part in the children's TV show *Tiswas* the same year, and joined the touring *Black and White Minstrel Show*, appearing alongside blacked-up white performers. He had written and starred alongside Tracey Ullman in television's *Three of a Kind*, and with Chris Tarrant in the late-night comedy series *OTT*, which stood for 'over the top'. He was also much in demand on the club circuit.

Born Lenworth George Henry on 29 August 1958 in Dudley, West Midlands, he was the son of Jamaican immigrants Winston and Winifred Henry. His mother had come to Britain alone in 1957, leaving her husband and four children behind in Kingston, and worked as a hospital cook until she could afford to send for them. Lenny, the fifth of seven children, was brought up in a comfortable semi-detached house in Buffery Park, Dudley, a home his parents worked hard to afford. Winston Henry was employed in the foundry at Beans Industries in nearby Cosley, making parts for British Leyland, and Winifred worked in various factories in the area. Money was tight; there was no pocket money for the children and clothes were handed down. Winifred Henry had no qualms about disciplining her children physically when they were naughty. 'It was a typical West Indian upbringing,' Lenny says. 'Getting hit was an important factor in it, which was horrible, but gave me a healthy respect for right and wrong.'

The young Lenny soon showed himself to be a talented mimic, and he began doing impressions to amuse his classmates. On leaving school, he took on an engineering apprenticeship, but in 1975 his life changed dramatically when he won a place on *New Faces*. His impersonation of Frank Spencer, from the hit comedy *Some Mothers Do 'Ave 'Em*, won him first prize. His six-foot-two frame and the fact that he was black made him virtually unique among his fellow comedians, and the nation quickly took him to its heart. By the time he met Dawn in 1981, he had become something of a darling with the press, who devoted acres of print to his every move.

None of which appeared to cut much ice with Dawn. 'I don't think she liked me at first,' he says. 'She said, "Ooh, you're the one who used to eat those dreadful condensed-milk sandwiches on *Tiswas*. Yuk!" I really did want her to write for me; it wasn't just a chat-up line. I saw her as an artist before I started seeing her socially.' But Dawn was not impressed, and her initial rejection of Lenny might have been the end of that, if it were not for the fact that the comedy scene is a very small world. It was inevitable that the two comics would bump into each other again.

They met for a second time in April 1982, in the foyer of the BBC's studios in Shepherd's Bush. They had gone to watch their friend Alexei Sayle record a show, and on this occasion they hit it off. 'We ended up sitting next to each other and talked throughout the recording,' says Lenny. 'Afterwards she suggested we went for a drink and we carried on talking. Then we went to a disco and carried on talking. It was the most I'd ever talked to one person in one night. It was clear there was something going on. I talked about things with Dawn that I'd never talked about with any other person, male or female. It was just so easy being with her.'

Each was forced to revise their initial opinion of the other. 'I'd always thought of him as the loud one on *Tiswas* and I didn't like him very much,' admits Dawn. 'And he thought I was a horrible snob. But then we did some snogging and that changed everything. We met again at a jazz club with some other friends and suddenly everybody started snogging and we were left like a couple of gooseberries. We just began to click, and I found out he's absolutely not a showbiz person at all. I just realised how funny and gentle and shy he was. He rang me later. And that was it.'

Having found herself a man, and a famous one at that, Dawn was determined not to lose him. With the memory of David's betrayal still painfully fresh in her mind, her old worries and insecurities started to kick in. Chief among these was Jennifer. Dawn was vaguely in awe of her posh friend, and considered her to be far more stylish and elegant than her. 'I was always scared that blokes would like Jennifer more than me, which they did,' she says. 'They were always after Jennifer. Blokes would chat me up and I'd think, "I'm going to get a snog here", and then they'd say, "Where's Jennifer?" When I first met Lenny I thought, "I must keep him away from Jennifer or he'll go for her instead". It's a natural reaction. If you love someone you expect they'll love the same people as you do. The first night Lenny stayed with me, sleeping in a sleeping bag on the floor, Jennifer happened to come round to see me first thing in the morning. I opened the letter box and shooed her away. I said, "Haven't you got any shopping to do?" '

As she got to know him better, Dawn discovered that she had a lot in common with Lenny, the most poignant being the fact that they had both lost their fathers when they were nineteen. But unlike the close relationship she had enjoyed with her father, Lenny had never really got to know his dad. Winston Henry was a remote and slightly forbidding man, who was already in his fifties when Lenny was born. He died in hospital from kidney failure when he was seventy-two, leaving his wife to bring up their youngest children single-handed. Lenny had been left devastated by his father's death, and in him Dawn finally found someone who could identify and sympathise with what she had been through.

Like Dawn, Lenny had enjoyed a happy childhood and had been an amusing child. Talking about their early life, they realised that they had also shared the same frustrating experiences of being teenagers, neither of them quite fitting into the dating scene in their respective home towns. While Dawn had been making the boys laugh in the pubs in Plymouth, only to watch them go off with her friends at the end of the evening, Lenny had been suffering a similar fate in Dudley. With Lenny, Dawn instinctively felt that she had found her soulmate. He was funny and clever and famous, and he was also good-looking. She couldn't wait to show him off to the folks back home in Plymouth.

Having realised the depth of her feelings for Lenny, Dawn was keen to introduce him to her mother. But, being Dawn, she chose a novel way to break the exciting news to Roma. She says: 'I rang her and said, "You know when I was little, you were always telling me about the big black bogeyman who would come and get me if I didn't go to sleep? Well, he's come and got me!" Mum laughed about it and I wasn't quite sure how to take it, but she was very sweet and keen to meet him. She had never met a black person, and rang just before we were going home to ask, "Just checking. Does he eat chicken?" She's a very open person and she loved Lenny straight away. But then he is Lenny Henry, and that makes a bit of a difference. It's not like he was some Rastafarian bloke. I think she felt she knew him anyway, like a lot of people do when you're on telly.'

Going home to Plymouth made Dawn realise that she and Lenny had yet another thing in common: both their mothers were obsessed with food. 'Lenny's mother tested me with food,' says Dawn. 'She gave me a lot of very hot, very spicy Caribbean food, piled right up to see if I was woman enough to take on her son. If I could get through that food, I was in the family. This was a test I could pass quite easily. And the funny thing was, my mother did the same thing to Lenny. She made massive great big pasties and tested him to see if he could eat them.'

That summer Lenny was booked to appear on stage at The Coliseum in Carlyon Bay, Cornwall. Dawn was in Plymouth staying with her mother, so instead of checking into a hotel in Carlyon Bay, Lenny made the one-hour drive back to Plymouth each night to be near her. But he did not stay at Dawn's family house in Old Ferry Road. Instead, in a rather quaint arrangement, he lodged with Tony and Ethel Hodge at their bed-and-breakfast establishment further down the road. 'Lenny stayed here with his road manager,' recalls Tony Hodge. 'He wanted to stay here rather than near to where he was working so he could see Dawn. He stayed about a fortnight.' Neighbour Charles Lawrence, who had given Dawn lifts to school, saw quite a bit of Lenny during this time. 'Tony used to let me use his garden, and Lenny often practised his act in the garden,' he explains. 'I'd talk to him quite a bit while I did the gardening, and he used to try out his act on me. If I laughed at the jokes, he figured it was good enough.'

For a while, Dawn's relationship with Lenny was the best-kept secret in show business. By the autumn of 1982, the *Sun* had got wind that he was dating someone, but knew only that his girlfriend was called 'Frenchie'. Lenny refused to enlighten them, enjoying the mystique. 'The last time I revealed something about a girlfriend we split up two weeks later,' he told their reporter. 'Now I have a new lady in my life, I'm not taking any chances.' But he decided to have a bit of fun at the tabloids' expense by waggling a carrot under their noses. As part of a private joke with Dawn, he told a *Sunday People* reporter in December 1982: 'She's a dancer from Blackpool. But I like to keep my personal life quiet.'

The news of 'Frenchie's' true identity didn't get out until September 1983, more than eighteen months after they had first started seeing each other. When the story broke in Fleet Street, Lenny came clean and admitted that he intended to marry Dawn. 'I don't believe in telling people the intricate details of my private life but I can tell you we got engaged two weeks ago,' he said. However, his exhilaration at being in love meant that he was unable to keep quiet on the subject. 'The way things are right now suits me,' he confided to several million readers. 'I have somebody I care for and who cares for me. There is no substitute for having a woman you can go to and talk over problems, get advice, laugh and cry with. That's what counts. We're very, very happy. I love her because she's just dead nice.'

His kid brother Paul was less poetic. 'We are all insane in this house and she's just like us, a nutter,' he told reporters. 'But she's great fun, we all like her.' He revealed that Dawn had been to the family house in Kingswinford, West Midlands, several times. 'Lenny has had a couple of girlfriends before, but he really loves Dawn,' said Paul. 'He's had his time running around. Now he wants to settle down.'

It was certainly true that Lenny had had his share of girlfriends. As a performer who spent a great deal of his time appearing at summer shows up and down the country, many of his conquests had been dancers whom he had shared the bill with. But when he met Dawn he wanted all that to change. 'I felt it was worth giving up whatever it is that goes with bachelorhood,' he said. 'I was very big-headed when I met her, very loud-mouthed, a bit cocky. I was just full of myself. When I met Dawn it was time to be doing something different, both personally and professionally. When I started going out with her my life went off into another direction.'

They got engaged in Plymouth in September 1983. Lenny had just turned twenty-five and Dawn was about to be twenty-six. It was the second time she had been engaged and she sincerely hoped that this time she would actually make it to the altar. A fortnight later, proudly sporting a diamond engagement ring, she told reporters what had attracted her to Lenny. 'He makes me laugh,' she said. 'He's a genius.' She later confessed that she had prompted him into asking her to marry him. 'Lenny proposed but I manipulated it,' she said. 'He gave me a huge diamond and sapphire ring as a surprise, all wrapped up inside three shopping bags. Lenny thought the way to show somebody you really loved them was to buy them the biggest diamond he could possibly find. When I asked him what it was for, he shrugged with embarrassment, pointed to my finger, and that was as far as he got. So I had to say, "I don't know what finger to put it on", then he pointed and that appeared to be the general direction we were going in.'

And thus did Dawn subtly yet stealthily snare her man. 'I remember when Lenny first introduced her to me,' recalls Robert Luff, the show-business impresario who had helped make Lenny a star. 'He didn't exactly say, "This is the lady I'm going to marry", but I soon cottoned on to the fact that he was going to. Knowing Dawn, it didn't surprise me at all when he decided to settle down. She is very determined. I wouldn't say she set her sights on him, but in her own way she handled it beautifully. She's a wonderful character, and I thought they made a very good pair.'

But at first glance, Dawn and Lenny were an odd couple. He was six foot two inches tall, while she measured barely five foot; he was relatively skinny, whereas she was plump. He was resolutely working-class, whereas Dawn had developed middle-class aspirations. The fact that he was black and she was white would invite little comment nowadays but was much remarked upon at the time. Many of the questions posed by reporters centred on this aspect of their relationship, and the potential problems they might encounter. Dawn stressed that it didn't trouble them in the slightest. 'We have talked at some length about the problems of having children in a mixed marriage, and we have decided we can deal with it,' she said. 'We don't worry about the difference in colour, and our families don't either. It doesn't come into our relationship at all, and I don't see why the public should care.'

The wedding was set for a date in October 1984. The previous month Dawn and Lenny teamed up on television in his debut solo series for BBC1, *The Lenny Henry Show*. 'It was a bit odd playing alongside each other,' he admitted. 'But we have a similar sense of humour, so why not?' Appearing in the show was practically all Dawn saw of her fiancé in the weeks preceding their wedding day. They had been forced to spend most of the summer apart while Lenny went to Blackpool to do the summer season, and Dawn stayed in London to concentrate on her own burgeoning career. When Lenny came off stage after his twice-nightly show at the town's North Pier, he would phone Dawn and sing Stevie Wonder's song, 'I Just Called To Say I Love You' down the phone to her.

To help take his mind off how much he was missing her, Lenny enrolled at a college of further education a few miles away in Preston to study O-level English language and literature. Dawn's influence was evident in his decision to do this. Having left school with hardly any qualifications, he was impressed and somewhat overawed by how clever and knowledgeable Dawn and her Comic Strip friends seemed to be. By contrast, he considered himself to be greatly lacking in this respect. 'A lot of people I know have got degrees and are supremely intellectual. Like my wife,' he said. 'They talk about the morality of art and things like that. I got my O levels just to prove I could.'

The 'Dawn Effect' was also noticeable in Lenny's refusal to judge the Miss Blackpool beauty contest that summer. Three years before he had been asked by a reporter how he would choose to spend a dream Sunday, and had replied: 'Basking on an Antiguan beach with a beautiful girl by my side – Miss America, Miss Jamaica, Miss England, Miss Japan. I'm not choosy.' But by 1984 his attitude had changed. 'I'm not that fussed about beauty contests,' he said. 'My fiancée is a feminist, and once you talk to somebody like her about it you see it's all a bit pointless.' Feminism had also made him a devout anti-fattist. 'I don't do sexist jokes because I don't find women's bottoms very funny,' he said, rather pompously.

Shortly before her wedding, Dawn went back to St Dunstan's Abbey to take part in an old school custom. 'There's a tradition at St Dunstan's that when you get married you pick some special myrtle from the school grounds to put in your wedding bouquet,' explains ex-pupil Marie-Louise Cook. 'Dawn came back to get the myrtle and to thank Miss Abley and Miss Abbott for the support they had given her. She brought Lenny Henry with her, and I remember it being hugely exciting because he was famous.' Former pupil Sarah Rawle also remembers Dawn proudly showing off her new love to her former teachers and classmates. 'Dawn came in with Lenny Henry to the bank where my sister worked, and said she had just been to school to introduce Miss Abley to her husband-to-be,' she says. 'From what I gathered it had gone quite well, but it could have been an interesting meeting because Miss Abley was quite prim and proper, and some of his humour might have been a bit brash for her.'

Like all brides-to-be, Dawn wanted to look good on her big day and she decided to lose weight. It was the first time in her life she had ever dieted. 'I suppose it was because every woman feels that her wedding day is the one day in her life when she should absolutely look her best,' she says. 'I suddenly thought, "All those people are going to be looking at me".' I didn't want to be a fat bride so I insisted my wedding dress be made in a size twelve.' Losing a bit of weight wouldn't have presented too much of a problem, even for a food-lover like Dawn, but she was a size 20 at the time and shedding a few pounds simply wouldn't be enough to enable her to fit into a size 12. When she had a fitting six weeks before the wedding, she realised that there was no way she would be able to squeeze into her dress.

With only a few weeks to go before she was due to walk down the aisle, Dawn took drastic action. She embarked on a crash diet and resorted to a series of injections to help her lose weight quickly. 'I panicked and went on one of those completely stupid quack diets,' she says. 'I was eating only fruit and meat – which made me smell like a corpse – and going to Harley Street for injections which cost a fortune. I was taking a load of slimming pills and having countless injections in the bum. I lost the weight over five or six weeks, which was really quick, and went from a size twenty to a size twelve. I probably lost about six stone but I felt awful – really odd and really weak.'

Although she had realised her goal and managed to fit into her dress on the day, Dawn bitterly regretted having succumbed to the pressure to be a slim bride. 'It was a trap and a lie,' she says. 'I was weak and stupid at the time. I had a moment of weakness, thinking perhaps I shouldn't look the way I do. I wasn't unhappy about my weight, but being on a diet certainly made me unhappy. You're a bit mad before you get married anyway, and even more so if you're fantasising about food all day. I was miserable for those six weeks, and Lenny didn't know why I was doing it, he couldn't understand at all. He loved me the way I was, and he still does. He thought I was mad, and I didn't understand my body. It became an alien thing to me. My personality changed. I was very depressed and all I could think about was food, which is not something I do usually. I got into the dress, but it wasn't my body at all. It wasn't me.'

Dawn and Lenny were married on 20 October 1984 at St Paul's Church, Covent Garden. They had both been so busy working they had almost postponed the wedding until the following year. As it was, Lenny arrived at the ceremony fresh from Blackpool where he had been on stage the night before. They had changed the wedding date once because the time and place had been leaked to the press, but there was still a scrum of photographers and reporters on the day. The guests included Jennifer Saunders, Rik Mayall, Nigel Planer, Chris Tarrant, Tracey Ullman and Robbie Coltrane. Dawn's former headmistress was there, along with her friend Janet Pearse and mum Sheilagh. Dawn's brother Gary gave her away, which was a bitter-sweet moment for them both.

In stark contrast to Lenny's zany TV image, both he and Dawn opted for conventional wedding-day attire. Dawn looked beautiful in a traditional white lace-edged wedding gown. She had flowers and ivy in her hair to match the lilies and roses in her bouquet, and wore a short lace veil, pearl-drop earrings and matching necklace. The groom wore a stylish three-piece wool suit with a tastefully spotted tie, and sported a double rose in his buttonhole. During the marriage ceremony a pigeon swooped over the gospel choir, leaving the 300-strong congregation in fits of giggles. Later the bird flew down and settled beside Lenny as he knelt at the altar, prompting more laughter.

The ceremony was followed by a lavish reception at the Savoy, which cost most of Lenny's salary from his summer season at Blackpool. It was a double celebration for Dawn: not only had she married the man she loved, she could also abandon her diet. Even when she had been standing at the altar she hadn't been able to stop thinking about food. 'I was so hungry that all I could think of all day was food,' she says. 'I was just so happy when the wedding was over so I could eat normally again. I was loosening the back of the dress immediately after the service, and started eating again at the reception. I couldn't see all that food and drink at the party and not have some. I had been so unhappy, it was a wonderful relief. I stayed a size twelve for about three weeks.'

The following year, another show-business pairing was made when Jennifer Saunders married Adrian Edmondson. It had been Dawn who was responsible for her friends finding love. 'Dawn's very good at putting people together, and it was her idea that I went out with Adrian,' says Jennifer. 'He and I had known each other a long time, but I was completely stupid and didn't realise that we should be together. When we first met, Ade was going out with someone else and I was too, so it wasn't a possibility. Not only that, but we were all like a family, touring and so on. It would have been a bit odd.' But Dawn told her partner not to be silly and to 'go for it'.

One thing that hadn't changed about Dawn's first impressions of Lenny was her dislike of the type of material he used in his stand-up act. He regularly told racist jokes to his predominantly white audiences; wiping sweat from his forehead and saying it tasted like chocolate, and threatening to move in next door to hecklers if they didn't shut up. All of which Dawn found deeply abhorrent. Soon after they met, she went to see him perform at an RAF club in Wiltshire, where he did his usual run of self-deprecating gags. He thought the show had been a great success, but she could not stomach much of his material. To her, watching Lenny verbally spar with his cabaret audience was like descending into a medieval bear pit. She later said that she had been 'utterly shocked' by the experience.

Dawn was dismayed and appalled to see the man she loved being subjected to such unashamedly racist heckling. 'The audiences were raw-meat-eating people who drank bones for blood,' she says. 'They would be shouting out, "Where's the sambo?" and Lenny would go on and gradually bring them round. It was like the Christians and the lions. No one from the alternative circuit could have survived until the end of the month, and that includes me.' She was adamant that he should not belittle himself in this way any longer, but it took a while for Lenny to come round to her way of thinking. At first he both resisted and resented her interference. 'I was very defensive at first,' he admits. 'I thought, "I've been doing this for years, I'm a professional, I'm a veteran".

But when I realised that she was right, I had to take a step back and think what I wanted to do.'

Lenny was initially a little intimidated by his wife and the clever, right-on crowd she associated with. If the alternative set stood for anything, it was to promote a new, politically correct humour that didn't rely on jokes about people's race, colour or sex to get laughs. Lenny's act belonged more to the old school, and Dawn and her contemporaries were hugely influential in changing the way he viewed his comedy. In a 1987 interview with the *News of the World*, he admitted he'd become a changed man since he'd met Dawn, and regretted ever trying to get cheap laughs by insulting his own race. 'I used to tell jokes about black people that were at my expense,' he admitted. 'After a while I had to examine why I was getting laughs, and it was for all the wrong reasons. They were laughing at me instead of with me. I was telling jokes that everybody was telling about black people but nobody ever said, "Don't do those jokes", until I met Dawn. She made me realise that it would be great to make people laugh without having to sell out. It planted a seed which led to me changing my act.'

Dawn also gave her husband the confidence to write his own material. 'I never believed I had the ability,' he admitted. 'Now I write a lot of my stuff, and it works great. But for years I tried to get on by rolling my eyes, making weird noises and doing frantic impressions. I just went on in front of those cameras and did daft things. I was just a kid mucking about. And suddenly I was a star – at sixteen. But I had no material or experience to sustain my success. It couldn't last. When the novelty of a young black impersonating people like Tommy Cooper wore off, I went through a very lean time. Nor did I have much money. Everyone thought I was making a fortune but if I was, it wasn't going into my pocket! I made a lot of mistakes when I turned professional. I wasn't mature enough to handle success. I got very big-headed and blew what money I did get on a good time.'

He had scrapped the racist jokes for good. 'I'll never do anything like that again,' he vowed. 'I grew out of it because I had some good advisers; it's all part of growing up. I have finally learned to relax and become a mature entertainer. I look back on the past few years as the period in which I grew up. Now I feel particularly concerned for new comics just coming into the business. They should be given some guidance about their material. And the moment they start saying things like, "My wife's fat" or telling gags about blacks or Pakistanis, the producer should say, "I think that's offensive". He went on to launch a blistering attack on comics who told sexist and racist jokes, suggesting that TV chiefs tell them to drop their offensive material. He knew he had once been guilty of telling some of the jokes that now angered him, but blasted comics like Jim Davidson and Gary Wilmot for stereotyping black people. 'I hate it when comedians encourage silly attitudes by putting forward stupid stereotypes for the sake of a cheap laugh,' he said. 'That's a real misuse of the art. Comedy should be clever and informative as well as funny. Anyone who uses it to reinforce stupid myths about blacks, the Irish, Jews or whoever, dishonours our profession.'

This last remark is one that many of the people who had listened to his act in the early days of his career would have been surprised to hear him make. But the reason Lenny had undergone such a major change in attitude is more complex than it at first appears. It wasn't simply that he had suddenly woken up to the fact that racist jokes were offensive to the vast majority of people, but more that he was still desperate to fit in with those around him. Just as he had sought to be accepted by the lager-swilling bigots from the working-men's clubs, so now did he want to be accepted by the right-on 'pseuds', who Dawn associated with.

But any suggestion that Dawn bossed Lenny around got both their backs up. 'Hints that she dominates her husband are met with an icy stare,' wrote a *Daily Mirror* journalist. 'If Lenny has stopped making sexist jokes, maybe it's just that he's grown out of them,' said

Dawn. 'I certainly wouldn't try to interfere with his work. Naturally we sit and chat to each other like any other married couple, so we're bound to have some effect on each other's lives. But anyone who knows Lenny knows that I couldn't kick him around even if I wanted to – we're both fairly headstrong characters.' At times Lenny felt the need to defend his wife. 'People have this idea that she's a Nazi in knickers telling me what to do all the time,' he said. 'But she's very sensitive, loving and caring, and would never, ever presume to say I had to change things.'

However, in subsequent interviews both admitted that Dawn had a major input in Lenny's work. In 1989 he paid tribute to her, saying that she was the secret behind his success. 'She understands the business and I really trust her judgement,' he said. 'I owe a lot to her. She comes to my shows and makes notes on what I have done, and we discuss them afterwards. Dawn can also criticise. She is very strong-minded and I respect her opinions.' He also started to use his wife in his act. 'The stairs have disappeared. She's chopped them up with her bare hands,' he said in reference to Dawn's apparently bad PMT.

'I write quite a lot of Len's stuff,' Dawn said the same year. 'I get paid in kind . . . in chocolate, and that's what I'm happy with.' Talking about when they first met, she added: 'He says his life was changed that night. He saw Alexei Sayle and Rik Mayall on stage – and he met me! He realised there was a different way of performing comedy. He'd done six or seven years of clubs by then, just nicking other people's jokes and revamping them. He'd been fourth on the bill with some dreadful racist comedian headlining. Lenny has changed, and he's shaped his act to suit his talents. Now, of course, he has an audience all of his own.'

Andy Harries, controller of entertainment and comedy at Granada Television, was one of the major influences on Lenny's career. As a young current affairs director, he approached Lenny with the idea of making a *South Bank Show* about him. 'Dawn and Lenny were young newly-weds living round the corner from me in Hammersmith,' he says. 'I met Lenny in the corner shop when I went to get a packet of fags and some milk. I was working at *The South Bank Show* at the time, and I thought Lenny would be a great subject. So I called him and said, "Hey, I live round the corner from you, do you want to do a *South Bank Show*? If you do I'll try to fix it with Melvyn." Then I rang Melvyn Bragg and he said, "Yeah, sounds great". So that's how I met him. I'd admired him for years because I just loved his work on *Tiswas*.'

Working closely with Lenny over many months on the film, *Lenny Live and Unleashed*, Harries got to know him well and witnessed at close hand the extent of Dawn's involvement in her husband's career. 'She undoubtedly had a huge influence, but it's not that surprising when you think that they are in the same business,' he says. 'When we were making the film it happened at least twice that we didn't go to the show for a couple of nights, and found that Dawn was going on those nights. Often the show was quite different after she'd been. Material that we were quite keen on would have disappeared; scenes that we were developing were out. He really listened to her. She would go backstage and give Lenny all the notes she'd made and say, "Cut this, cut that". But comedy is a collaborative thing and Dawn is in the business, so it's not surprising that she's influencing his set and would have a strong view on what he should or shouldn't be including for posterity in the final film. I'm sure Lenny does the same thing to Dawn when she's working.'

Harries believes Dawn's influence was more subtle than many people think. 'His act evolved,' he says. 'The way he performed and the sort of material didn't massively change, he just rounded off the edges. His material became more "him". He found his voice, and I'm sure Dawn helped him to find that voice. She played a huge part in polishing Lenny's act.' Dawn's friends also had an effect on his decision to change the way he worked. 'There was an explosion of young comic talent which was perfect for him to get involved in, but not over-involved in,' says Harries. 'It excited him and interested him, but he married into it rather than becoming part of it.

The Comic Strip wanted to eradicate the prejudices that were prevalent at that time. Lenny had been part of those prejudices because he was a very young lad when he became famous, and was easily influenced. He was unaware and there was no one there to guide him. He had a very old-style manager and his mum, who just wanted to see her lad do well. I think it was the general influence of all the Comic Strip performers that opened his eyes. Lenny was very close to Alexei Sayle, and Ben Elton is a big mate of Lenny and Dawn's too.'

Comic Malcolm Hardee also saw the change in Lenny. 'Lenny was not at all PC when I first knew him,' he says. 'It was only when he met her and got in with The Comic Strip set that he decided to turn into what he thought was PC.' Not everybody believes that the change has been completely for the better. 'Lenny came and appeared at the Comedy Store and he was pretty sharp in those days,' says Don Ward. 'For me, he has somewhat dulled off over the years, but he was extremely hungry then. If Dawn hadn't been around he would have been the way he was – one of the lads. But he became a thespian somewhere along the line.'

Just as Dawn had helped to change the public's perception of Lenny, so too had their marriage made people see her in a different light. 'Before Lenny, I know a lot of people misunderstood me,' she says. 'I think once you've been established as the kind of joker in your gang, it's very hard to lose that. Guys were a bit frightened of me because they couldn't see further than that shell. I didn't want anything too gooey. I just wanted proper people who didn't take me for my image. Lenny and I laugh together a lot. But I was glad that he was someone who could tell when I'd had enough of a good laugh.'

In interviews, Lenny happily told reporters how marriage to Dawn had tamed him. 'We manage to be supportive of each other and we try to be home together every night,' he gushed. 'We cook or watch the telly; we don't have to be out on the town. I went through the partying and discoing three or four times a week since I was fifteen, and I had various relationships with different girls. I was coming to the end of that curve about the time I met Dawn. It was getting boring. My marriage is a very, very wonderful thing. She makes me laugh a lot. She's a very funny woman, on and off stage. She's good at listening too, and tells me off when I make corny jokes.' Vaguely aware that he perhaps shouldn't give the press chapter and verse on his love life, he nonetheless didn't seem able to stop himself. 'It's wonderful, and the greatest thing in my life,' he said. 'But I'm such a chatterer I might say too much, and that's not fair on our private lives. I'll just say that Dawn's terrific and funny, and I agree with her strong feminist views – feminism is a way of looking at life, not rushing round the kitchen reading bits out of Spare Rib.'

Dawn and Lenny began married life in a five-bedroom, end-of-terrace house in Agate Road, Hammersmith, for which they paid £150,000. It had a thirty-foot L-shaped living room, marble bath-room and roof terrace, and the couple were initially very happy there. Dawn loved the area and spent her weekends shopping at the market in nearby Shepherd's Bush. 'I love living here, it's dead good,' she said in an early interview. 'It's so colourful, really loud and very alive. I've always felt that wherever you live you just create your own village. We're all like little tribes, and we get our own tribe together. Our tribe is in our area, and it's very friendly.' The couple acquired two cats: Aretha, after the soul singer Aretha Franklin, and Merkin, which Dawn delighted in telling people was the name for a pubic wig.

But while they were living in Agate Road something happened that threatened to destroy their enjoyment of their home. The couple were targeted in a vile campaign by racist bigots who objected to their mixed-race marriage. They received hate mail and sinister visits in the middle of the night, and Dawn became frightened to be in the house by herself. 'Lenny would be away on tour and I would often wake up at three a.m. to hear them clattering downstairs,' she told Neil Kinnock in a chat show for BBC Wales. 'People would appear in the garden. It got so that I couldn't sleep at night. I took a stand for a long time. I decided to stand firm. I used to dig my heels in and tell myself, "I will deal with this, it's not going to worry me". Then one night I came home and someone had decided to leave faeces over our front door. People like that don't leave a calling card so you can go and smash them in the gob. That's what I'd like to do. They are cowards that do it, and they leave you with the fear of wondering when they are going to come back.'

A picture of St George had been pushed through their letter box with the words 'You have been visited by the Ku Klux Klan' written on the back. 'I couldn't believe something like that could still happen,' she says. 'I was terribly upset for about a minute, but then I was angry. I just ripped it up and threw it in the bin. It was horrible hate mail. Lenny was angry too, but he's had to cope with racist nastiness all his life and deals with it a lot better than I ever could. I think it's a shame that he has to go through that, but as long as we have bigots in this country then it'll happen. It's disgraceful, but what can you do?'

During a show in 1988, Lenny told his audience about the attacks. 'I know about the National Front, I know what these people are like,' he said. 'I came home with Dawn one night and noticed that the letters NF had been smeared in excrement above the door.' He said he had also received a poison-pen letter from a racist. The sender had branded him a coon, but spelled it wrongly. One theatregoer said: 'He was poking fun at the National Front for being so thick, but was obviously angered by what had gone on. The tittering stopped. We realised he was being deadly serious.'

Dawn had nothing but disdain for their persecutors. 'Some people have a go when they see us in the street, but usually it's under their breath, nothing I can actually confront them about,' she said contemptuously. 'Others do it openly, thinking it's funny – look at all the racist comedians there are. People make jokes about Lenny's blackness more than anything else when they meet him. I find that so juvenile and ignorant. I suppose we are a fairly public mixed-race couple, so if anyone's got a hang-up about that, we get it. I got a letter at the theatre from someone who writes to me regularly as 'Nigger Lover'. These are tiny-minded people who have nothing better to do than be vitriolic.'

CHAPTER EIGHT

Lashings of Ginger Beer

Dawn was a virtual unknown when she met Lenny Henry, but it would not be long before she would become just as famous as her husband. Like the majority of the alternative set with whom she associated, Dawn was destined to have a spectacularly quick rise to fame. Within a few short years of starting out, she and her contemporaries would all have their own television shows – something that was almost unheard of previously.

In the past, comedians had trodden the traditional path of apprenticeships spent doing the rounds of working-men's clubs and seaside summer seasons, graduating to a slot on the television show *The Comedians* if they were lucky. As Don Ward pointed out, people didn't play the Comedy Store hoping to get on television because that simply didn't happen. What changed things for Dawn and her contemporaries was the birth of Channel 4 Television. Launched on 2 November 1982, the station set out to be different from conventional TV channels by catering for a younger, more cosmopolitan audience. It was irreverent, daring and new – and was dogged by controversy almost from day one. Within weeks the Conservative Home Secretary, Willie Whitelaw, voiced his concerns about 'the bad language, political bias and many other undesirable qualities' which he said people had found in the new programmes. Established to cater for minorities, the channel was heavily criticised for being too concerned with 'homosexuals and feminists'.

With its avant-garde brief, Channel 4 was the perfect showing ground for the Comic Strip team. Peter Richardson pitched his ideas to Channel 4's senior commissioning editor of entertainment, Mike Bolland. A planned spoof of Enid Blyton's *Famous Five* adventure stories was a zany concept, but one that tickled Bolland's fancy. 'What he was proposing were quite elaborate pastiches, but having seen the acts at the Comic Strip club, and knowing the people involved, I thought it was a really exciting prospect,' says Bolland. 'It was the very first thing I ever commissioned. It fitted the brief perfectly for what Channel 4 should be doing at the time.'

Six Comic Strip films were planned for the station's opening winter season. 'It was a real chance thing that Channel 4 started at that time, and we were a new name,' says Richardson. 'Everything just coincided in a way that I couldn't have planned.' The first of *The Comic Strip Presents . . .* offerings, *Five Go Mad in Dorset*, went out on Channel 4's inaugural night. Dawn starred as Blyton's tomboy heroine George, Jennifer was cast as the girly Anne, Adrian Edmondson played Dick and Peter Richardson was Julian, the five's self-appointed leader. The film was a witty parody of Blyton's precocious child detectives. Brilliantly observed, the cast mimicked perfectly the speech and mannerisms of the characters, sending them up hilariously with references to 'wizard' picnics and 'lashings of ginger beer'. But while it unashamedly took the mickey, it did so in a rather affectionate manner and managed to remain peculiarly true to the original.

However, good clean fun it was not. The unsavoury subject of bestiality was hinted at between Dawn's character and the dog, Timmy, and early on in the film the children had a black railway porter arrested on suspicion of being foreign. Controversially, the team also decided to make the ubiquitous Uncle Quentin of Blyton's novels gay. In an inspired piece of casting, *Crossroads'* David Hunter, aka actor Ronald Allen, was chosen to play the mysterious uncle. He had one of the best lines in the film when he explained to the outraged children the truth about his relationship with their aunt Fanny. 'She's an unrelenting nymphomaniac and I'm a screaming homosexual,' he said, impressively managing to keep a straight face.

When they got wind of the film, the guardians of Enid Blyton's wholesome image were understandably concerned. 'There was an eleventh-hour meeting with a couple of barristers from Blyton's estate and a relative,' reveals Mike Bolland. 'We sat down in a room in the Channel 4 building in Charlotte Street and watched it. You could have cut the atmosphere with a knife. But it was actually wonderful because the woman barrister's folder started shaking. She was trying to hide her face but at the end of it they were all laughing and they were fine.'

Five Go Mad in Dorset was followed by four more films: *War*, *The Beat Generation*, *Bad News Tour*, and *Summer School*. The sixth film in the series, *An Evening with Eddie Monsoon*, about a television chat-show host, was cancelled amid fears that it might prove libellous. Richardson's plan was for each film to be completely different to the last. He and fellow writer Pete Richens wrote most of them, but the other members of the team were encouraged to come up with ideas too. *Summer School*, about a group of university students studying prehistoric village life, was written by Dawn. 'If you had an idea you submitted it and clenched your buttocks a bit to see if anybody liked it, and if they did you went away and wrote it,' she says. 'It was quite simple really.'

The Beat Generation, in which Dawn played a spoiled sixties model, contains one of Lenny Henry's favourite Comic Strip scenes. 'I love Dawn in *Beat Generation*,' he says appreciatively. 'I love that shot of her legs in stockings as it goes down. Fantastic!' Despite the fact that The Comic Strip was deemed to be right on and therefore presumably anti-sexist, Dawn and Jennifer were encouraged to wear sexy clothes. 'We were always made by Peter to wear quite short skirts and fishnet tights and high shoes,' says Dawn. 'Even if you were playing a lumberjack that would be a suitable costume. It was just Peter's fancy, I think.'

The films attracted a cult following. 'The viewing figures were never very good; three and a half million was about the most,' says Robbie Coltrane, who appeared in several. 'But having said that, most of that three and a half million could recite the whole show the next week. It was quite a dedicated following.' Despite the modest ratings, Mike Bolland believes The Comic Strip was hugely significant. 'It was important in that it actually stamped a personality on the channel in the early days,' he says. 'They brought a new irreverence to the whole sense of pastiche. They were ground-breaking because they were shot on film, and because somebody somewhere was prepared to put money into a bunch of people who were virtually unknown.' That someone was Michael White, a theatrical producer who had been involved with members of Monty Python and The Goodies. He and Peter Richardson set up the company that financed and produced the Comic Strip films in association with Channel 4.

A second series of The Comic Strip Presents . . . kicked off in November 1983 with another Blyton spoof, Five Go Mad on Mescalin. Transmitted exactly a year after Five Go Mad in Dorset, the film featured the same cast as before. This time the 'Famous Five' were on the trail of Uncle Quentin, who had escaped from jail and was in hiding on Love Island. As an in-joke, the five were staying with a 'Mrs French' at Hot Turkey Farm. And in a most unlikely Blyton storyline, the innocent Dick was seduced by a beautiful sex goddess, played by Candy Davies, who took his virginity and fed him drugs.

The same year, French and Saunders made their television debut as a double act in the Channel 4 series *The Entertainers*. Created as a showcase for new performers, Ben Elton, Chris Barrie and Helen Lederer were among the people who made their earliest television appearances on the show. By 1983, Dawn and Jennifer had honed their stage act and built up a respectable following at fringe theatres around the country. Their routine for *The Entertainers*, broadcast on 6 October 1983, included the 'Psychodrama' sketch, one of the staples of their act. This resulted in a major headache for Channel 4, however, because of the use of the word 'clitoris'. It was deemed a no-no, even for a channel that was prepared to shock — and despite the fact that the previous week's programme had mentioned 'penis'. Initially scheduled for 8.30 p.m., the show was put back to 11.15 p.m., losing most of its audience in the process. 'We'd been trundling along nicely at two and a half million, and the figures never recovered,' says producer Paul Jackson. '*French and Saunders* got about nothing.'

Jackson, who went on to become head of entertainment at the BBC, was a big fan of the alternative comedy scene and played a key role in getting many of the acts on to mainstream television. 'In a way it became the new punk,' he says. 'There was a connection with punk; there was an anger and a kind of attitude about it. They did not wear safety pins but they would have gobbed on the audience if they had thought it was a good idea.'

The second series of *The Comic Strip Presents . . .* also featured the films *Dirty Movie*, written by Rik Mayall and Adrian Edmondson, *Slags*, written by Jennifer Saunders, and *Susie*, in which Dawn drew on her previous life to play a randy schoolteacher. In *Gino — Full Story and Pics*, one of the best Comic Strip films, Dawn murders her unpleasant cripple husband, Rik Mayall, pinning the blame on Gino — played by Keith Allen. It was no secret among the other actors that Dawn and Allen did not hit it off. 'I didn't get on with the members of The Comic Strip,' Allen admits. 'It wasn't my game. I didn't belong to that. I always thought that character-based stand-up comedy was a cop-out. I believed you had to stand up on stage and reveal yourself, that's what you did, and in so doing you could have an influence or an effect. Whereas all these guys came down to, basically, was that they were comic actors. And I wasn't that impressed.'

In a television documentary about the history of The Comic Strip, Allen told how he had advised Dawn to go back to teaching. 'I was talking to Dawn and she was very worried; I'm sure Dawn would agree that in those early days it was rubbish,' Allen recalled. 'She said, "What shall I do?" I think she was a primary-school teacher, and I said, "Oh, give up, just give up and go and be a primary-school teacher". It's probably the best case of ignored advice ever.' Despite the albeit backhanded compliment, Dawn shot back. 'He's a very cocky person, Keith,' she responded testily. 'He just likes to be loud, really. Quite a lot of people with small genitals do that, don't they?'

She and Allen were thrown together in 1983 during filming of the spoof western *A Fistful of Travellers' Cheques*. Many of the Comic Strip movies were filmed in Devon, near to Peter Richardson's family farm, but for *A Fistful of Travellers' Cheques* the team decided to treat themselves to a trip to sunny Spain. A take-off of Clint Eastwood's *A Fistful of Dollars*, Richardson starred with Rik Mayall as a pair of would-be gunfighters who bragged about what bastards they were, when in fact they were simply ordinary West Country boys. Dawn and Jennifer played Australian tourists.

'There wasn't much hard work involved,' laughs actor Christopher Malcolm, who appeared in the film. 'It was the end of the series, and they wrote the script in order to give themselves a holiday. It was filmed in San Jose, near Almeria, which is a beautiful spot and a famous area for movies. It's where virtually all the spaghetti westerns were made, and there's even a Hollywood town there. We went for a couple of weeks and it was fantastic.' The Spanish trip was the first time he had met Dawn, although he would subsequently put her on in her first West End stage play and the two would become friends.

Christopher soon spotted what Malcolm Hardee had noticed: that the key members of the group were a select clique and weren't always welcoming of 'outsiders'. 'They all knew each other so well, so it was slightly difficult,' he admits. 'I've come across it before on film sets, so I just didn't pay any attention to it.' Malcolm Hardee, who also appeared in several of the Comic Strip films – including Supergrass, The Strike, and The Yob – says Dawn usually kept a low profile during filming. 'She kept herself to herself and just came out to do her bit,' he says. 'I hardly saw her; she didn't come out of her hotel room, and she wasn't very outgoing. There are two types of people in this business: the type who get pissed and have a laugh, and the other type like Dawn who come along, do their act and then pack up and get home. She's not the party type.'

Christopher Malcolm, who would also later appear with Jennifer Saunders in Absolutely Fabulous as one of her ex-husbands, was left with much the same impression. Although a light-hearted holiday atmosphere prevailed on the set, he says Dawn and Jennifer were not really a part of it. 'They were around but they kept themselves to themselves,' he recalls. 'It was very much work for them. They are very professional and when they go to work, they work.'

Dawn, however, claims that she didn't take her Comic Strip work seriously enough. 'Peter is a fantastic director, who's very original and ahead of his time,' she says. 'He knew what he wanted to do but we didn't; we were all just larking about. We hadn't made very many films, so it was like when you come back off holiday and you send your pictures to Boots and you can't wait to see them again; that was the feeling. It was like, "Oh, look at me in those shorts!" Nobody's thinking, "Welcome straight to film-making".'

While Dawn kept a low profile in Spain, Keith Allen painted the town red. His antics did little to impress Dawn. 'I don't think many women like Keith Allen – he's a bit of a lad,' observes Christopher

Malcolm. 'He was on pretty riotous form in Spain. There was a lot of drinking and a lot of bad behaviour. We had a notorious poker game in a pub near the hotel, where he kept doubling up the bets and losing. He owed me something like fifteen hundred quid by the end of the night but he didn't pay. Dawn and Jennifer weren't involved in the game, but they were there. It was quite funny; Allen was very drunk and the locals got really pissed off with him. The whole thing was coming to a head and I knew there was going to be fisticuffs. We were all wondering when the fight would start, when Keith did something brilliant. He dropped his trousers and showed his dick and they all had a laugh and that was it. It defused things. The locals had a laugh and got the beers in.'

With this kind of behaviour going on, it was perhaps unsurprising that Dawn and Jennifer chose not to stay with Allen and the rest of the team in the local *pension*, but instead rented an apartment nearby. But the decision came close to costing them their lives. The block of flats they were staying in had a potentially deadly gas leak, and the French and Saunders partnership was very nearly ended before it had properly begun. The women arrived back at their apartment after filming one evening and collapsed exhausted into bed. But while they were asleep, toxic gas filled the flat and the fumes were on the verge of sending them into a coma. They were roused by a member of the crew who smelled gas and realised they were in danger. Dawn and Jennifer were left shocked and terrified by what had happened, but thankful that they had escaped with their lives.

'Dawn and Jennifer almost died out there,' reveals Malcolm. 'Their apartment had been recently constructed and something had gone wrong with the gas supply. Fortunately somebody smelled gas and broke into their room and found them lying there. They managed to rouse them – they were caught just before they both went off to sleep for ever, or were blown up. They were OK once they'd got some air but it was very near to being a disastrous situation.'

Apart from being a great deal of fun to make, gas leaks notwith-standing, the Comic Strip films were also hugely influential. They made television executives sit up and take notice of the new-style comedy, and it is questionable whether many of the alternative comedy shows would ever have made it on to mainstream TV if The Comic Strip hadn't existed. Its particular brand of humour, along with the people who were involved in it, would come to dominate television comedy for the next two decades. Shortly before the launch of Channel 4, the BBC had been showing interest in some of the new comedy stars – namely Rik Mayall, Adrian Edmondson and Ben Elton – and was considering their idea for *The Young Ones*, a sitcom about four delinquent students sharing a house. But the corporation didn't appear to be in much of a hurry to commit itself – until word got around about Channel 4's interest in The Comic Strip. Worried that they might lose out to the new station if they didn't act decisively, the BBC commissioned *The Young Ones* in the autumn of 1982. Starring Rik Mayall, Adrian Edmondson, Nigel Planer and Chris Ryan, the only non-Comic Strip member, the show quickly became one of the most popular comedy series of the eighties.

The following year, Dawn and Jennifer also landed their own television series. *Girls On Top*, made by Central Television, was initially intended to be a female version of *The Young Ones*. The idea came about because there were no parts for them in *The Young Ones*, and they knew they could come up with a wealth of material from their flat-sharing days at drama school. They met American actress Ruby Wax at a party and discussed their ideas with her. She was keen to be involved and the idea took root. Lenny suggested they meet with Tracey Ullman, his co-star on *Three of a Kind*, and having met her, the *Girls On Top* team was complete. The show was written by French and Saunders with Ruby Wax, with contributions from Ullman. Their friend Ben Elton acted as script editor.

It was commissioned in 1983, but was beset by production

difficulties and didn't actually go out until October 1985. Dawn played Amanda Ripley, a domineering left-wing feminist and bossy-boots; Jennifer was old school friend Jennifer Marsh, a complete dimwit; Ruby Wax played Shelley Dupont, a rich American would-be actress; and Tracey Ullman was Candice, a hypochondriac, tart and liar. Lady Carlton, the girls' batty landlady, was played by the late actress Joan Greenwood. 'It's women's comedy,' said Dawn. 'It's cruel and real. We delve into the inner thighs, plucking the bikini line – that sort of thing.'

Dawn and Jennifer had found the world of television very different to what they had been used to. 'Sitcom is another world entirely,' said Jennifer. 'We're finding it hard work. And Ruby Wax is a tyrant. We write three alternatives for every line in the script. You just have to regard it as a job – sit down and get on with it.' Dawn was the one who galvanised them into action. 'She is a great motivator, which provides a useful asset in our working relationship as I lean more towards the apathetic and lazy,' admitted Jennifer. Dawn explained why Jennifer appeared to have fewer lines in *Girls On Top* than the other characters. 'Jennifer fell asleep during most of the writing,' she revealed. 'I'd say, "We've got to scene three and you haven't said anything yet!" then she'd say, "I'll say this here", and go back to sleep for another two hours.'

Girls On Top was destined to be short-lived. By the time the second series was made in 1986, Tracey Ullman had left to forge a career for herself in America, and at the end of series two the remaining characters and the entire house were destroyed by an explosion. Like *The Young Ones*, which also ended after only two series, the writers were determined not to be sucked into a long-running series. This attitude represented something of an about-turn within the industry, and was met with a great deal of surprise by TV executives. Normally artists were delighted if they could tie themselves in to a long-term deal. 'The days when you walked in with a contract and people fell at your feet were gone,' explains Paul Jackson. 'People didn't want to know how much and how long, they wanted to know who was writing and how it was going to be done. All the television companies found this very difficult to cope with.'

The mid-eighties was an extremely busy time for Dawn as her career well and truly took off. In 1985, at around the same time as *Girls On Top* was being shown on ITV, she and Jennifer appeared on BBC1 for the first time in *Happy Families*. Written by Ben Elton, the six-part serial told the rather complicated story of the search for the four missing girls of the Fuddle family. It was chiefly a vehicle for Jennifer Saunders, who played five parts in the show – including all four daughters and the girls' octogenarian grandmother, Granny Fuddle. Rik Mayall, Adrian Edmondson, Nigel Planer, Stephen Fry and Helen Lederer also appeared, along with Dawn as the Fuddle family cook. Given the not inconsiderable sum of money it had cost to make, the show wasn't judged a huge success. It attracted a rather modest six million viewers and Paul Jackson, who had produced and directed the series, later admitted that it had been wrong for peak-time viewing on BBC1 and should have been aired on BBC2. Jennifer and Dawn received praise for their performances, but some of the others were criticised for 'wild overacting'.

The same year, Dawn appeared on the Channel 4 entertainment series, *Saturday Live*, hosted by her husband. She enjoyed working with Lenny and in April 1986 she joined forces with him and their celebrity friends for the first-ever televised Comic Relief. An off-shoot of Bob Geldof's Band Aid fund-raising work for the starving in Africa, Dawn and Lenny were key members of the initiative to raise money with laughs. Shown on BBC1, the new talent represented by people like French and Saunders, Nigel Planer, Ben Elton and Rowan Atkinson rubbed shoulders with the more established acts such as Billy Connolly and Ronnie Corbett. The highlight of the evening was provided by Cliff Richard teaming up with *The Young Ones* to perform his song 'Living Doll'.

In a 1992 interview, Dawn admitted that she had been too scared to go to Africa to see the suffering for herself. 'Lenny's visited a few times and been very moved,' she said. 'I haven't been yet. I'd like to go but I'm a bit frightened. I'm quite good at doing what I have to do here, but I'm not sure how well I'd cope over there.' But Comic Relief wasn't just about helping the people of Africa. 'Two-thirds of the money goes to charities in this country – the homeless, the physically disadvantaged, the young and those with drug or alcohol problems,' Dawn explained. The latter is a cause close to Dawn's own heart because of her mother's involvement with Trevi House, a rehabilitation centre in Plymouth for mothers with addictions to drink or drugs.

In February 1987, Dawn and Lenny once again found themselves at the centre of a racial storm. The *Sun* reported that the couple were being forced out of their weekend home in Wiltshire because of 'race-hate comments by neighbours'. They had spent more than £125,000 buying and refurbishing an old Victorian schoolhouse in the village of Erlestoke, near Devizes, but were apparently being victimised by a whispering campaign against them.

Dawn had chosen Wiltshire for their country retreat because it was halfway between their home in London and her family in Plymouth. Although they did subsequently sell up, she and Lenny were furious about the story and accused the *Sun* of stirring up racial hatred. 'I care when our whole village has to suffer allegations of being racist,' she fumed. 'Nothing could be further from the truth. We have a great relationship with all our neighbours. They've been protective and kind.' Her husband echoed her feelings. 'I've been to places where they don't like black people, so I know what it's like,' Lenny said. 'But this village isn't one of them. It's a shame because these reports soured something that was potentially good. It's more of a slur on the village than on me, and that's sad. Naturally I'm sensitive to racism – I'm a black man. Much of it is water off a duck's back. But some things do cut through and when it affects your family, friends and private life, it's a different matter.' The paper later admitted the story was untrue and apologised.

In 1987, Dawn hit the jackpot when French and Saunders got their own television show. Being given a series on the BBC really made Dawn feel that she had made it, and she has described it as her biggest thrill. 'I couldn't believe having our own show with the globe going round and Morecambe and Wise on afterwards,' she marvelled. More accessible and less shocking than the brand of humour embodied by *The Young Ones*, *French and Saunders* became the show watched by everyone and their grandmother. Quirky enough to be different and new, yet comfortingly reminiscent of old-style comedy acts, they managed to bridge the gap between mainstream and alternative television.

The first series – which Dawn would later condemn as 'dreadful' – consisted of their usual tried-and-tested format of sketches, centring around a fake TV variety show. Raw Sex – aka comedians Simon Brint and Roland Rivron – provided the music. The first of six shows began on 9 March 1987 on BBC2, and the channel remained their home until they were 'promoted' to BBC1 in the early nineties. The first series pulled in five million viewers – a respectable figure for BBC2 – but the duo admitted that they found preparing for their own series daunting. 'We've never written it down before,' Dawn said. 'We've always done it from improvisation.'

She said it was impossible to concentrate on work if they met at home, so they forced themselves to go into an office at the BBC every day. 'If we met at home we'd never get anything done,' she explained. 'I'd be saying, "Have you seen my new curtains?" or, "Do you think I should re-cover that chair?" and we wouldn't write a word. We use the BBC as a torture chamber.' A typical workday involved sitting at a desk, gossiping and being silly, until eventually a sketch idea came to them. On days when nothing came, they talked about their husbands and holidays.

Dawn was reluctant to leave Jennifer to write unsupervised

because of her partner's tendency to daydream. 'One day I left the house and she was sitting there drinking a cup of coffee and looking into the fire,' Dawn recalls. 'I came back seven hours later, *seven hours*, and there she was. The fire had gone out but it was the same cup of coffee. And I can remember thinking, "What is going on with this woman?"' Daydreaming apart, the women claim never to have fallen out over a script. Instead, they have acquired a series of codes over the years which lets the other know if she is being unfunny or going on too much. Should either one of them utter the words, 'I say, is that the tea trolley?', for example, the other knows it's their cue to shut up.

Having been somewhat spoiled, artistically speaking, by the indulgent atmosphere of the Comic Strip team, working for ortho-dox television companies came as something of a shock to Dawn. In Peter Rosengard and Roger Wilmut's book, *Didn't You Kill My Mother-in-Law?*, she is critical of the BBC, making remarks she would be highly unlikely to utter today. 'We'd love to use technicians from drama, our stuff is much more drama-based, but the big TV companies don't ever let you do it,' she complained. 'Which is why The Comic Strip is great, because you have the freedom to use people in the crews that you respect. People in those crews will give you suggestions, whereas at the BBC there are obstacles. People have been trained by the BBC to be clever dickies, and to have a snappy, sharp show – there are lots of shows that are right to be like that, but our stuff is much better when it's all languid and gentler.' Jennifer agreed. 'You're not expected to be in certain meetings, you're not expected to suggest certain things,' she said. 'I'm sure we were considered terribly difficult, but if you write something and perform it, you obviously have an idea of how you want it to look.'

In April 1987, Dawn's career took another turn when she made her West End theatre debut. Christopher Malcolm was staging Sharman MacDonald's play, *When I was a Girl I Used to Scream and Shout*, a poignant Scottish comedy about the growth of sexual awareness. It had been playing at the Whitehall Theatre with Julie Walters and Geraldine James in the lead roles, and when the actresses finished their stint Malcolm cast Dawn to replace James. 'I asked Dawn to do the role of Vari and she jumped at it,' he recalls. 'I didn't have to persuade her. She went and saw it and subsequently joined with Sharon Duce. It must have been daunting for her to take over from Geraldine, and it certainly was her first West End appearance, but she didn't seem nervous. She was amazingly confident. I thought she was excellent, a natural, and she got very good reviews.'

It was the perfect opportunity for Dawn to spread her wings without her co-star because Jennifer was at home expecting her second baby. She and Adrian Edmondson had become parents for the first time in 1986 when their daughter Ella was born. Dawn admitted that it was strange being without Jennifer. 'I find it really weird to be working so intensely on something that Jen isn't in. I feel nervous but at the same time really excited.'

She did other solo work that year, beginning a pattern of working sometimes with Jennifer, sometimes on her own that continues to this day. She made a fashion show, *Swank*, for Channel 4 in 1987, despite claiming to dislike the subject. 'I hate fashion, but the producer kept asking so in the end I thought, "Why not?"' she says. This was followed in 1988 by *Scoff*, a series about a subject much closer to her heart – food. At one point she had to report from the Smarties factory. 'I thought I'd died and gone to heaven,' she laughs. But she quickly nipped in the bud any worries people might have about her 'abandoning' her double act with Jennifer Saunders. 'If we do separate things, we have more to bring back into the act,' she pointed out.

As the members of the Comic Strip team pursued their individual careers, they inevitably worked together less and less. But when Peter Richardson was making a new film they would usually endeavour to drop everything to take part. 'We wouldn't do anything for months, for anything up to a year, and then we'd all come together again,' says Robbie Coltrane. 'It was like family reunion time – it was great fun. It was all on location, so we'd just all appear at some hotel in Devon and get pissed for a week.' Christopher Malcolm explains how people participated in the films because they were fun to do. 'It was absolutely not for the money,' he laughs. 'Although funnily enough, I still get little cheques from them because they're all shown endlessly.' Dawn agreed that having a good time was often their motivation. 'The Comic Strip team are the best fun you can have,' she says. 'In the early days, we used to have to put our mortgages and savings on the line to make the films, but now they have a life of their own and can attract finance. They're always a good laugh and they only take ten days to make!'

The third series of *The Comic Strip Presents* . . . did not go out until 1988, but in the intervening period Dawn worked with the team on three specials for Channel 4. *The Bullshitters*, a spoof of the TV show *The Professionals*, was shown in 1984, followed by *Private Enterprise* and *Consuela* in 1986. The latter, starring Dawn in the lead role as the sinister housekeeper and written by her and Jennifer, was a take-off of the Hitchcock film *Rebecca*. 'We wrote it because of the pressure,' explains Jennifer. 'We felt we had to keep up in some way, and that was the only way to do it. And when you say you'll do something, occasionally you actually have to go through with it. I don't know why we chose it, except that we probably saw *Rebecca* the night before.'

In between the showing of the three specials, The Comic Strip made its first foray into full-length cinema with *The Supergrass*. Released in November 1985, the film starred Adrian Edmondson as a nerd who pretends to be a drug smuggler in order to impress his girlfriend, played by Dawn. In February 1988, the third series of *The Comic Strip Presents* . . . started its run on Channel 4. The first film, *The Strike*, was a send-up of how Hollywood might portray the miners' strike of 1985. Peter Richardson played Al Pacino, who in turn was playing miners' leader Arthur Scargill. Jennifer was Meryl

Streep, aka Mrs Scargill. Dawn played a film director's secretary and appeared as an Elizabeth Taylor lookalike in the award ceremony scene. Life mimicked art in this respect as *The Strike* won a prestigious Golden Rose award at Montreux. It was followed by *More Bad News*, *Mr Jolly Lives Next Door*, *The Yob*, *Fun Seekers* and *Didn't You Kill My Brother*, all of which Dawn had little or no involvement in.

Also in February 1988, Dawn took part in *A Night of Comic Relief* on BBC1. It ran for six hours and involved virtually everyone in show business – mainstream and alternative – and raised more than £13.5 million. Dawn made newspaper headlines when she was accused of swearing on live television. She shocked millions of viewers by apparently calling newsreader Michael Buerk 'a fucking ninny' when he appeared in a sketch with her and Jennifer. Dawn asked him who he was and he whispered, 'I'm Michael . . . Buerk.' Dawn then blurted out, 'Don't call me a berk. I'm Dawn, you fucking ninny.' Lenny and co-host Griff Rhys-Jones were 'visibly embarrassed' by her outburst, according to press reports, but Dawn has always denied using the F-word.

The second series of *French and Saunders* began on 4 March 1988 and was markedly better than the first. The variety-show format had been scrapped in favour of their preferred sketch-based approach. 'This show still gives us major poo-pants,' Dawn said. 'We've only just learned how to write a comedy show, and you can try and fail so quickly. The tacky variety theme has gone because it forced us to get too caught up in logic and story. That's not our strength, and it never has been. This series is more disjointed but we've tried to do things that we think are funny, as opposed to things that make sense, and that's been a huge relief.'

The series included a sketch in which the pair pretended to be young girls, discussing sex and contraception in wildly inaccurate terms with mind-boggling references to 'Philippine tubes' and 'UFOs'. There were also frequent appearances from the team of *French and Saunders* 'extras' – singers Lulu, Toyah Willcox and Kirsty

MacColl, and actresses June Whitfield and Stephanie Beacham.

Once they had secured their own television series, Dawn and Jennifer were keen to distance themselves from the alternative tag. 'We feel we owe a lot to the tradition set by Morecambe and Wise,' said Dawn. 'A lot of people still see us as alternative comedians – whatever that means – but we're not. We're about variety – and that's much closer to Morecambe and Wise than anything alternative. Our comedy is very earnest, trying to put together a good show, and packing it full to the brim with family entertainment.' The BBC, too, was keen to stress their wide appeal. 'They've always had their loyal fans,' said a spokesman. 'But in this series people who've never seen them before are waking up to their talent at last.'

But the *French and Saunders* Christmas special threw their claims about being family entertainment into question when they were accused of making insulting sexual remarks about the Queen. It was the second time Dawn had landed in hot water that year. According to the *Sun*, hundreds of viewers had bombarded the BBC switchboard to protest, and furious MPs had called for the show to be scrapped. The cause of the row was a sketch in which Dawn and Jennifer appeared as lager louts watching the Queen's Christmas message on TV. Dawn acted out 'obscene' gestures against the furniture and said, 'Do you reckon she gets a bit?' Jennifer writhed in her chair and panted, 'Queen or no Queen, she's got a woman's needs.' Dawn then said the Queen was not like her sister Princess Margaret who 'goes like a bunny'. Tory MP Anthony Beaumont Dark, who could always be relied upon to be suitably outraged when asked by the press for a comment, called it 'pathetic and offensive filth fit only for the gutter'. He said the show's producer Geoff Posner should lose his job 'at once' and that the BBC should launch an immediate enquiry. The BBC, announcing that there were no plans for an enquiry, found that *French and Saunders* could be described as alternative when it was prudent to do so. 'It wasn't meant to be upsetting,' said a spokesman. 'It should be seen as alternative comedy.'

The highlight of the Christmas special was their hilarious send-up of the successful eighties all-girl band, Bananarama. Dawn and Jennifer demonstrated their brilliant observational skills when they transformed themselves into singers Lana Nee Nee Nu. The take-off was so good they were asked to release the song as a single. 'We thought about releasing it but decided no one would buy it,' said Jennifer. Early in 1989, however, they decided they *would* cut a record – but with the real-life Bananarama girls – to raise money for Comic Relief. The singers had apparently loved the way French and Saunders had sent them up, and agreed to record a cover version of the Beatles classic 'Help!' with them.

The following year, French and Saunders took their show on a nationwide tour of thirty-one provincial towns. It consisted of a string of ruthless mickey-takes, including jibes about their friend Ruby Wax and the boy-band sensation Bros. Dawn outrageously claimed to have undergone a liposuction operation to remove flab, performed by Janet Street-Porter's lips. 'I rather enjoyed it,' she said. 'She sucked it from my cheeks and blew it up my bottom.' Dawn revealed that pre-performance jitters were essential to get them into the right frame of mind, and that the one time they had gone on stage feeling relaxed they had given an 'awful' show. She also cheerfully admitted that it was a silly tour, with a lot of childish material. 'We did set out to do some grown-up material,' said Dawn. 'But it just seemed so incredibly pretentious and self-indulgent.'

By the end of the eighties, French and Saunders had firmly established themselves as mainstream television stars. They were the most successful women to emerge from the alternative scene. 'French and Saunders were innovative on two levels,' explains fellow comic Arnold Brown. 'First being female: apart from Maggie Steed and Pauline Melville, and later on Helen Lederer, there were very few female stand-ups in the business; and also in that they were a double act. Double acts, even in male comedy, are few and far between. With female comedy you have to go back to Gert and Daisy, who were music-hall acts in the fifties.'

Dawn, however, maintains that she was never interested in the 'women in comedy' label. 'We knew that our advantage in the beginning had been that there were no women about,' she says. 'But when we fell in with The Comic Strip, nobody was making a point to us about being "the women".' Nor was she a fan of the term alternative comedy. It is something she found both puzzling and annoying. 'We were labelled as the alternative comedy group, and you couldn't have had a group of people more offended by being called alternative,' she says. 'Because we hadn't invented the phrase, we didn't know what it meant. The press had decided that that is what we were. And it was the press in the long run that decided that was what we weren't – that we'd sold out. Within minutes of realising it was hip, it was really un-hip to be this thing called ' "alternative" – and I still didn't know what it meant.'

In the summer of 1989, Dawn and Lenny sold their London home after a year-long wait for a buyer. It had initially been for sale at £415,000, but they ended up having to knock £115,000 off the asking price because of the property slump. They also decided to sell their weekend retreat in Wiltshire, and put the cottage on the market for £185,000 – £110,000 more than they had paid for it two years before. They had spent little time in the property, and said that they found commuting 'too exhausting' and wanted something nearer to London. In August, they found their dream home – an exquisite late Queen Anne period home in the upmarket Berkshire village of Shinfield, near Reading. The location was ideal: within easy reach of the M4 and London, yet pleasantly countrified. They paid £1 million for Hyde End Farm, situated at the end of a 400-yard tree-lined drive and surrounded by farmland. It boasted its own swimming pool and tennis courts, and the high stone wall surrounding the back garden promised total privacy.

When Dawn and Jennifer started work on a third series of *French and Saunders* the following year, the duo suffered their first attack of writer's block. Instead of coming up with new ideas, they spent their time cutting out people's heads from *Hello!* magazine and pasting them on to the shoulders of other celebrities. 'We gave ourselves five months to write the series and after three months we had nothing at all that we were proud of,' admits Dawn. 'We either had to pretend we'd died and go to live in another country, or pursue it and shit it out however bad it might be. I used to think people were just lazy when they said that, until we had the Big Block ourselves. Finally fear and a looming deadline pushed us through.'

She put their momentary lapse in creativity down to four years of working together, day in, day out. 'I hadn't been on holiday for three years,' says Dawn. 'Nor had Jen. You run out of ideas and the freshness of it – and as soon as you get jaded you shouldn't do it any more.' In the event, they overcame their lack of inspiration to produce a series they felt happy with, and ten million viewers regularly tuned in. The duo relied heavily on send-ups of famous movies, including *The Sound of Music, Gone With The Wind*, and *The Exorcist*. In one of the series' most memorable sketches, they did a brilliant parody of the classic *Whatever Happened To Baby Jane*, with Dawn playing Bette Davis's character and Jennifer as Joan Crawford's cripple.

One of their best creations was the tough old country women who were unperturbed by even the most horrific injuries – decrying everything as 'fuss and nonsense'. In order to play them, Dawn and Jennifer had to be trussed up in foam-rubber latex and endure four-hour make-up sessions. For her role in *The Exorcist*, Dawn wore special contact lenses to give her white eyes, and had tubes full of gunge taped to the side of her face to make it appear as though she was throwing up. The last episode of the series included a sketch in which Jennifer played an irresponsible, party-loving mother with Dawn as her sensible daughter. The skit

would subsequently become the inspiration for Jennifer's hit solo TV series *Absolutely Fabulous*.

The downside of Dawn's new-found success was that by 1990 she and Lenny were in danger of becoming ships that passed in the night. The fear that they were not spending enough time together led her to suspend her own work plans in the spring of 1990 to accompany Lenny to America. He was due to make his Hollywood debut in *True Identity*, a film about a black man who disguises himself as a white man in a social experiment to see how the other half lives. They were both enormously excited about the movie, hoping that it would propel Lenny into a new league of superstardom. Dawn was desperate to go along for the ride. 'I thought I'd go with him for a month, or however long I could stand it; he was scared and he needed a chum,' she says.

'I wouldn't have gone unless I knew that he wanted me to be there, but I wouldn't have liked it if he had wanted to go without me. I don't think you can be apart for that long and enjoy your marriage. And when you're doing something where your ego is on the line so much and you're so vulnerable, you need your chum with you. I couldn't imagine leaving Lenny to deal with that on his own. When I got there and saw the pressure he was under I knew I'd have to stay for the whole time. I didn't want him stuck in a hotel; I wanted to be sure he had a home after his seventeen-hour days so he could sit down with a beer and read his comics.' In the end she spent four months with him in Los Angeles, during which time she fought on his behalf for time off when he was working too hard. He later said that she had become 'his backbone'.

But any thoughts they might have entertained of a movie-star lifestyle in Beverly Hills bit the dust upon arrival in LA. There were no limousines or plush hotel suites – she and Lenny were met at the airport in a Honda Civic. 'And we had to find a house to rent ourselves,' she says. 'It was pretty but small.' Filming was scheduled to begin in April but in the event nothing happened until November. 'It was a very weird year of hanging about waiting for something to happen,' says Dawn.

She spent some of the summer back in Britain, where she and Jennifer filmed their roles as pigs Porcas and Dorcas in the TVS film adaptation of Beatrix Potter's *The Tale of Little Pig Robinson*, transmitted that Christmas. 'We were perfectly cast,' laughs Jennifer. 'Two pigs who can't stop talking.' Dawn joked that no make-up was needed, but in truth the women had to be encased in sweltering rubber suits. 'It all sounded very exciting but when you're filming at sea in an old schooner, surrounded by pig padding, it's very different,' Dawn says. 'It was like wearing two sofas all day. And since make-up started at five in the morning and we didn't start filming until ten, we had to let our minds go blank to the discomfort. Poor Jennifer was eight months pregnant at the time and I kept on asking her, "Are you sure you want to go through with this?" And she said to me, "Yes, it will be a good laugh".'

Back in America, Dawn and Lenny decided to renew their marriage vows to commemorate their sixth anniversary. But their 'second wedding' couldn't have been more different to the first. Instead of a smart suit and tie, the groom looked more like a pizza-parlour waiter in a white T-shirt and red waistcoat, and in place of the beautiful wedding dress she had worn the first time around, Dawn wore a cassock-like shirt and trousers. And instead of the elegant venue of St Paul's Church, Covent Garden and the Savoy Hotel, the couple opted for one of the tackiest places in the world – Las Vegas. They booked the Silver Bell Wedding Chapel for the bizarre ten-minute ceremony, which cost £45, and were serenaded by an Elvis impersonator who sang 'Love Me Tender'. The only lip-service paid to tradition was provided by Dawn's bouquet of red and white roses. 'It was meant to be romantic,' says Dawn. 'But I wet my knickers I laughed so much. It makes a mockery of everything you think about marriage – plastic flowers, Velcro-fastened dresses and a preacher who had to look at a prompt sheet to remember your names.'

Dawn was not impressed by the time she and Lenny spent in Los Angeles, branding the city 'evil' and 'a cesspool'. 'It's like Blackpool but with bigger cars,' she says contemptuously. 'Everything you hear about Hollywood is true. So many liars and cheats who'll welcome you then stab you in the back the next day. The place and the people are completely mad. It's full of greed and desperation. The people that do come from there are hidden away in terrible ghettos, and those who don't are orphans living in a place which is blanketed by a poisonous fog. It's just a tiny Mexican town that got bloated.'

Her impressions of the industry weren't helped by the fact that no one paid any attention to her. 'It's the first time I'd ever gone anywhere as The Wife,' she says. 'I was ignored a lot, I wasn't the star. Actually, it was rude. I didn't expect anyone to know me, but I did expect some good manners.' Everywhere she went, movie moguls treated Lenny as a star and ruthlessly cut Dawn out of their conversations. 'I was treated like some fluffy thing on the arm of his jacket,' she moaned. Finally, during yet another dinner at which she was being ignored as usual, a rather inebriated Dawn had a cringe-making showdown with her hosts. 'No one was speaking to me at all,' she explained. 'I just got angrier and angrier and was drinking and drinking, to the point where I stood up and told them what I was about and how I had my own TV show in Britain. The next day they sent a car to pick me up for the first time. Suddenly, I was a person and valid because I was on telly here. That said it all: I mean, how pathetic.

'They only talk to people who are successful. They all expect you to tell them who you are, and they couldn't understand why I hadn't told everybody I had my own television show. In America if you're not openly, verbally proud of yourself, then fine, you're a failure and you'll be treated as a failure. I found that quite hard to take.' In a candid moment she admitted: 'The American businessmen who control the film industry don't like little, fat girls.' She then cheerfully went on to detail all that she had eaten during her stay, admitting that she had taken full advantage of film-set catering. 'They have an enormous trestle table covered with sweets and bread and peanut butter and jam, and huge bowls of bubblegum and lollipops for people to have all day,' she said in wonderment. 'So I was on set most of the time even though I wasn't in the film. I was just on the set, grazing. I also spent an awful lot of time on the beach, swimming, eating peanut-butter thingies, Mexican food and Hershey bars.'

Dawn naturally hoped that the film would be a hit for Lenny and that America would prove to be where it was at. 'I don't think I'd like to live there, but I'd quite like to visit and take from it what it can offer, especially since we can't be offered those chances in this country,' she said. 'Nobody here would give Lenny a feature film to star in, whereas the Americans do value their comedians.' She was understandably hurt, therefore, when superstardom failed to materialise and *True Identity* flopped on both sides of the Atlantic. 'Lenny didn't get bad reviews, although the film did,' she said defiantly. 'He did incredibly well out of it, and there are now other offers on the table for him.'

She pinned the blame on the Americans. 'When he went over there he had a really good script, but by the time twelve producers had got to work it wasn't,' she said. 'Lenny had a horrid time because he wasn't in control.' She later admitted that Lenny had been bitterly disappointed when *True Identity* bombed. 'It was a dream thing for him,' she said. 'He wanted to make it over there, maybe because most of his heroes are American comedians.' Dawn told reporters she had written a script while she was in America that had been snapped up by one of the big studios. 'I have an idea for a film which I hoicked around and they liked, so that may happen,' she said. 'Mel Gibson has read the script and really likes it.' But the film failed to come off.

Dawn hadn't gone to America just to support Lenny. In truth, she rather hoped that the trip to Hollywood would open some doors for her too. But when she got there she felt distinctly out of her league. As a big fish in a small pond back home in Britain, she had never appeared to suffer from shyness or a reluctance to talk herself up. But in the city of the beautiful people, her confidence deserted her. She became suddenly self-conscious and shy of approaching people in the industry with her ideas. 'I knew that if I just turned up they'd say, "Who is this little fat girl? She must be an English Roseanne Barr. Let's put her in something about mad people",' she says.

Their brush with writer's block had made Dawn and Jennifer realise that they shouldn't necessarily work together all the time. 'It was coming to the stage where we'd had no experience outside each other,' Dawn explained. 'We'd sit down to write and there was that old face again. Now we want to take time off to do other things. To be honest, the friendship I have with Jen is more important than the work – I'd rather be her friend till I die than keep the act till I die.'

With this in mind, early in 1991 Dawn followed up her success in *When I was a Girl I Used to Scream and Shout* with another West End theatre role. Her pal Ben Elton chose her to play the lead in *Silly Cow*, his play about a bitchy newspaper columnist. It was a role he had written specially for her. 'People think it's nepotism, but nobody else ever asks you to do any plays,' Dawn said. 'Perhaps there is a gang. But it's a successful one.' The play opened on 26 February at the Theatre Royal Haymarket with Dawn starring as the wickedly witty Doris Wallis. 'She's a lady with a bad attitude, but funny, feisty and ballsy,' she said. 'I'm going to have fun being a bitch. Doris is thoroughly unpleasant and amoral!'

Both she and Elton refused to say who the character was based on, but Dawn admitted enigmatically: 'I've had to find a truly unpleasant person to draw upon for my performance.' She was relishing the challenge of being on stage again. 'This role is nerve-racking, terrifying, to be honest,' she admitted. 'It feels like a massive mountain to climb. This is The Big One. The fact that it was written for me makes it a weightier prospect.' Labour leader Neil Kinnock turned out for the show's opening night, along with Jonathan Ross, Peter Cook, Bob Geldof, Jennifer Saunders and, of course, Lenny. 'I think it's a great play,' he gushed. 'I think Dawn's brilliant.'

After the play, Dawn went straight into filming her new BBC2 series *Murder Most Horrid*. It was a collection of six self-contained murder mysteries, with Dawn playing a myriad different characters. It began transmission in November 1991, and her solo television debut was judged a resounding success. The show won a prestigious British Comedy Award for 'Best Comedy Drama'. 'I enjoy the challenge,' said Dawn of her new role. 'With each of these shows you start afresh. If you're a show-off, the best fun you can have is playing lots of different characters – lots of dressing up with the dressing-up box.'

By the start of the nineties, Dawn was feeling pleased and contented with her lot. And rightly so. In the space of just ten years she had gone from being a drama teacher in a London school to being one of the most popular and in-demand comedy actresses of her era. But being a comedienne and an actress were only some of her talents. Dawn had another role lined up for herself: that of a high-profile ambassador for the larger woman . . .

Size Matters

By the start of the nineties, Dawn had become a rich woman. A lucrative contract with the BBC was topped up by other television work and theatre roles, and she was also in demand for advertising voice-overs. As part of a successful double act, and half of a high-profile show-business marriage, she was frequently invited to parties, and there were premieres and award ceremonies to attend. As such, she needed to dress the part of the glamorous celebrity but one thing never seemed to change: she still had nothing to wear.

As thousands of women can testify, it is depressing to see rails full of beautiful clothes and not have the money to buy them. Equally frustrating is to have the money but be unable to find anything in your size, and this is the problem that Dawn continually faced. Because she was famous, she was in the fortunate position of being able to call upon top designers like Vivienne Westwood and Jasper Conran to run her up one-off creations for special occasions. But on a day-to-day basis she still had difficulty tracking down nice clothes. It was the same old problem she had encountered all her life, and one that only became more annoying the older she got.

She couldn't understand why more manufacturers didn't make clothes for large women. After all, she wasn't the only woman in the country who was bigger than a size 14. It didn't take a mastermind to work out that if she was experiencing difficulty finding fashionable clothes in her size, thousands of other women must have the same trouble.

For years the only shop that catered for the 'fuller figure' was Evans Outsize, a chain of stores supplying cheap, mass-produced clothes which, to put it kindly, were functional rather than glamorous. Even by 1990, larger women who wanted something a little bit different still had to rely on finding a tailor. Some designer clothes were starting to trickle on to the market in bigger sizes, such as the Italian label Marina Rinaldi which went from a size 12 to size 26, and Harrods had a Big is Beautiful range. But outside of London and the major cities, smart designer garments were almost impossible to come by.

For those who could afford to travel, America proved to be one solution to the problem. In a country raised on hamburgers and fries, US designers have had to cater for big men and women for years. Dawn discovered the US gold mine of outsize clothing when she spent her scholarship year in New York as a teenager, and flew there to shop whenever she could. 'In the States they have wonderful clothes even in huge sizes, so you can try on clothes that are too big just for a change,' she says. 'In New York there's a department store six storeys high, selling underwear and belts and big shoes – things people forget that big women need.'

Back home in Britain, she was infuriated by the apology for clothes offered to her. She realised that there was a huge untapped market out there, and was at a loss to understand why designers couldn't see it. Half the reason, of course, was that most designers don't want overweight people wearing their clothes because in Western society fat isn't sexy. Fashion design is a glamorous and vain business, and image is all.

'The shopping options here seem to be confined to dark little shops that are as furtive as porno places, and stores full of clothes designed for fifty-five-year-olds,' Dawn complained in 1990. 'Sixty per cent of British women are larger than size 14, and they're not all middle-aged. I would be very interested to know how I would have developed a sense of style if I had somewhere to shop other than Evans Outsize, confronted by a lot of middle-aged nylon frocks. I'm thankful for Evans when it comes to knickers and bras, but too much of the rest is like shower curtains. As any fat person will confirm, every time you enter their portals you desperately hope no one you know will see you. They are not a hip place to be. It gets me so angry that sassy, proud girls get stuck in that horrible stuff chain stores think fat women should wear – or have to buy their clothes in menswear departments. My sister-in-law, Sharon Henry, is one of the sassiest girls I know, and she certainly doesn't want to be concealed under a crimplene tent!'

Dawn had found a kindred spirit in Lenny's youngest sister, and the two women became firm friends. Both were large women, and in 1990 Sharon helped Dawn model sweaters to publicise her first foray into outsize fashion. It was a book called, appropriately enough, *Big Knits*, and featured knitting patterns by designer Sylvie Soudan. Dawn loved wearing jumpers, but had been forced to buy men's extra-large ones until she met Sylvie. 'We hit it off immedi-ately and she made me a sweater which I just wore and wore non-stop,' she explains. 'So many big girls were asking me for her number, and it seemed so unfair that if they couldn't afford to pay over £200 for a designer sweater they didn't have the options I had.' The book represented a cheaper alternative, whereby people could wear Sylvie's designs but save money by knitting them at home.

Participating in the knitting book and modelling the jumpers in magazines set Dawn thinking about becoming more involved in the fashion business. That larger women should have a choice of decent things to wear was something she felt passionately about, and it was her dream to open a shop for big women. As she trundled around the shops trying to buy clothes, growing ever more depressed when the largest sizes she could find were size 16 or – if she was lucky – an 18, she often fantasised about how great it would be to have her own store where nothing would ever be too small. She had it all pictured in her mind: there would be large aisles and dressing rooms to make customers feel comfortable, and the mannequins would reflect the shoppers' figures rather than the usual model-sized 10. Best of all, there would be a milk-shake bar in the corner – because after all, one could always go for a bigger size.

Inspired by *Big Knits*, she started to wonder if there was any reason why her dream shouldn't become a reality. She knew there was a market and explained her ideas for dressing French-style. 'I want a big, proud shop with lots of space, loads of choice, no communal dressing rooms – one of the greatest forms of cruelty to women – and big women serving,' she said enthusiastically. 'Big women don't want to be served by stick insects. It would have really well-fitting swimwear and underwear – and cotton knickers that aren't made for PE instructors. Also sportswear – I used to go riding a lot but I couldn't buy jodhpurs in my size. Sixty per cent of the population is currently not being catered for. Gradually, some stores such as Marks & Spencer have begun to go up to size 20, but that's where big girls *start*! It's a shame because most big girls simply give up in despair and spend their clothes money on boxes of Kleenex to sob into, and big cream cakes to eat.'

She embarked on an in-depth investigation into what launching her own fashion company would entail. But after looking into it she was forced to admit that she simply could not afford it. No matter how hard she looked at it, the figures always added up to the same amount. She would need a hefty £750,000 to finance her fantasy. 'I never dreamed it would cost so much,' she announced sadly. 'But I wouldn't want to do it unless I could do it right.'

That might have been the end of her dream if clothes designer

Helen Teague hadn't read an interview with Dawn in which she talked about her hopes. Teague, who had her own shop and mail-order business specialising in clothes for the fuller figure, was keen to expand but needed capital and publicity – both of which Dawn could provide. She sought the actress out when she was appearing in the West End play *Silly Cow*, and went to see her in her dressing room. 'I'd written to her on impulse, asking if she'd be interested in buying a share in the shop,' Teague explains. 'One evening I went backstage to broach the subject. She'd already made up her mind, so it seemed. We ended up chatting very quickly about children and all that personal stuff, and at the end of it I wasn't sure whether she'd said yes or not. I said, "Are you up for this, then?" and she said, "Yeah, I'll give it a whirl".'

Like Dawn, Helen Teague was a big woman, and she shared Dawn's frustrations at the lack of stylish clothes on offer. She had lived in Ghana until she was twenty and came to England to do an architecture degree. 'When I arrived in England I found it hard to believe that people couldn't see the beauty of the different sizes, shapes and ages of women,' she says. 'Similarly, fat women usually don't see themselves as beautiful because they are bombarded by stereotyped magazine images and can't equate themselves with beauty. It's just not like that in Ghana.'

Dawn had met Helen briefly the year before when she visited her shop, Big Clothes. 'I was buying loads of stuff – doing that panic-buying that big women do,' recalls Dawn. 'I could hear someone downstairs working on a sewing machine. Then it stopped and Helen came up the stairs, looked at me and said, "I've been waiting for you to come here". She is very spiritual and thinks that everything has its place, and believes fate brought me to the shop. I had approached various designers but it would have meant remortgaging the house, and I'm too cautious to risk everything. When Helen came along she was the answer, really.'

Launched in London's trendy Primrose Hill in November 1991,

Dawn and Helen's new shop promised to give big women an equally big choice of beautiful clothing. They called it 1647, after finding out that forty-seven per cent of British women were a size 16 or over. The name also referred to the fact that their sizing went from 16 to 47 – although they were classed as Small, Medium and Large. For the first time in her life, Dawn was able to utter the immortal words, 'I think I'll have a small'. The vital statistics were impressive: the clothes were designed to cater for up to a 66 in. bust, 60 in. waist and 70 in. hips. 'I wanted a shop that big girls could be proud to go to,' explained Dawn. 'We sell the biggest clothes in the world.' The garments were made in Ghana, where Helen spent much of her time.

As Dawn had planned in her daydreams, the shop was customer-friendly, with tea and coffee and a comfy sofa to settle into. Unfortunately the milk-shake machine idea never came off, although there were bowls of chocolates scattered around for shoppers to dip into. Customers were encouraged to make appointments, and there was also a mail-order service selling tops from £25 and trousers from £30. Dawn found having her own clothes shop to be even more rewarding than she'd imagined. 'We've had women crying because they've found a pair of trousers that fits,' she said, clearly awed. 'One of the greatest bonuses of finding clothes that fit and flatter is the self-confidence they can engender in women who have never before enjoyed that experience.'

She spoke from bitter experience on this point, recalling with a shudder the type of clothes she had previously been forced to buy. 'I've got blouses with a bow at the neck, you know, like Margaret Thatcher wears, because it's the only thing that would fit me,' she says. 'You see big women in smocky dresses or in orange velour because it's all they can get.' By contrast, 1647's clothes were well cut and designed to make big women feel comfortable, using fine fabrics like silk and jersey which were cool to wear – 'because big women sweat', Dawn pointed out. 'It's not that we want to be fashion victims,' she insisted. 'Big women simply want to be able to get dressed!'

Dawn modelled most of the clothes herself, realising that the shop stood more chance of attracting publicity with a famous face involved. Newspapers and magazines were glad to offer her some free publicity for the new venture, in return for an interview. It was an arrangement that suited both parties, with the papers filling their pages and Dawn plugging 1647. Not all the coverage was flattering, however. The *Sunday Times* described the clothes as being 'closely based on the wardrobe of Andy Pandy'.

The early days of the new business were a thrilling time for both women. 'It's a dream come true,' admitted Teague. 'Our business makes me feel like a pioneer. Although somebody said the clothes were like pyjamas, I'm very pleased that we've got a style people can recognise. We always discuss designs in detail; it's a collaborative process. Dawn has strong ideas about what she likes – we definitely don't do frills and flowers.' Dawn, however, drew the line at designing the clothes herself. 'Helen and I have very similar tastes,' she explains. 'We both like a simple but sophisticated look and beautiful fabrics. She lets me see all the designs and takes on board my comments but I don't ever help do design – that's Helen's bag. Helen runs the shop; all she requires from me is a bit of money and a bit of publicity to encourage people to go there.'

The 'bit' of money, however, was to mount up considerably over the years. Dawn's initial investment was £100,000, and by 1998 she had yet to see a return on her money. Moreover, she has continually had to put more cash into the business to keep it afloat. In 1994 she claimed that turnover had increased tenfold since they'd started trading, but two years later big losses were revealed when the company accounts were filed. They showed that 1647 had piled up losses amounting to more than half a million pounds. There was a deficit for 1995 alone of £226,470, following smaller losses in previous years. In 1992 the firm had lost £70,288, followed by

£88,909 in 1993 and £145,844 in 1994. But Dawn was in it for the long haul, and Helen Teague insisted that everyone was 'very happy' with the firm's progress. 'Our figures don't make it look as though we are making a profit, but we are expanding and investing,' she said.

Part of this expansion involved landing a concession at Liberty in Regent Street. The prestigious store took 1647's designer line, French & Teague, in August 1995 and the launch was celebrated with a catwalk show and champagne reception for VIPs and the press. The collection was made from luxurious fabrics such as velvet dévoré and satin, and was designed mainly for evening wear. The garments were far more expensive than the standard 1647 range; a sumptuous velvet jacket, for example, cost £1,000. 'I want to sew a very tiny little label inside that says "Sorry",' Dawn said apologetically at the launch.

It was a coup for Dawn to have her clothes on sale at Liberty, especially as they were displayed on the store's main designer floor – alongside those of John Galliano and Issey Miyake – and not confined to the 16-plus section. The following year, 1647 also had its clothing in the 1996 autumn/winter Littlewoods catalogue. Dawn naturally wore the clothes herself, although for special occasions she still indulged herself in the luxury of having items made for her by her favourite designers Betty Jackson and Jasper Conran. She became a fan of Conran's when he made her a fabulous red dress to wear to Lenny's thirtieth birthday party in 1988. 'I think he looked on it as a real challenge to dress a body like mine,' she says. 'And he came up with quite a sight. It had a very tight bustier with a skirt that went into a big peacocky thing at the back, and it had a bolero top – which sounds like something a big woman should never wear. But it was just wonderful. It had a bustier by Rigby & Peller, which hoisted my tits up and out so that – wham! – when anyone came up to talk to me they were right there, in their face. I had to have a couple of gins before I could walk into a room in it, but when I tried to leave the house to go to the party with Lenny, we had to stay a bit longer at home than planned, so it did the trick!'

That she had the courage to wear such a sexy dress says a lot for Dawn French. Many women who are larger than a size 14 or 16 would never dream of wearing such a revealing outfit, let alone revelling in it as Dawn so obviously had. She proved again that she has guts in 1995 when she appeared in a copy of Elizabeth Hurley's infamous Versace safety-pin dress for Comic Relief. Her self-assurance has grown over the years. Her father's words to her when she was fourteen stayed uppermost in her mind and gave her an unshakeable confidence in herself. Marriage to Lenny Henry only served to bolster her ego further. She in no way doubted her attractiveness or sex appeal, and seemed genuinely happy to be the size she was.

She had a right to be proud of herself. She has succeeded where others have failed – making it to the top in show business without dieting or changing the way she looks. Her size has also helped to further her funny-girl image over the years. She has claimed that she's never used her weight to get laughs, but in truth many of her comedy sketches rely on the fact that she is fat in order to be amusing. Witness her, for example, wearing an outsized tutu and masquerading as a ballerina in a *French and Saunders* skit. She has never been afraid to expose herself to mockery, and as a result she has won many admirers – as well as a few detractors. When French and Saunders did a take-off of Jane Russell and Marilyn Monroe from the movie *Gentlemen Prefer Blondes*, Dawn put herself well and truly up for ridicule. Dressed as a rather unlikely bunny girl, complete with fishnet tights and lacy body stocking, her ample curves were displayed for the whole world to see.

The concept of a fat woman who isn't ashamed of her weight is one that the media has never been entirely comfortable with. Inevitably, some sectors couldn't resist taking a pop. The *Sun* had fun using a publicity picture of Dawn and Jennifer in costume, describing how 'the jelly-like jokers squeezed into trawler-sized fishnet stockings before wobbling through the TV sketch'. Two days later, the paper's slimming editor Sally Ann Voak dubbed Dawn 'young, gifted but fat'. 'Roly-poly comic Dawn French has declared that she would rather be fat than kick her passion for chocolates, chips and jam butties,' she wrote. 'But I bet she shed a few tears after seeing her own wobbly bum and cellulite-dimpled thighs in Monday's *Sun*.' It went on: 'Dawn's take-off of Jane Russell relies heavily (*sorry!*) on the fact that she looks like a two-ton tuna thrashing around in her fishnet tights. Come off it, Dawn – you are too talented to have to use your bloated body to get a cheap laugh. Despite all your joky protests that big is beautiful, I just don't believe that you are happy as a fatty. No one who is as overweight as you is ever happy about it, or healthy.'

Regardless of Dawn's protestations to the contrary, many people refuse to believe that she is happy being the size she is. 'I think she must be mindful and conscious of the fact that she's very fat to be making a reference to it,' says Don Ward, her boss at the Comedy Store. 'If she wasn't, and if it didn't somewhat concern her, she surely wouldn't bother to speak about it. I think it's a defence mechanism kicking in.' Sally Ann Voak was of a similar opinion, and invited Dawn to contact her for a personal exercise and diet programme – which she promised would include a daily ration of chocolates. 'Why not shed a couple of stone?' she urged. 'You'll be just as funny when you're slimmer. With a sensationally pretty face like yours – underneath those chubby chops I'm sure there's an Ava Gardner struggling to get out – you'll have even more targets to send up. All that blubber is just clouding your performance as a fantastic funny girl.' Needless to say, Dawn did not pick up the phone to the *Sun*'s Wapping HQ.

In an interview with the *Sunday Times* in February 1990, Dawn revealed the trials and tribulations she had encountered as a famous fat woman. 'People tend to stereotype you as a fat slob if you're my size, but I actually lead a pretty active life,' she said. 'Interviewers often describe me to my face as "rotund", "ample" or "happy" – never fat or big – and that's far more offensive. They want to know how I "cope" with my size, as though it were some terrible physical disability; I feel like asking them how they cope with their sagging knees, or whatever. As I've grown older I've been able to measure my self-confidence against other people's, and found I have more of it. It must be because I have a great family and good friends.' One can only imagine her horror, however, when the interview was picked up by the *Sun* the next day and turned into a full-page feature under the headline 'I'm A Plump Lump And Just Love It!'.

Back in the early nineties, Dawn was determined not to become a zealous advocate for 'fat lib'. 'I'm not a missionary,' she insisted. 'I just get on with what I do.' Her remarks on the subject of size were reasonable – along the 'everyone has the right to be the size they want' line. 'I'm not saying that everyone should be fat, or that if a woman's health is endangered she shouldn't do something about it,' she said. 'But I think that if you're happy to be big, you shouldn't be swayed by what the media tells you. It takes courage to keep your size.' To convince an often disbelieving world of how content she was with her weight, she would take along a large bucket of biscuits to photographic shoots, and always made a point of ordering cake when being interviewed.

'Women have to remember that in many parts of the world to be big is to be regarded as beautiful,' she reminded. 'It's all to do with confidence. I do have confidence, but I'm not sure why. I think it comes from having a happy upbringing where size was never brought into question. I was shocked when I started to notice people's prejudices, as I never thought of myself as fat Dawn. Coming from a family that was short and wide and marrying into a big one probably helped. Both my parents made me feel good about myself. You are supposed to feel you are ugly because you are fat.

Well, I never thought I was ugly. When I was six I decided I'd be big and happy, as opposed to dieting and unhappy. I thought, "Either I'm going to stay the way I am and be happy, or diet and be miserable". I suppose I made the easy choice.'

But by choosing not to diet, Dawn did not stay the way she was. She got progressively bigger over the years, and her views about her weight grew stronger. In the early days of her fame, her main complaint was that there should be nothing wrong with being overweight. But in the mid-nineties she suddenly became far more strident in her views, turning from somebody who opposed discrimination against fat people, into someone who appeared to be actively against thin ones. She managed to polarise the debate completely to the extent that in her opinion there were only two types of women: fat women like her who made the brave decision not to diet, and thin women who were permanently on diets and desperately unhappy into the bargain.

She now makes no acknowledgement of the millions of women who are neither excessively fat, nor model-girl thin; or to those who are overweight and unhappy and desperate to lose weight. She pays scant regard to the crucial question of balance, even though it is widely acknowledged that to be either too fat or too thin is not good for a person's health. Neither does she appear to have considered the possibility that her parents might have done her a disservice by encouraging her to overeat.

Many of Dawn's comments regarding how much she eats are of the kind many overweight people make: 'I don't think about food much', 'I only eat when I'm hungry' and – the perennial excuse – 'I must have a slower metabolism than other people'. She is famous for her love of chocolate and once admitted: 'I love chocolate more than life itself.' She sets aside part of her fridge just for storing the stuff, and once drove for over an hour to get hold of a Crunchie bar. She was therefore the perfect choice to advertise Terry's Chocolate Orange, which she promotes with the memorable catchphrase: 'It's not Terry's, it's mine'. She has a chocolate bar every afternoon, but apart from that treat claims to eat 'just the usual three meals a day'.

At times, her forthright opinions appear to have increased along with her girth. In March 1994, she caused a stir by claiming that fat women made the best lovers. This was not to say that large women could be just as good in bed as slim ones, but that they were actually *better*. It was a sweeping generalisation, the type of which – as a feminist – she should have been against on principle. She went on to say that most men secretly fancied large women, and contemptuously referred to non-fatties as 'coat-hangers'. 'They love to sink themselves into softness, to sleep wrapped around curvy hips and swollen bellies, to rest their heads against delicious, ample bosoms,' she said in a no-holds-barred interview with the men's magazine *Esquire*. 'They keep their desire for big women a dark secret. They are seen out with coat-hangers because fashion dictates they should.'

She boasted that her former boyfriends had found her ample curves irresistible. 'I have never felt grateful, like many big women do, for the mere attention of a man,' she said. 'I have never felt that I only deserved the leftovers that thin women rejected. I always felt the right to be choosy, and my choices were the kind of men who rejoice in the fleshy, soft, sensual luxury of a generous body. In fact, I haven't shagged one yet who didn't like it. Big women do sex fantastically well. We know how to use our mighty weight; we know the considerable power of a full and voluptuous body. Our ample embraces are mere tastes of the pleasures men are on this earth to enjoy. There is a whole feast we can provide. Yum, yum.'

Obviously out to shock, she spoke candidly to the interviewer about erotica: 'Agonising, dark and very pornographic,' she leered. 'You only have to peek at erotic art, or even porn – Readers' Wives are my favourite – to know that I am right. There's something extremely delicious about flesh, and women who are confident about having it are very alluring. We won't eat you. Well, actually, we will – but you'll enjoy it!'

Every bit as surprising as her comments were the photographs that accompanied them. In a move that was to shock many of her fans, Dawn volunteered to put her money where her mouth was and pose nude to prove that fat could be sexy. She also elaborated on her view of sex. 'Big women have an abundant amount of sexual fantasies, more so than thin ones,' she said, clearly professing to be some kind of expert on the subject. 'We have enormous amounts of sex – we pump more oestrogen, so we want it more.' She didn't have much truck with the medical reports that claim excess weight can reduce libido. 'Big women want more sex, get more sex and fantasise more about sex than thin ones,' she insisted. 'I think we're more beautiful than thin ones. But bigger women aren't allowed to be sexy, they aren't portrayed as sexual beings. Yet I know from letters I've received, and from my own experience, that that's not the case.'

In the category of 'things-we-don't-need-to-be-told', she confessed that her secret fantasy was 'a major licking from a well-hung man'. 'I'm much juicier now,' she revealed. 'I cannot believe how randy I have become over the past three or four years. I am more interested in sex today, much more.' Of her decision to strip off for the camera she said: 'Of course it was a bit embarrassing in the studio, but fuck it.'

But despite her nonchalance, Dawn would later bitterly regret taking her clothes off, especially when the photographs found their way into the tabloids. The pictures and the remarks that accompanied them became a feature of virtually every newspaper in Britain, and her words came back to haunt her big time. Dawn's size had always attracted attention in the press, not all of which was complimentary. The *Independent* once remarked: 'Jennifer Saunders is the one who hides her looks behind a grumpy sneer; Dawn French is the one who hides her looks behind a roll of fat.' Once she had thrust herself so forcefully to the forefront of the big is beautiful crusade, the tigers were well and truly unleashed. She found herself on the receiving end of some wincingly cruel remarks.

'We're not fooled, are we?' asked Margot Norman, writing in *The Times*. 'Flipping through these photographs we don't see the outlines of a siren for the nineties. We see Ursula, the sinister and enveloping underwater witch of Disney's *The Little Mermaid*.' Norman criticised Dawn for not being satisfied with being loved as a comedienne and insisting on becoming a sex symbol. 'Insatiable types, these, and definitely alarming,' she wrote. 'Tell me I'm beautiful or I'll bash you.' She said that Dawn's remarks about how great big women are in bed were 'enough to send the average Englishman scuttling for cover', and went on to describe Dawn in the *Esquire* magazine pictures as 'reclining in wisps of white muslin, ostensibly like an Ingres odalisque but with an unmistakable undercurrent of beached whale'.

Dawn was appalled by the coverage the *Esquire* feature received and admitted that she had been naive. 'I was trying to prove that big women can also look great with their clothes off. What I didn't expect was for the photographs to turn up in every fucking tabloid under the sun,' she complained. 'If I could sue someone about it, I would.' She felt cheapened when one newspaper ran a phone hotline alongside her picture. 'So people could ring up and say whether or not they wanted to fuck me,' she scorns. 'I don't want to find out what they said, I think it would be too painful.' She was also upset when a *Sunday Times* journalist rubbished her theory, and claimed that in order to cover her in kisses he would need to take a week off work. 'Obviously written by a man with a very small penis,' Dawn concluded.

That she should be shocked by the reaction to the article is somewhat surprising, as it should have been obvious that the *Esquire* piece would cause a stir. But it didn't appear to have crossed her mind that her vociferous and opinionated remarks would be questioned. 'I did not expect the attacks at all,' she said, clearly upset. 'It was quite extraordinary and very hurtful. I didn't realise how virulent body fascism was. People seemed to think I wanted to grab headlines with the pictures but that wasn't the point. I did it because I think everybody is entitled to have the body they want without being ridiculed. Big women have not been allowed to be regarded as sexual beings, and I'd like to see that change.'

Dawn's body made plenty of headlines, and stoked up a national debate on the fat issue. Shortly after she stripped off for *Esquire*, she took part in a special edition of *The South Bank Show* called 'Big Women'. She also posed nude again, this time in a reconstruction of a Rubens painting. Many of her comments on the show made sense. 'What role models do big fourteen-year-old girls have?' she asked, speaking from first-hand experience. 'Everyone has to be thin. No wonder they all get anorexic. If they are never presented with the way to show themselves as attractive and sexy, they will never see themselves as such. We accept the large Renaissance women, but at some stage in history it all changed. People can't cope with the nineties image of a big sexy girl.'

Warming to her theme, she embarked on an attack on the fashion world. 'Fashion models are stick-thin and there is a reason for it,' she said. 'It's an old chestnut, but it's probably true, that the majority of fashion designers are gay men and they design for boys. They want models who are flat-bellied and flat-chested. Men should celebrate what we are, rather than looking at photographs of Kate Moss, aged sixteen and six stone, and making us feel like social misfits.'

Pertinent points, and ones which no doubt had women nodding in agreement at their television screens up and down the country. Dawn's concern for impressionable young girls was laudable, but once again she took things a step too far, insisting that fat ladies weren't simply every bit as attractive as slim ones, but were *more* attractive. 'Large women are more relaxed and more sexy,' she hectored. 'All erotic art is about big women. If I was alive in Rubens's time, I wouldn't have to be a comedienne for a living – I'd be celebrated as a beautiful model. In those days Kate Moss would only have had one use – as a paintbrush. He'd be painting me and I'd say, "What's that in your hand, Rubens?" He'd say, "It's Kate Moss. I'm using her as a paintbrush".'

Dawn also 'outed' a fellow fatty for refusing to appear on the show. She'd invited famous women who were a size 16 or over to take part, including the journalist and novelist Julie Burchill. But Burchill refused point-blank, so Dawn reaped her revenge at the end of the show. As the credits rolled she screamed: 'Big women in history have included Diana Dors, Joan of Arc, Marilyn Monroe, Julie Burchill, Julie Burchill, Julie Burchill.'

Defending women for being overweight was one thing, being rude about thin women quite another. Dawn had succeeded in opening the issue up to debate, but that she wouldn't like a lot of what she heard was only to be expected. 'Just when you thought you'd seen all there is to see of Dawn French – here she is again, trussed up like a box of chocolates in this month's *She* magazine,' said the *Express*. 'Britain's biggest comedy star tells us yet again why it's fab to be fat.' Richard Burton's widow Sally decided to hit back on behalf of thin women everywhere. 'I have had about as much as I can take of Dawn French's big is beautiful campaign,' she wrote in the *Mail on Sunday*. Under the headline: 'Forget It Dawn – Fat Isn't Sexy', Burton vented her indignation. 'Barely a publication has resisted the temptation to jump on her accommodating, politically correct bandwagon,' she said. 'She comes out with lines like, "There are two types of women: the ones who like chocolate and complete bitches". I'm tired of this fattism, and I find her arguments unconvincing. I refuse to believe that she will persuade anyone that it is a great idea to pile on the pounds.'

She poured cold water on Dawn's claim that men secretly desire fat women. 'This may bring some comfort to the forty-seven per cent of women in Britain who are a size 16 or over, but it is not actually true,' she wrote. 'In Dawn's definition I must be a bitch. Well, it takes one to know one. *The South Bank Show* has Dawn and a few of her tubby friends on one long bitch. If a thin woman released such venom at a large woman she'd be laid to rest. Everybody has a right to be who they are. Don't bitch at me for being thin, and I won't bitch at you for being fat.' Burton also accused Dawn of being too aggressive. 'Dawn can't understand why the appreciation of Rubens women has not carried through to the modern age,' she said. 'I can tell her. Rubens's models were feminine. By politicising the issue, size is now being used as a challenge; it's used aggressively. Size has become part of the feminist arsenal – "I'm big, I make jokes and I talk dirty. You listen to what I've got to say, dammit, or I'll thump you with one of these".'

Once again, Dawn was all innocent indignation. 'The programme was meant to be a celebration of big women, it wasn't a placard-waving thing,' she insisted. But she had learned a bitter lesson: if you dish it out, you've got to be able to take it. What she had said about thin women had been construed as offensive and rude. If thin women had made such disparaging remarks about her in print, she would not have hesitated to accuse them of fattism. *Daily Express* writer Alice Woolley found herself barracked by Dawn and Helen Teague for daring to admit to being on a diet. They even rather rudely suggested that she needed therapy. 'Tyranny, of course, can come in all shapes and sizes,' Woolley noted sagely.

But for all those who criticise Dawn for being outspoken, there are others to whom she is a heroine. They applaud her bravery and seek to emulate her confidence. Having initially claimed not to want to be an ambassador for large women, she nonetheless has become one. For millions of women in Britain, Dawn French is a role model: one of the most famous large women in the land. 'I get letters all the time from big women saying they're so pleased that I'm in the public eye because it shows you don't have to be skinny to be successful,' she says proudly. Many of her comments on the weight issue have been wholly responsible, especially her concern for young girls' eating habits. In 1995, she was a key member of a campaign to stop children from dieting, and she has frequently spoken out against the fashion industry's preoccupation with too-thin models. 'It should be balanced,' she argues. 'Teenage girls have no role models. We're only used to seeing high fashion on stick insects. Why aren't fashion designers interested in the challenge of designing things that would only look good on big women?'

She notched up another small triumph against her detractors when she was named as one of the world's sexiest women in a survey for *Company* magazine. She was listed alongside supermodels Naomi Campbell and Claudia Schiffer and David Bowie's beautiful wife Iman – proving that large women can be just as attractive as their thinner sisters. In another survey, Dawn and Lenny romped home with the dubious title of 'Tastiest Twosome'. Mr and Mrs Henry, according to the poll in *Forum* magazine, were voted the couple men and women would most like to have a sexy threesome with – beating glamorous screen stars Hugh Grant and Elizabeth Hurley hands down.

Despite criticism, Dawn continues to sound off on her pet subject. 'It's a losing battle for me even to try to be skinny,' she told *She* magazine in one of her numerous 'big is beautiful' sermons. 'It makes me so angry to see beautiful big women dieting – everyone's brainwashed.' She was outraged when she was invited to *The Clothes Show Live* event in Birmingham and the organisers refused to use big women to model 1647 clothes. 'I got so angry,' she says. 'The Clothes Show were not prepared to offer big models, but I wouldn't dream of showing my clothes on small women.'

Dawn has always maintained that she is happy being the size she is. 'I like the way I am,' she insists. 'A lot of women would regard me as damaged because in their eyes I've let my body get too big. But they're unable to see the damage they're doing to themselves –

mentally and physically – by trying to be thin. They're destroying their bodies with crash diets, and paying good money to do it too!' This, of course, is a reference to Dawn's first and only diet when she was trying to slim for her wedding, and shows her one-sided view of dieting. The fact that she resorted to a crash diet and expensive slimming injections in Harley Street appears to have given her a somewhat lopsided view of what losing weight is all about. She pays no attention to the fact that millions of people manage to diet sensibly and safely.

It is clear that her one-off diet had a traumatic effect on her, and she often harks back to it. 'I can't say if I liked being a size twelve,' she admits. 'It was different. I'd look in the mirror and think, "Oh, this is what a waist is supposed to look like". But to stay like that would have meant being unhappy for the rest of my life, as I'd always have to diet severely and never eat anything I liked at all.' She jokes that she started her wedding day as a size 12 and left the reception a size 14. Whether she has ever thought seriously about dieting sensibly and losing weight slowly is highly unlikely. Once asked how much she weighed, she replied defiantly: 'I haven't a clue and I don't give a toss.'

She says she keeps fit by swimming and playing tennis in the privacy of her home, but admits that her size *is* a bar to her doing certain things. She doesn't work out with Lenny in his gym because she finds it too uncomfortable. 'Exercise is painful when you've got big bosoms,' she points out. 'Sex is really the only kind of exercise I'm interested in. I think it gives you energy, yet it burns energy. If you've had a really long day, it's a nice way to go to sleep, but it's also a nice way to wake up and it gets you going in the morning – gets the blood pumping round.' She says she's also in good health. 'I've had my general health checked for mortgage insurance and stuff, and I'm completely healthy,' she says. 'My heart's fine and I never get sick. If a doctor told me I had to lose weight for my health, he'd have to show me some very conclusive proof that my life was in danger before I'd go on a diet and start exercising. I have no blood-pressure problem, no breathing problem and no heart problem, because my body accepts my weight. Look how unhealthy skinny women are! You can't say that women are unhealthy just because they're big. It's possible to be fat and healthy.'

Dawn insists that it is only when dealing with the media and the TV industry that her size becomes an issue. 'I've always felt that people who have a problem with you because you're fat aren't worth knowing,' she says wisely. 'Lenny has never asked me to lose weight, and I'm not sure I'd be with him if he had. He loves me just the way I am. But where it matters – in the media – fat is still a bad thing. And until we see a nice big round woman presenting the news and sitting on the TV-AM sofa, that's not really going to change much.' She has found Fleet Street picture editors particularly resistant to change. 'They've got a picture of me as a forty-year-old Iron Age woman, with a hessian jacket and dirt on my face,' she says. 'It was a photo from a Comic Strip film called *Summer School*. And they use it all the time, usually with the caption "Lenny's spunky wife Dawn . . ."'

Television reviewers, too, rarely fail to make some reference to her girth. 'They seem to regard it as some sort of physical disability,' she complains. She long ago grew tired of journalists' obsession with her weight. She and Jennifer even did a sketch about it, in which Dawn played a doctor who was doing a radio interview, but nobody wanted to talk to her about her work, only her weight. But the thing that drove her to distraction was getting job offers that sought to show her size in a poor light. 'If my agent gets calls for me to do anything, it's still mad, fat girls, people with eating problems, mothers of eight, or matrons,' she says. 'All fat parts. It has to be in the job description, either fat and depressed, or retarded. The producer from *Inspector Morse* will ring up and say, "Will you be the sort of weird one who eats too much?" Then I suddenly see how other people see me.'

All of which goes a long way to explain why Dawn comes up with so many of her own projects. 'I'm so glad I've created the work that I do,' she says. 'I just don't see myself like that because I never put myself in a category. In the Comic Strip films I would wear fishnet tights and little skirts. It never occurred to me that it was totally unsuitable for me to do that. It felt perfectly all right. Peter Richardson cast me as a mother, daughter, sexy girl or whatever, and none of those men ever thought twice about it.' In March 1990, Dawn claimed that she had turned down £40,000 to star in a British version of the hit American comedy *Roseanne* because she was afraid it would make fun of her size. 'They wanted me to be the leading role,' she said. 'But I get offered a lot of parts where the joke is that I am a big woman. I don't find that very funny.'

She also rejected an offer to reveal all for *Playboy*. 'They offered me an awful lot of money but I said no,' she revealed. 'I don't like the magazine because they turn women into sex objects. I'm not a sex object, though I am a sexy woman.' She featured in the TV documentary series *Fat*, which looked at the advantages and posi-tive aspects of being big. 'I'm not criticising thin women – some of my closest friends are thin and, even though they can snap easily without careful handling, I still like them,' she joked on the show. 'I'm just saying let's open the choice up a bit at the other end of the aesthetic scale. I long for the day of the fatter supermodel – when it won't be token and curiously circus-like.'

But within the same interview she once again insisted that fat women were better than thin. 'There's something more alluring, more powerful, more abundantly lovely about our full and splendid bodies that shouldn't be ignored,' she bragged. 'Softness, warmth, depth, comfort, ease. And all in abundant quantities. Not that I'm boasting, of course. Fat may not be fashionable, but it's inviting. It symbolises a love of life. It's sexy.'

By the start of the new millennium, Dawn was arguably just as famous for being a professional large woman as she was for her television work. And once that other pioneer for big women, Vanessa Feltz, 'sold out' and lost six stone, Dawn's position as a role model became more important than ever. Her fans can rest assured that she will *not* be following Miss Feltz's lead.

She remains passionately committed to her fashion business, although it continues to be something she has to invest in, rather than becoming the money-spinner she had hoped it would. While directors of successful companies can expect to draw hefty dividends, Dawn has regularly had to put in her own money in order to keep 1647 afloat. The company accounts for 1998 show that it had lost a quarter of a million pounds up to 1997. 'On paper, the company would appear to have traded at a loss for a number of years,' says accountant Bernie Hoffman of London firm Edelmans. 'It could not continue to trade without the support of its bankers and its directors, who appear to have guaranteed bank facilities and put in their own funds. The directors keep pumping money in to support it for whatever reason – whether it's a hobby or a love or something they think is going to come right in the long term.'

The shop in Gloucester Avenue is still open, along with the 1647 mail-order service. Liberty no longer stocks French & Teague clothes, but the label is now on sale in Evans – ironically the very store where Dawn made so many unhappy shopping forays in her teens.

CHAPTER TEN

A Girl Named Billie

If there was one thing that riled Dawn more than constant questions about her weight, it was continually being asked when she was going to have a baby.

With Jennifer Saunders producing three in quick succession, it was perhaps only natural that people would wonder when Dawn would follow suit. During interviews to promote their TV work, talk would inevitably turn to children and parenthood – particularly when the pair were talking to women's magazines. From 1985 to 1991, Jennifer was either pregnant with, or had just given birth to, one of her three daughters, so there was always scope for baby talk. Ella, Dawn's goddaughter, was born in 1986, followed by Beattie in 1988 and Freya in 1990.

Jennifer found the direction interviews often took to be mildly irritating, grudgingly answering that yes, Ella was teething, or no, Beattie wasn't walking yet. But for Dawn it was downright infuriating. During a joint interview with the *Daily Mirror* in 1987, she groaned out loud when the reporter ventured to ask Jennifer about the baby she was expecting. 'Do we have to talk about babies again?' she asked crossly. 'I want to talk about the new series.' It was a persistent problem and Dawn's frustration was tangible. 'It's annoying when you set aside a few days for interviews, and you give all the journalists a glass of wine and attempt to explain what you're trying to do with your new series,' she complained. 'And then a few days later an article appears saying, "Dawn and Lenny go to the Seychelles for their holidays and Jennifer's got two lovely kids and Dawn loves them . . ." and you think, "Oh, well, I can't be bothered to do that again".'

At times she handled the situation better than at others. In humorous mood, she once suggested a headline for an article: 'Dawn's not ready yet, but the egg's inside her and ready to burst'. But it was clear that such personal enquiries were beginning to gall. In October 1987 it had been reported that she was pregnant, having apparently become broody after spending time with her goddaughter. She and Lenny were said to be expecting their first child in April 1988, but after the initial story of her impending motherhood there was no further mention of a baby. Whether this was because Dawn had suffered a miscarriage, or had never been pregnant in the first place, is something she has never divulged. All she has said on the subject is that she and Lenny were going to have children shortly after they met in 1981 'and then didn't'.

But her childlessness was obviously a sensitive subject for Dawn. 'It's so predictable,' she groaned in 1988. 'People don't think you're normal until you've had a baby. These days I'm the hard, career-minded bitch and Jennifer's the lovely fluffy one because she's a mum. At least people don't think we're gay any more! But I'm still the threatening career woman – they'll only be really happy when I've had a baby too. Then I can be soft and cuddly like Jennifer.' For the first time since their partnership began, there was the merest whiff of jealousy of Jennifer in Dawn's remarks. Jennifer appeared to have it all: a loving husband, three beautiful children and a successful career. And she seemed to juggle motherhood and work with effortless ease. Of the two, it was usually Jennifer that female journalists empathised with because she was the one who fitted into the 'married with kids' norm. Despite her apparent anti-children stand, Dawn felt more than a little left out at times – hence her prickly attitude.

By 1991, it looked as if Dawn and Lenny would never become parents. 'I have so many friends who have such a flame, then they have a baby and suddenly it goes out,' she told the *Observer* that year. 'That frightens me. Lenny and I have great times together, doing what we want, when we want.' In another interview at the same time she said: 'I wish you could start having kids when you're sixty. We were going to have them ten years ago and then didn't. Now I've stood back and watched other people, and it's so disillusioning seeing what happens to them. The light goes out of their eyes, the fire that attracted you to them in the first place has gone and I'm saying, "Hello, HELLO?" I'm scared of it; is it a chemical thing that you have to turn into a jelly brain?'

But even as she uttered those very words, Dawn had a big secret up her sleeve – or, more accurately, a little one. She was about to become a mum herself. Watching Jennifer and her other friends with their children had had a profound effect on Dawn. Like many women reaching the big 3-0, she suddenly became aware of her biological clock and began to feel broody. To her great surprise she realised that she did have a maternal streak after all. But after more than two years of trying for a baby there was still no sign of her and Lenny becoming parents. Eventually they started to explore other avenues and, after much soul-searching, made up their minds to adopt.

While Dawn was busy telling journalists that she and Lenny were happy as they were, the couple were in fact in the middle of lengthy discussions with the adoption service. They had to go through the same strict screening procedure that all prospective adoptive parents face. But as a famous couple they were ironically at a disadvantage. Despite their wealth and lovely home, they had to overcome the prejudices that some people have about celebrities.

They had to convince social workers that their marriage was stable enough to raise a child, and that their lifestyle didn't involve going out partying every night of the week. They had to prove that they could give a child a normal upbringing, and allay fears that their careers involved lengthy working trips away from home. In short, they had to prove how 'ordinary' they were.

After undergoing more than forty hours of intense questioning, the couple were finally approved for adoption in March 1991. They managed to keep their plan a closely guarded secret during this time, terrified that if word got out their hopes would be dashed. Having been given the go-ahead to adopt, they began the long wait for a baby to become available. They were warned that this could take anything up to three years, and were also told that if they were lucky enough to be given a baby, it would be a year before they could legally adopt it as their own. In the event it was eight months before the call came through. In November 1991, they got the news they had been waiting for: there was a two-week-old mixed-race baby girl who would be just perfect for them.

It is a time of strong mixed emotions for adoptive parents. On the one hand they are ecstatic with excitement and cannot wait to see the baby and take it home. But on the other hand there are the same worries that many new parents experience: what if they don't love the baby? What if the baby doesn't like them? What if they aren't any good at being parents? Would they be able to cope? But unlike other mothers-to-be, Dawn hadn't spent nine months bonding with her baby and this made her extra nervous. 'It can be very traumatic because you could take an instant dislike to the child, or the child could dislike you,' Dawn later explained. 'It's awful – not like birth, where a baby has come from your body and belongs to you. Here's a little child that has already been formed and made somewhere else. You might only have found out about the child a week before, then suddenly you come face to face.'

But in the event, she didn't feel any of these things. It was love at first sight, and in a television interview with Mavis Nicholson she movingly described the magical moment when she first laid eyes on her daughter. 'Our social worker sat us down in a little room and told us she was going to get the baby,' she said. 'It seemed like she was gone for ten years, and Lenny and I sat staring at the doorknob. Then she brought in this little thing that could have been our natural child. I thought she looked just like Lenny, and at the same time he was thinking she looked like me!'

Dawn had been nervous in case she didn't immediately love the new baby, and worried what she would do if she failed to 'bond' with her daughter. But her worries proved groundless and she and Lenny fell in love with the baby the minute they saw her. 'She's an angel,' Dawn told *Hello!* magazine. 'It's quite extraordinary how beautiful she is. I expected to see a little wriggling thing, not a beautiful little wriggling thing!'

The rest of the day was an emotional blur for Dawn and Lenny. They took their daughter home and celebrated with a handful of close friends who were privy to their big secret. They raised a glass of champagne to their as-yet-unnamed daughter and wept tears of joy. After a few days of deciding what name would suit her, they decided to call her Billie. Dawn explained that they thought she was going to be very tall and figured that a flowery name like Emily or Rose wouldn't be suitable.

Once the initial euphoria was over, the couple faced a nail-biting wait for the adoption to become final. They had been warned that Billie's natural mother could change her mind at any time during that period and demand her child back. The thought that their beloved daughter could be taken away from them was too dreadful to contemplate, and the threat hung over them like a death sentence. They could scarcely wait for the 'danger period' to pass, and wished they could fast-forward the clock to a time when Billie would be one hundred per cent theirs.

As a safeguard against anything going wrong with the adoption, the couple resolved to keep their new daughter a secret. The last thing they wanted was the news breaking in the media. In this respect Dawn and Lenny achieved the nigh-on impossible. Not only did they manage to conceal their adoption plans from all but a tiny handful of close friends and family, they also had Billie at home with them for four months before word got out. In order to do this, they embarked on a cloak-and-dagger operation worthy of the secret service. They didn't take Billie out with them in case they were spotted, and Dawn even persuaded a pal to pretend she was pregnant so that they could avoid suspicion on trips to Mothercare. Shinfield is a tiny village, but Dawn and Lenny made sure that even the locals did not set eyes on little Billie.

They did well to keep her under wraps for as long as they did, but inevitably Fleet Street finally got wind of the new addition to the Henry household. 'Lenny and Dawn's joy as they adopt a baby,' trumpeted the *People* on 13 March 1992. 'World exclusive. Billie makes their dream come true.' It transpired that their neighbours hadn't been as blind as Dawn and Lenny had thought. Newsagent Rasmi Patel told reporters he'd heard rumours of a baby and had seen a buggy when he delivered papers to the house. Bizarrely, it transpired that even Lenny's own mother hadn't seen Billie. 'I still haven't seen the little girl,' Winifred Henry told reporters as she emerged from church. 'I don't know what she is like yet. I live over two hundred miles from Lenny and Dawn but I hope they will bring her to see me in time.'

Furious that their news had leaked out, the couple went to extreme lengths to keep the press at bay. The adoption had yet to be finalised and they went into a major panic, terrified that the publicity might somehow endanger their hopes of Billie becoming theirs. As two of the nation's most popular comedians, there was naturally a great deal of interest in the story. Everybody wanted to wish them well and they were inundated with requests to pose for a family photo and talk about their happiness. But from the way they reacted to their secret getting out, one would have thought their daughter was at risk of being kidnapped by the Mafia. One of the problems about where they live is that Dawn and Lenny do not own the driveway that leads up from the road. This is owned by the adjacent stud farm, and strangers frequently drive past the couple's front door. Paranoid that every car contained press photographers, Dawn and Lenny hired a burly fifteen-stone minder to check all cars approaching the house.

While their desire to protect their daughter was natural, the way Dawn and Lenny handled the situation was over the top by anyone's standards – even for two inhabitants of Planet Celebrity. Famous people have children all the time – almost always without the press laying siege to their home. Ironically, it was the very cloak-and-dagger way in which Dawn and Lenny chose to behave that was responsible for turning the event into such a media circus. A delightful human-interest story suddenly became a major news event, something that could have been avoided with a little judicious planning by the couple. As experienced show-business stars, they would have been fully aware of the tried-and-tested way in which the rich and famous can deal with such situations. They can contact the Press Association with a prepared statement and if they so wish, they can also pose for a single photograph which is circulated to every newspaper and magazine. That way everyone is happy: the press gets its story and the celebrity is left in peace. Dawn and Lenny instead embarked on a game of cat and mouse with Fleet Street. And subsequently granted an interview to the fawning celebrity tome, *Hello!* magazine.

News of the couple's adoption took everyone by surprise. Everyone, that is, except Mystic Meg, the *News of the World*'s resident psychic. The week after the story broke, the paper claimed that Meg had foretold the whole thing. 'Comic Lenny Henry's a dad, and it was our Mystic Meg who told you first,' it exalted. It went on to explain how Meg had written in December that 'Virgo Lenny' would be 'rocking cradles by autumn'. And his stars for March foretold 'good news about a child'. However, it didn't take a mystic to see that Dawn's attitude to motherhood had softened. Looking back at her comments in 1991, the clues were there for all to see. The fact that she had talked about being frightened of becoming like the other parents she knew showed that she must at least have been thinking about parenthood. She also gave a hint in another interview. 'Len has a large family with loads of kids around all the time,' she said. 'I know he would be very supportive and I know he'd help.' Lenny too had spoken about fatherhood, and had been quoted as saying, 'Married life is fabulous and we want to have a baby. We're still practising. At the moment I'm still trying to get her dressing gown off, but I'm sure we'll have a baby soon.' He added that any baby he and Dawn might have would be 'double-caste, not half-caste'.

Once the adoption was finalised later that month, Dawn and Lenny decided to explain why they had cast such an astonishing smokescreen over the entire affair. Showing their new daughter to the world, they appeared on the front cover of *Hello!* and over numerous pages inside, beaming for the camera. 'There's something very special to protect when there's a child involved,' Dawn explained earnestly. 'So we've kept completely quiet about this, and have managed it for a lot of months.' She said they hadn't even told some members of their family because they didn't want them to have the burden of the secret.

Desiring a reasonable amount of privacy was wholly understandable, but it was still unclear why the couple had taken things to such extreme lengths. As Dawn explained the full story of Billie's arrival, it began to resemble one of French and Saunders's more far-fetched sketches. Dawn claimed she had to do the nursery in 'complete secrecy', and had felt unable to go shopping for baby clothes in case it gave the game away. Instead, she recruited one of her women friends to act as a decoy. The pal turned up at Dawn's home with a large cushion stuffed up her jumper, looking for all the world like an expectant mum. The scene having been set, she and Dawn set off on a marathon shopping spree to buy things for the new baby. Dawn felt completely relaxed as she walked around the baby shops, picking out romper suits and bootees for the new arrival, safe in the knowledge that anyone seeing her would assume she was just helping out her extremely pregnant pal. In Mothercare, a thoughtful shop assistant sat her friend down and made her a cup of tea and Dawn had to bite her lip to stop herself from laughing. But she admitted she felt guilty for pulling the wool over people's eyes. When the women arrived home they 'gave birth' to the cushion, ceremoniously laid it in the cot and welcomed it as a member of the family.

Dawn also revealed that for several weeks she and Lenny hardly took Billie out of the house because of the need for secrecy. They relied on trusted friends to take the baby on outings into the big wide world and had only taken Billie out with them 'under wraps'. She admitted this had been a terrible strain but said she had felt so protective of her new daughter that she hadn't been able to behave normally. 'It's been a question of looking twice to see who's there every time I've walked through the front door,' she told *Hello!*, although quite what she meant by this rather odd remark, or who she was expecting to see, was unclear.

Dawn and Lenny knew that until the adoption was finalised by the court, Billie's natural mother could ask for her back at any time. And whilst they realised it was unlikely that that would happen, they didn't want to run the risk of anything going wrong. Dawn was worried that if the judge saw stories in the newspapers it might give the impression that they were unsuitable adoptive parents and they would be turned down. Another reason for the secrecy was that Dawn and Lenny naturally wanted to get to know their daughter and spend time together as a family.

Billie's nursery had been lovingly decorated by her mum and dad with an eclectic selection of pictures, including a photograph of Neil Kinnock and one of Lenny meeting Nelson Mandela. Dawn and Lenny held two christening ceremonies for her: a Church of England ceremony near their home in Berkshire, and a second one at Lenny's mother's gospel church in the Midlands. Dawn also revealed that her family had a history of adoption, explaining that her grandmother had gone to an orphanage, picked a baby and taken her home in a basket 'like a kitten'. 'She went to court two years later to sign the papers,' Dawn said. 'There were no visits from social workers or anything like that.'

Dawn and Lenny planned to tell their daughter she was adopted as soon as she was old enough to understand. 'There has to be total honesty,' Lenny explained. 'We'll tell her that she was specially chosen by us, and how very much we wanted her.' He touchingly revealed that he had written her a series of notes, which he would give to her once she could read. He planned to write her more letters as she grew older so that she would have a complete record of her life form the very beginning.

It was obvious that the couple were besotted with Billie, and Dawn was clearly overjoyed to be a mum at last. She told how Billie had opened up a new world to them. 'It's as close to heaven as you can get,' she said happily. 'We've had a lot of dancing in the kitchen, singing and much baby-bouncing. She likes Lenny's variation of "There Once Was An Ugly Duckling", which now runs "There Once Was A Lovely Billie". She finds it highly entertaining when he sings her nursery rhymes reggae-style.'

Dawn and Lenny were both struck by how many similarities there were between them and their daughter. Dawn said Billie looked a lot like Lenny and was already showing signs of showing off – 'as her parents occasionally have!' she laughed. She echoed Lenny's remark about their child being 'double-caste' rather than half-caste, and said as far as she was concerned, Billie had a 'double dose of everything that's good'.

But like all new mums, Dawn found caring for a baby tiring. After thirty-four years of pleasing herself, she was suddenly at the beck and call of a helpless infant. She was surprised at how exhausted she felt, but admitted it was a pleasant feeling because she was weary from doing something worthwhile. She said she felt like Billie's 'proper' mum and although she didn't know how well she and Lenny were fulfilling their role as parents, she knew they were doing their best.

The couple refused to say whether they had chosen adoption by choice or necessity. 'I think you can at least keep your internal workings private,' Dawn said testily during an interview. She later described her frustration at people's fascination with the subject. 'Everyone wanted to write about my barren womb and my sorrow. I thought, "Hang on, you don't even know whether it's me or Len that has the problem". And I don't think people should automatically assume you can't have kids. There are all sorts of reasons for adopting. Surely there have to be some things that only belong to you, and what goes on inside your own body is your own business.'

But she admitted that they had talked about adoption from the very beginning of their marriage because 'it seemed a good thing to do'. And Lenny gave the distinct impression that any further additions to their family would happen the same way. 'We would definitely like more children,' he said. 'We'll be happy to have them – if we're allowed to.' His trips to Africa for Comic Relief had made him acutely aware of how many children in the world needed a home, and he was keen to do what he could to help. 'When I came back from visiting Ethiopia in 1987, I told Dawn I wanted to adopt a whole orphanage,' he told the *Daily Mail*. 'People are wrong when they say we can't have our own children – we don't know we can't.'

Because of the couple's well-publicised connection with Africa, rumours abounded that Billie had come from abroad. In the *Hello!*

interview, Dawn said she was aware of what people were saying, but left readers none the wiser.

Dawn and Lenny were put through an intense screening procedure before they were judged to be suitable adoptive parents. 'Obviously they want to know you're not involved in anything dark and awful,' Dawn explained. Social workers had wanted to know everything about them – their personalities, plans for the future and the stability of their marriage – and also spoke at length to the couple's family and friends. Dawn said they were happy to have the necessary enquires made because they trusted their social worker implicitly. 'She made it clear that our jobs and wealth had nothing to do with whether we were suitable adoptive parents,' she said. 'It was rigorous but it wasn't hard to go through because we wanted to do it.'

Dawn and Lenny's main concern was that their occupation might cast a shadow over their chances of adopting a baby. Aware that certain institutions, like car insurers, often assume that showbusiness personalities lead racy lifestyles, they were determined to show how ordinary their lives were. 'We had to make sure the people who were going to judge us as prospective adoptive parents would understand what our lifestyle is, rather than what they thought it might be,' she explained. 'We are not a glitzy duo who go out clubbing every night.'

Dawn and Lenny had no worries on that front. Well known for shunning the show-business lifestyle, they prefer to spend time at home relaxing with family and close friends. Jennifer Saunders was one of the few people in on Dawn's big secret, and she too was quizzed by social workers. The adoption service wanted to know how Dawn planned to balance motherhood with her career, and she could give them no better illustration of how to make a success of the juggling act than her partner Jennifer. 'The agency met Jennifer and saw that she has some help and that she manages to have plenty of time at home as well as her career,' Dawn said. 'Jen's the most capable woman I know. She manages it all incredibly well. She likes the fact that she can be a mother and she can write.' It was obvious that Dawn considered her partner a perfect role model, and she said Jennifer's children were so well brought up that if she only did half as well with Billie she would be pleased.

But speaking a couple of months later, Dawn admitted that the adoption procedure had been far more stressful than she had at first let on. 'It sounds sanctimonious, but I really believe that if some people who had decided to get pregnant naturally had gone through the process of adoption instead, they might have thought twice about the whole idea,' she said. 'They put you through an awful lot and make you question all sorts of things about yourself. You have to talk very openly together and about each other in front of another person. Unless you go to marriage guidance, that's not something you would be used to. People do back out of it because they suddenly have to listen to each other and be incredibly open. I'm sure that if a lot of natural parents were put through that process they would be told, "Sorry, you're not suitable to be parents".'

Once Billie was legally theirs, Dawn could relax. But she confessed that she was already dreading the day when her daughter might ask to meet her real mother. She accepted that it would probably break her heart, but was confident she would be able to do the right thing for Billie. 'The social worker counselled us very closely about telling a child from the moment they ask anything about babies or children that they came to you in a slightly different way – that they were adopted and why,' she said. 'The child has to know, and mustn't find out from another kid or adult. I couldn't imagine anything worse. I think we'll make Billie stronger by telling her, and making her understand. Surely the most important thing is to make sure she knows how much she was wanted and that she wasn't rejected by her mother – that her mother had to give her up for a certain reason.

'Children can understand things if you explain right away. I'm sure Billie will ask lots of questions, including quite a lot that I can't answer. She may have to find out for herself exactly why certain things are the way they are. I'll be there to support her, and I hope I'll be able to do it right so that the day comes when she might want to meet her mother. Then I'll have to stand back and help her to do that if she wants to. My own emotions will have to take a back seat while she does that. But quite often children who are encouraged all the way through don't feel the need to find their parents. It's usually the people that have had a mysterious gaping hole who need to fill it in. She will know that the desire to have her in our family was enormous, and how precious she is to both of us.' Dawn also hinted that she and Lenny would not allow Billie to blame any problems she might have in her life on the fact that she was adopted. 'It's a lovely excuse, isn't it?' she said. 'I have a friend who was adopted who always wanted to believe his natural parents were really royalty.'

As well as watching how Jennifer did things, Roma French was a strong role model for Dawn. She remains extremely close to her mother, and considers her 'an inspiration'. It was Roma's influence that determined the way Dawn set about raising Billie. 'You only have one upbringing and if you've had a happy, confident one, you've got a pattern, something you can copy because we are all our mothers,' Dawn explained. 'You only know what you have experienced. Now I hear my mother in me and I think, "Well, she did OK".'

Within only a few months of becoming a mum, Dawn's attitude to children appeared to have gone full circle. Where once she would have been infuriated when journalists mentioned the B-word during interviews, it was now she who steered the conversation round to babies. Noticing that a reporter from *Today* newspaper was seven months pregnant, she immediately proffered some motherly advice. 'Let me tell you now – don't bother buying a room full of pink fluffy toys because they are just not interested,' she said knowledgeably. 'We've got rows and rows of soft cuddly things, and all Billie does is play with a spoon or a milk-bottle top. She gets bored with her toys in one minute flat. She looks at them fleetingly, then turns away in favour of something that clanks.'

The old Dawn, who had scathingly remarked that babies made women's brains turn to marshmallow, would surely have run screaming from such a conversation. 'Mummy Dawn', however, seemed perfectly happy to indulge in a spot of baby talk. 'Billie is actually doing very well now,' she said in another interview. 'She is "going through the night", as mothers say. It's amazing when women get together and say things like, "What time does she go down? Has she got any teeth yet? Is she crawling?", I'm just getting used to all that.'

But she admitted that she sometimes found her daughter hard to cope with. 'She's a little devil, and she's got a real temper and a forceful personality,' she said. 'Billie is a very angry child if she doesn't get her way – which she doesn't quite often. I think she is going to be quite a handful – but a pleasurable handful.' She naturally worried about her new infant, and the anxiety took its toll on her. 'The first year with a baby is hellish, and no one can understand it unless they've been through it,' she explained. 'There's the tiredness and the constant worry that they're going to die. It leaves you with no energy for anything other than that.' And Billie, it seemed, was running circles around her mum and dad. 'We have one of those baby intercoms that we have glued to our ears at night,' Dawn explained. 'Billie has realised that simple crying doesn't always bring us running, so she has developed this alarming choking noise. You're really tired and you've gone to sleep, and it's about three in the morning. Suddenly you hear this gasping, this choking coming through the speaker next to your ear. It's really awful. We run into her room and she's there with a smug smile on her face.'

By the beginning of 1994, Billie was well and truly in the grip of the Terrible Twos. 'She is acting like the enemy at the moment,' a despairing Dawn told *Today*. 'She is a creature from another planet. It's such a shame because we have time together and she is being really horrible. They are all horrible at that age, so everyone tells me, but I have never been pushed by another human being this much before. She matches me in anything. She stands up to me. She is not afraid of anything. I am not going to beat her, but I do everything but and she laughs at me. She laughs at Len too. In fact she laughs at him more.'

As a backlash against the strict West Indian upbringing he had experienced, Lenny was something of a softie where his daughter was concerned. 'He's great, much more patient than me,' Dawn explained. 'He's not good on the discipline side of things, but he's very good at spoiling Billie. She dotes on him.' It was left to Dawn to lay down the law when necessary. This should have presented no problem for such a self-confessed bossy-boots, but to her complete surprise she discovered that in her angelic-looking toddler she had well and truly met her match. It was an experience she found deeply unsettling. 'I thought you could bully small children and I had every intention of doing that,' she admitted. 'I thought that I am bigger and older and I know more, so surely I can intimidate her. But no. It's like she's been alive for a hundred years. She knows everything. She knows every trick. Do you remember at school there was always one girl in the class who would tell the teacher to fuck off, and all the rest of the girls were going, "I don't believe she said that"? Well, Billie is the one who will do it.

'I get into complete furies at how belligerent, mischievous and naughty she is. I'm sure I was as conniving and manipulative at that age – maybe I'm jealous – but I find it very unattractive. But she gets away with a lot of it because of her looks. She's a real head-turner of a kid.' Certain naughtiness, however, would not be tolerated – looks or no looks. 'I just insist on proper behaviour,' Dawn explained. 'Drawing on the walls of our house is something I consider unacceptable.' If all else failed, there was one sure-fire way for Dawn to get through to her daughter – by showing her a video of Mummy being cross. 'She just laughs at me when I put on my nastiest voice,' she said. 'But if she sees me shouting on *French and Saunders*, she bursts into tears!'

Asked if she and Lenny had any plans to add to their family, she admitted that she was undecided. 'Billie's at such a difficult age at the moment, the thought of another one fills me with terror,' she said. 'But we almost certainly will get around to it.' She added that she was secretly glad Billie was so spirited. 'I'd rather have a confident kid – the quiet ones are scary.'

By the time she was four, Billie knew she was adopted. 'She knows she wasn't in my tummy but in someone else's,' Dawn told the *Daily Mail* in 1996. 'And if I say to her, "Why are you so special?" she answers, "Because I was adopted". We gave her a book which has her whole life in it. There are pictures of her birth parents, all the information about her birth and where she is from. She knows what was going on in the world when she was born because we have written it all out for her. Lenny writes to her every birthday, and we put all the letters into her book. It is her personal book, and it stays in her bedroom. She even shows it to people. Sometimes I wish she wouldn't, but it is hers to do what she likes with. We have told her everything we can, but I know we are going to go through a sticky patch one day when she might want to explore further. I don't know how wise I'm going to be when we reach that stage. I may well fall apart. There are things that matter to adopted kids. I can't imagine what it's like not to know my grandparents, what illnesses they had, what they looked like, what their natures were.'

On balance, Dawn was pleased she had waited a few years before adopting. 'I'm glad I left it late because Lenny and I had already done everything we wanted,' she said. 'I said right at the beginning that I couldn't have a child unless Lenny took on half of what was involved. Which he has done. He's been absolutely brilliant.' She admitted that their lives were now more restricted, but that having Billie more than made up for that. 'We can't just pack our bags and go off like we used to,' she said. 'Now we have to spend hours organising bottles and nappies and toys, but I don't mind. We don't go out much, but I don't want to go to parties when I can be at home with Billie instead. That's the great thing about having a baby when you're older. You want to spend more time at home, and I made sure that a baby didn't happen until I was ready to ease off the work a bit. I also think you have to have a great marriage or partnership with someone so that they can help out.'

Dawn and Lenny had easily met the standards laid down by the adoption service, but their hopes were almost dashed at the last minute when a doctor told Dawn that she was too fat to be a mum. The adoption service is reluctant to place children with parents who are fat, and has on occasion barred overweight people from adopting. The reasoning behind this is that being overweight has health implications, and children with fat parents often grow up to be overweight themselves. Dawn was no exception, and her size was a potential barrier to her being accepted as a parent. The doctor who assessed her case was concerned that she was not fit enough to look after a young baby, and told her she would have to lose weight. With something so important at stake, Dawn was not in a position to argue and had to bite the bullet.

For the second time in her life she embarked on a diet, but once again it was purely as a means to an end. She gritted her teeth and lost weight, but vowed to go back to eating what she liked as soon as she was given a baby. However much she was prepared to listen to social workers' advice about the ins and outs of adoption, there was little chance of their changing the way she viewed her size. Seven years on, she was still furious about the enforced diet. 'Lenny and I passed all the criteria,' she explained crossly. 'It was the doctor from the adoption agency who felt she could halt the whole procedure – purely because of my weight. I had to promise her I would lose x stone in order to fit into this strange chart on the wall.'

Dawn passionately believed the authorities should have considered it a *bonus* for Billie to be brought up in a household where weight was not an issue. 'There's the strange fascist world of the charts you have to fit into in order to get a mortgage or adopt a child,' she said. 'You have to be pretty strong to remain big, if you are naturally big, which my family is. I think that's something to celebrate. But somehow having a fat mum is not OK.' She was determined that Billie should grow up free from inhibitions about her weight, and if that meant her daughter becoming fat, that was fine by her. Somewhat disconcertingly, Dawn gave the impression that she would encourage Billie to eat as much as she wanted, just as her mother had done with her. 'I hope that living with me will mean she won't have a hang-up about herself, whatever size she is,' she told *Woman's Own*. 'She's going to eat what she likes when she likes, and look just the way she wants.'

She later described how Billie had begun to be interested in her self-image and liked to take her clothes off and look at herself in the mirror. In an anecdote that would no doubt appal the health lobby, she told of how Billie had looked herself up and down and said: 'Oh, I hope I get fat soon.' Dawn says she glowed with pride at that moment, saying, 'It was so great that she can value me as her fat mum,' but many would seriously question her judgement.

She tried to give Billie healthy food, but admitted to a guilty secret. 'I do have to confess I did something incredibly stupid,' she revealed. 'When she was about seven months old, I was eating a Mars bar and I looked at her, and of course she didn't even know what a Mars bar was, but I just thought, "I'd love to witness that virgin moment when a baby first has chocolate". And I did it very quickly, so that she'd hardly know what had happened – and then I saw that little look on her face, as she obviously thought, "What is all this rubbish you've been giving me? Give me chocolate". I can see it won't be long until I have to hide my stash of Twix!'

In 1999, Dawn said she was trying hard to make sure her eight-year-old daughter grows up with a healthy attitude to body size and food. 'What I am doing is making sure that she doesn't think that being fat is a bad thing, and I challenge her on that if she thinks it is,' she said. 'And I make sure that she's not ashamed or embarrassed about me being big. I don't lecture her about it but I keep my eyes open. I would be sorry if she became a body fascist like so many other people. But I would hope that, living in our house, she wouldn't do that.'

◀ ▲ Hamming it up as Baywatch's Pamela Anderson for a *French and Saunders* sketch.

Mistress of disguise –
the different faces of
Dawn French in
Murder Most Horrid.

◀ Daughter Billie joins mum on set of *The Vicar of Dibley*.

▼ Clowning around with Emma Chambers, who plays the dippy verger Alice in *The Vicar of Dibley*.

CHAPTER ELEVEN

Holy Hilarious

Despite the joys of motherhood, after six months of being at home with Billie full-time, Dawn was itching to go back to work.

A workaholic whose greatest fear is of being unemployed, she had spent ten years diligently building up her career. And while Jennifer Saunders had taken time out to have her children, Dawn had not let up for a minute. *French and Saunders* was by no means the only string to her bow. She had twice tried her hand on the West End stage, devised and starred in her own award-winning television series, *Murder Most Horrid*, and launched her fashion business 1647. To find herself suddenly cast in a new role, that of housewife and mother, was a strange experience for Dawn. Although she initially enjoyed spending time with her new baby, it wasn't long before she realised that she missed the buzz of being involved in show business. She also had a terror of turning into what she described as a 'jelly brain', and in May 1992 she announced that she was 'ravenous' to return to work.

As a wealthy couple, Dawn and Lenny could afford to pay for professional help with caring for Billie. In addition, they decided to take it in turns to pursue acting work, so that one of them would be available to look after their daughter. But at the same time as declaring that Billie came first, Dawn said she didn't believe children should take over one's life completely. 'I've got a friend who will fill in at home for me when I'm not around, or Lenny or I will take Billie to work with us,' she explained. 'One way or another we'll work it out. I do feel strongly that you can't let your kids control every single step of your life. They have to fit in with you. I think every mother should do what she feels comfortable with in terms of whether to go back to work or not, if they have a choice.

'Spending time with children is such fun, but I just hope that you can hang on to your brain. I can see why you sometimes don't because you do get so tired. Often I just sink into a chair and think, "I don't want to do anything except put the telly on". You don't have the energy to think, "Oh, I'll just develop that idea I had".' She appeared to have no truck with the guilt that many working mothers feel at being parted from their children. 'Guilt shouldn't come into it – stay at home if you feel guilty,' she said. 'I don't want Billie to grow up to find this hollow woman and wonder what I've ever done with myself.'

Dawn was excited about resuming her career and was particu-larly looking forward to working with Jennifer Saunders again. The pair had been in the middle of writing a new series of *French and Saunders*, scheduled to go out in 1992, when the call came through from the adoption service. Work had to be hastily abandoned as Dawn dropped everything to prepare for her new baby. Because of the secrecy surrounding the adoption, she wasn't able to explain to the BBC why the new series of *French and Saunders* would not be forthcoming, and it was left to Jennifer to square things with them. This Saunders did by vaguely promising to 'come up with something'.

Bad as she felt at leaving her partner in the lurch, Dawn's priorities lay elsewhere at that time and there was little she could do about it. She was immensely grateful to Jennifer for handling the situation with the BBC. 'Jennifer really helped when we adopted Billie,' she says. 'She knew that I was waiting for this call from the adoption agency, and that when it happened I would have to go into action immediately, regardless of what was going on. It was very weird because we couldn't stop any of our work, we couldn't plan around it, we just had to go on as though it wasn't happening. But we knew in the back of our minds that when it did happen we had to move fast. When the call came I rushed off and left them with the studio booked, and a producer and director lined up but no product.

'Jen was wonderful. I didn't want the BBC to know why I was suddenly dropping out, but you don't suddenly drop a key commitment without an explanation. I knew I couldn't tell anyone because it would have got out. So what Jennifer did was simply to say, "Right. We can't do the series, and I will do what I've been meaning to do for ages but have been too lazy to do. This will give me the kick I need to write a sitcom. Therefore we don't need to explain too much because I'm going to be giving them a product". That enabled me to slip off. No one said anything at all. But if it hadn't been for her, I wouldn't have been able to get away with it. It was the act of a true friend.'

But when the time came that Dawn was ready to resume work, she discovered to her disappointment that her partner was not available. For, in the few short months that she had been off the scene, Jennifer's career had gone ballistic. For the time being at least, Dawn was surplus to requirements. In truth, her disappearance had proved to be a blessing in disguise for Jennifer. With Dawn preoccupied with changing nappies, and the BBC needing something to put out in place of *French and Saunders*, Jennifer had the perfect opportunity to try her hand at writing a series of her own. The idea she came up with was inspired by the *French and Saunders* sketch about a neurotic, self-obsessed mother and her sensible teenage daughter. She called the series *Absolutely Fabulous*, and it was to become one of the hottest shows on TV.

Jennifer played the lead role of the selfish and spoiled Edina Monsoon, and with Dawn out of the picture, looked around for a co-star. In an inspired piece of casting, she picked Joanna Lumley to play her fast-living, toyboy-loving best friend, Patsy Stone. Julia Sawalha was cast as Saffron, the role played by Dawn in the original *French and Saunders* sketch, and the veteran actress June Whitfield was chosen to play Edina's dimwitted mother. Within a couple of weeks of beginning transmission on BBC2, *Absolutely Fabulous* was the most talked-about show in the country.

Nobody, least of all Jennifer, could ever have imagined what a runaway success it would be. The cast, who with the exception of Julia Sawalha were already household names, suddenly found themselves elevated to a whole new spectrum of fame as the nation went *Ab Fab* mad. The biggest sensation was Joanna Lumley. Nobody had ever thought of casting the glamorous actress in a comic role before, but she was terrific as the alcoholic Patsy. And June Whitfield, for ever associated with her role in the seventies sitcom *Terry and June*, was amused to discover that she was now something of a cult star. The BBC was delighted with the show's success, and immediately commissioned a second series, promoting it from BBC2 to a prime-time slot on BBC1.

For Dawn, sitting at home in Berkshire with her new daughter, it was an unsettling time. Seeing her partner's career take off before her very eyes was a strange and not wholly pleasant experience. On the one hand she was pleased for Jennifer, but on the other there was a certain amount of jealousy that she had played no part in her partner's new-found success. That Jennifer's triumph should come at a time when Dawn was 'resting', albeit voluntarily, did not help matters. Of the two, it was Dawn who had always been the more prolific outside of the partnership. But now, when she had turned her back for only a few months, Jennifer was the one people couldn't get enough of. Suddenly everyone was talking about Jennifer and Joanna, not Jennifer and Dawn.

The newspapers and magazines were full of articles about *Absolutely Fabulous*, and spread after spread was devoted to interviews with Jennifer and Joanna Lumley. Where once Dawn's photo would have accompanied Jennifer's in the press, it was now Joanna's beautiful face that smiled out at Dawn. The impact of *Absolutely Fabulous* on the public consciousness was such that, with just one series, Jennifer managed to eclipse completely Dawn's solo achievements. The balance would later be redressed, but for a while in the early nineties it was Jennifer who was deemed to be the more successful of the pair. Any ambitious person would find that hard to cope with, no matter how fond they might be of the other person. Show business is a notoriously competitive industry, and the majority of the people in it have huge egos that need constant massaging. Dawn is no exception, and she experienced bitter-sweet emotions at her partner's triumph.

'I was hoping she would fail miserably,' she joked. 'I was a bit surprised that she had any talent whatsoever and could do it on her own.' But, jokes aside, Dawn admitted that she was suffering an attack of the green-eyed monster. 'When you like someone as much as I like Jennifer, you have a cocktail of emotions about them,' she explained. 'I'm ferociously proud and furiously jealous at the same time. *Absolutely Fabulous* is great. I've always known Jennifer is talented, but that's what makes you do your own work better. We are competitive, but it's a kind of friendly competitive. Besides seething with jealousy about how funny *Ab Fab* was, and being very annoyed that she could be that funny on her own, I took so much pride in it on her behalf because I really love Jen. I don't believe there's a bone of jealousy in Jennifer's body. It's probably because she's so confident about her own talent, and has good reason to be. It's only recently, though, that she's been able to show the public how talented she is, and in *Absolutely Fabulous* she had the chance to show the wilder side of her character.'

But Jennifer's preoccupation with her new 'baby' meant that although Dawn was keen to get back to work, Jennifer was not free to work with her. Dawn's main plan had been to begin writing a new series of *French and Saunders* with her partner that April, and with that now out of the question she found herself at a loose end. She stayed at home and continued being a full-time mum, but where she had initially found it exhilarating and fulfilling, she now felt frustrated because she really wanted to be working. Jennifer was so busy throughout 1992 that Dawn saw very little of her. They got together socially when they could, and that summer they went on holiday together to Italy with their families, but work-wise Dawn felt hugely left out. She busied herself with promoting her fashion company, and with looking after Billie, but being absent from the world of television was beginning to have a detrimental effect on her.

In the end, she was away from work for eighteen months, a situation that resulted in her suffering a dramatic loss of confidence. Acting, by its very nature, is an insecure business. In a world where image and trend is all, there is the constant fear of being passed over for someone younger and better-looking – or the indignity of being overlooked in favour of the Next Best Thing. Such neuroses affect even the biggest stars; in many ways they are more susceptible because the more successful they are, the further they've got to fall. That someone as seemingly confident and level-headed as Dawn could suffer from insecurity is not as surprising as it at first seems, especially given Jennifer Saunders's high profile at the time.

The longer she was at home – and the more successful Jennifer became without her – the less confident Dawn felt about her own abilities. She knew she had to get back in the saddle soon, or she might never do so again. But for the first time in her life she started to doubt herself. The prospect of returning to work became less appealing, and increasingly she found herself thinking of opting out of showbiz life and returning to teaching. She had enjoyed the year she'd spent at Parliament Hill, and knew she was a good teacher. Her experience in television would mean she'd have more to share with her pupils, and she wondered if perhaps that was where her destiny lay after all.

Dawn was practically on the point of quitting show business when a script landed on her mat early in 1993. Almost uniquely, it didn't seek to portray her either as retarded or as someone with an eating disorder. In fact, *Tender Loving Care* – a film for the prestigious BBC Screen One series – looked promising from the outset. Written by top television-drama writer Lucy Gannon – the pen behind popular shows like *Soldier, Soldier* and *Peak Practice* – its subject was the decidedly dark world of mercy killing. Dawn was offered the lead role of a harassed psychiatric nurse who murders her elderly patients. It would be her first straight acting TV role but, more importantly, it would get her back to work.

Dawn immediately accepted. In fact, she was sufficiently keen to secure the role that she even cancelled a family holiday to Barbados. Instead of sunning herself in the Caribbean, she decamped to windy Cardiff to begin filming. And because there was now Billie to consider, Lenny had to make himself available to take over the bulk of the childcare. In the end, the easiest thing was for Lenny and Billie to go to Cardiff too, and the whole family stayed in a hotel for six weeks. 'We both agreed it had to happen that way,' Dawn explained. 'Only one of us can be in the driver's seat at one time. Your mate has to be there, but in a supporting role. When Lenny was making *True Identity*, I was the one playing the supporting role. Now it's his turn to look after me.'

She was extremely excited about her new role. It would mark her debut as a serious television actress, and it was also an opportunity for her to prove to herself that she still had what it took to be successful. It was certainly a sharp contrast to anything she had done before. Laughs were distinctly thin on the ground in the grim story of Elaine Dobbs, overworked nurse and mother. Exhausted by crippling hours in a Welsh geriatric ward and the strain of running a home and family, Nurse Dobbs decides to help her patients on their way with her own brand of 'tender loving care'. 'I wanted someone who looked normal, whatever that is, and also someone you automatically want to like,' explains Lucy Gannon. 'Dawn was absolutely right for the role. She is known and loved by millions and has an image of being kind and caring, which makes her character's behaviour all the more sinister. People think murderers and killers have horns and look like the Devil, but a lot of them are just like you and me.'

Dawn has strong views on the subject of mercy killing. 'I'm completely in favour of euthanasia in controlled circumstances, after consultation with family and doctors,' she says. 'I've had experience of people with dreadful terminal illnesses who might have wished for euthanasia if it had been available. I have seen people dying very cruel deaths, and I know they would not like to die that way if they had a choice. I believe it happens all the time in hospitals.' She admitted that she had reservations about working on the set of a straight drama, because *French and Saunders* and the Comic Strip films had always involved plenty of larking about. 'I thought I'd have to act "grown-up" all the time as it was a drama,' she says. 'But thankfully the rest of the cast and crew were a riot. Off screen it was a good laugh, which helped enormously.'

On the first morning of filming, she told director Dewi Humphreys to be firm with her. 'I said she must be very strict with me and not allow me to use any of my comedy tricks because my instinct is to make everything funny,' she says. 'I had to put away my comedy antennae because I automatically look out for jokes and laughs. I needed all the discipline I could muster in one gruesome scene, where I put on surgical gear and then whack someone over the head with an iron weight. I had to resist the temptation to turn it into something comic.'

Dawn took her role in *Tender Loving Care* for what it was: a chance to play it straight for a change and an opportunity to get back to work again. She assured her fans that she had no plans to turn off the comedy path she had been treading for twelve years. 'I hadn't been fishing for a straight role, but I knew I wanted to do this as soon as it was offered,' she said. 'The subject is powerful and it's very well written. I just said, "Let me have it". I think I'm perceived as a funny girl completely by accident because that's the job I seem to be able to do. It doesn't necessarily mean that I can't follow another road. I'll be sad if I don't get other dramatic offers because I enjoyed the experience so much, but it's not a conscious career move.'

It was only once she had made *Tender Loving Care* and recaptured her self-esteem that Dawn admitted how close she had come to giving up her career. 'I lost a lot of confidence,' she said. 'Not in a sort of "let me talk to Anthony Clare in the psychiatrist's chair" kind of way, it was just that when you start thinking about why you work and how you do it, it gets scary. I had never, ever been lacking in confidence before that. At one stage, trying to get back to work, I can remember thinking, "Well, I'm not going to do this any more, I'll teach, maybe that was my role all along". It was the very thing I was afraid of about having children. I'd watched the spark go out of so many women's eyes. I now understand why. You're exhausted and you have to start thinking in an entirely different way. It's quite hard to suck yourself back into firing on all cylinders. Luckily I was surrounded by people who were very encouraging.'

She admitted that being offered the Screen One drama was a crucial turning point. 'It turned out to be exactly what I needed because it took me off in a fresh direction,' she explains. 'You are only the result of the opportunities you grab. If I had gone back to working with Jennifer straight away, I think I would still have been at a very low ebb. Whereas by the time we did start working together again, I had regained this confidence.'

In April 1993, Dawn teamed up with Jennifer for the first time
in eighteen months to join their old mates for a new Comic Strip
film. Called *Space Virgins from the Planet Sex*, it starred Dawn and
Jennifer as sex-mad aliens who travel to earth to kidnap men for
lust. In a marked departure for The Comic Strip, the film did not
go out on Channel 4, but instead appeared on BBC2. By the
summer of 1993, Dawn's career appeared to be back on track, and
she was over her little blip of insecurity. She was pleased with her
performance in *Tender Loving Care*, and it was well received when it
was shown that autumn.

In June, her position as a big-league player was well and truly
cemented when she and Jennifer signed a record-breaking five-
year contract with the BBC. The deal, worth an estimated £2
million, was the biggest of its kind in the history of television
comedy, and elevated the duo to the television superleague. It was
the first time the BBC had signed such a large 'golden handcuffs'
deal with individual entertainers, and it was a clear indicator of
how highly they were rated by the corporation. Alan Yentob, the
controller of BBC1, paid tribute to Dawn and Jennifer. Yentob had
nurtured *French and Saunders* when he was controller of BBC2, and
was determined not to lose them to commercial television.
Speaking at the Montreux television festival, where an episode of
French and Saunders had been entered for a prestigious Golden Rose
prize, he said: 'Their range and talent make them a one-off. In
these days of hop, skip and jump deals, this contract represents a
real commitment.'

The commitment cut both ways, and Dawn and Jennifer admitted that they felt hugely grateful to the BBC for supporting them
through the early days of their careers. They said their decision to
sign the five-year deal was partly a thank-you to the corporation.
'We have enjoyed being there, and they stuck with us through
some very bad things we did early on,' said Dawn, self-
deprecatingly. 'The first series of *French and Saunders* was atrocious,

but they didn't sack us. We like working at the BBC. They are very paternal and allow us a lot of control, and they have always had complete faith in us.'

Their big-bucks deal gave Dawn and Jennifer a great deal more clout, something that clearly meant a lot to them both. 'It's taken time to get here, but now kind of what we say goes,' Dawn said proudly. 'Both Jennifer and I had so many years of seeing sketches we'd written and performed in being edited or shot wrongly, or good ones thrown out and bad ones left in. When you have put so much effort into something it really hurts. There were times in the past when they wouldn't even let us into the editing suite. So we thought, "We've got to have more control". I can take the blame for my mistakes, but not somebody else's. You cannot tell the public, "Look, it *was* great but this twit ruined it". We're very bossy bitches these days, and we want all the reins. Not many people will allow you to do that.'

The new contract made Dawn and Jennifer the highest-paid female double act in British television history and – crucially – provided for them to work alone as well as together. This was just as well, for no sooner was the ink dry on their agreement than Jennifer went off to record a second series of *Absolutely Fabulous* and Dawn started work on a new series of *Murder Most Horrid*. As one of the BBC's hottest properties, Dawn now enjoyed certain perks while filming. One of these was a large trailer which she transformed into a temporary nursery for Billie, so that her daughter could be on set with her most days. She also insisted on working a five-day week so she could spend weekends with her.

Dawn did her research for *Murder Most Horrid* by poring through a library of horror, reading books on Charles Manson and other notorious killers. She confessed she found them fascinating. 'Murder is a tricky subject and must be handled carefully,' she explains. 'You must make sure the right people get their come-uppance, and you can't be too grisly. The minute you murder kids or old people, or the reason for the murder isn't funny enough, you've got a problem.' *LA Law* actress Amanda Donohoe guest-starred in the series, along with Kathy Burke and *French and Saunders'* favourite actress, Jane Asher. The show followed up its successful first series with another British Comedy Award, winning 'Best Comedy Series' – the viewers' telephone vote.

But although it was well received by the critics and popular with viewers, *Murder Most Horrid* failed to grab the public's attention in quite the same way as *Absolutely Fabulous* had. If anything, the second series of *Ab Fab* was an even bigger smash than the first. And while it went out at peak time on BBC1, *Murder Most Horrid* still languished on BBC2. The media was keen to speculate on the unspoken rivalry between Dawn and Jennifer, and the duo devised a stock reply to deflect such questions. During joint interviews, the standard procedure was often for Jennifer to warn Dawn to remember that she was the funny one, and for Dawn to joke back: 'I think you'll find Joanna Lumley is the funny one.' But just as she had felt left out in the early days when journalists quizzed Jennifer about her babies, so Dawn now felt left out when people insisted on talking about *Absolutely Fabulous* all the time. When the two did a radio interview together to promote *French and Saunders*, the interviewer spent ten minutes talking solely about *Absolutely Fabulous* and at the end, Dawn could not refrain from chipping in: 'And *Murder Most Horrid* is coming back too!'

In December, *French and Saunders* won the 'Top Female Comedy Performers' prize at the British Comedy Awards. Dawn appeared to be making up for lost time in 1993, and took on a huge amount of work. She made a cameo appearance in *Absolutely Fabulous*, playing the role of Kathy, and filmed *The South Bank Show* special on big women. She was the voice of Jim Hawkins in an animated TV version of *Treasure Island*, and was much in demand for advertising voice-overs. She also devoted plenty of time to her clothing company.

At Christmas she topped off a busy year by reuniting with Jennifer to appear in their first West End stage play together, *Me and Mamie O'Rourke*. Written by Mary Agnew Donoghue, the play was about female friendship and not, as the tabloids gleefully reported, about lesbianism. To a great deal of hype, it was revealed that Dawn and Jennifer would kiss each other – *on the mouth!* For Dawn, who had once boasted that she had snogged every member of The Comic Strip except Jennifer, it was an opportunity to complete her score. 'I've lots of plans for funny ways to do it,' she said mischievously. 'We've never kissed for any length of time before. Not consciously, anyway. They attempt lesbianism in a big, carnal way. We have a full on-the-lips kiss. It's a thing a lot of women have thought about.' But Jennifer played it down. 'It's been blown out of all proportion,' she insisted. 'It's not really a snog – more of an embarrassed peck. The characters say they have such fun together, wouldn't it be great if they were gay? Then they get very drunk, and the embarrassed kiss is all they can manage.'

Both women admitted that they found the prospect of appearing in the play daunting. This was mainly to do with the fact that they had by now become used to being in charge of everything at work. Having written and performed their own material and been involved in every stage of production, they were unfamiliar with being directed. This was less of a problem for Dawn, who had appeared in *When I was a Girl I Used to Scream and Shout* and *Silly Cow*, so it was unsurprising that of the two, Jennifer was the more nervous. 'Jennifer is quite a calm person,' Dawn explains. 'She doesn't really get panicked about anything until the last minute. Whereas I will panic from the day we accept the commission, so that I am in a complete state of high fear most of the time. Then when we actually come to do the show, I'm sort of in control of my fear because I've been like that for weeks. Jennifer doesn't get the fear until half an hour before she goes on stage, and then she tries to hail a cab and get out, and I have to stop her. I have known her try to leave the building. I completely expect it now. In fact, the cooler she is in the run-up to an appearance, the more I know it is going to get to her just before we do it.'

In interviews to promote the show, Dawn revealed that despite her prestigious contract with the BBC, she still wasn't a hundred per cent confident. Again, much of this appeared to be down to the success of *Absolutely Fabulous*. 'I am much more of an introvert now, but only at the moment,' she mused. 'Jennifer's very helpful with that: she senses that I'm a bit more timorous and vulnerable. There is also the fact that while it's perfectly natural that we both do individual projects, when one of you does *Ab Fab* you have a curious mix of emotions. There's pride there, but you have this raging jealousy as well. But that's OK, it doesn't come between us or get to be an issue. It's a good thing because it spurs you on a bit.'

It was this feeling of being continually judged against Jennifer's success that drove Dawn to take on so much work in 1993. She gave every appearance of being a supermum – someone who really could have it all. She announced that while she was doing the play with Jennifer, she was able to put Billie to bed at home in Berkshire before driving into the West End to perform on stage. 'Not many working mothers can say they do that,' she said triumphantly. And she bit the head off a *Radio Times* interviewer when he dared to ask her if it was difficult being a working mother. 'I wonder if you'd ask Lenny that question,' she replied frostily.

But in truth, Dawn *was* finding it hard being a working mum. 1993 was an exhausting year, and the demands of a West End stage play, coming on the back of a gruelling twelve-week shoot for *Murder Most Horrid*, proved to be simply too much. Instead of driving home to Berkshire from the Strand Theatre on a post-performance high each night, Dawn spent the journey sobbing her heart out. The play was generally poorly received by the critics, but it wasn't this that had her in tears. She was well and truly exhausted, and was forced to admit that she wasn't superwoman after all. 'I was driving home from the play every night weeping in the car for no reason and thinking, "Why am I weeping? I'm perfectly happy",' she explains. 'I was just so tired, the tiredest I had ever been. I was at the end of my tether, exhausted with trying to juggle all these plates and realising that I was not juggling any of them particularly well.'

In addition to her television and stage work, she was heavily immersed in promoting her clothes business, and there were also Billie and Lenny to devote time to. Dawn could have managed her gruelling workload just fine in the days when she didn't have a child to take care of, but with an energetic toddler in the house there was no respite. The unsociable hours of the theatre brought home to her how hard it was to try to juggle a career with motherhood. 'Theatre would be wonderful if you had the life of the old-style thespians who woke up at three in the afternoon and had lovely long suppers after the show,' she explained wistfully. 'But it isn't like that. I have a two-year-old who wakes me up at five-thirty a.m. and I find I can't get to sleep until two, so I've been managing on three and a half hours' sleep a night for the past three months. I'm knackered.'

Suffering from a debilitating throat condition didn't help matters. Six months of appearing on stage in *Me and Mamie O'Rourke* had ruined her voice and left her with nodules on her vocal cords. Driving home in tears, she realised that something had to give. She saw that she had been trying to cram too much into a frantic schedule and accepted that it would have to stop. 'I absolutely loved making *Murder Most Horrid*, but I found the hours really difficult,' she admitted. 'Maybe it is just me getting older. I had to leave home at five a.m., and if you are going to be as bossy as I can be and involved in everything you end up not leaving until eleven at night. Then after learning the next day's lines you finally get to sleep two hours later. It was like that for three months, but I just can't do it any more. I'm not the young thing I was.

'Taking on the play was a big commitment because you need to be at the peak of your energy when you are performing at eight o'clock at night and have to put everything into it. That's normally when I'm having a cup of cocoa and watching *EastEnders* and winding down. Of course you can't sleep immediately afterwards because you're so hyped up, so that's when you eat. That means you don't get to bed until around two a.m., and Billie wakes up at the crack of dawn. Doing the play and looking after Billie would be enough to fill most people's day, but I took on *The South Bank Show* too, which meant filming all day. And although I have a partner who runs 1647 day-to-day, there's all the extra stuff like the hiring and firing, money problems, premises and all that kind of stuff. Plus a little thing called a marriage that has to exist somewhere in your life!

'I'm a great one for agreeing to things because I get excited about them, but I don't think them through or consider what it will make my life like. I like doing many things at once because it makes me think faster, but to take on that amount of work was counter-productive and stupid. It was entirely my fault. Once I finished filming I thought, "That's it for a while". Billie comes first, and if I was given a choice to come in and do a voice-over there's really no competition. She wins.'

Dawn admitted that it was fortunate she and Lenny were in the same business because other men may not have been so understanding. 'Len has been brilliant,' she praised. 'He knew that while I was doing the play he'd be on baby duty a lot of the time. We swap about. Of course, every now and then you don't get it right, but one of us is always there as often as we can. I think it would be quite tense if one of us wasn't in the business, because it would be very difficult to understand the hours and the stresses. I can imagine that if I was married to an accountant working nine to five, he'd get pissed off with my hours.'

Early in 1994, Dawn was offered the role that would indelibly establish her as one of Britain's most popular actresses. Her good friend Richard Curtis, co-founder of Comic Relief and creator of TV comedy series *Blackadder* and the smash-hit film *Four Weddings and a Funeral*, had written a show especially for her. *The Vicar of Dibley*, a comedy about the newly ordained female vicar of a small English parish, was destined to become one of the BBC's top-rating shows. Eleven million people tuned in to watch the first episode in November 1994, and its success quickly grew.

Dawn was perfectly cast as Geraldine Granger, the jolly, chocolate-loving vicar of St Barnabas. Known as Gerry to her parishioners, the Reverend Granger spends her time caring for the spiritual needs of her somewhat eccentric flock. In stark contrast to the cutting wit of *Blackadder*, *The Vicar of Dibley* had a decidedly old-fashioned, traditional sitcom feel to it. 'Richard has tried to write something about goodness, which is a supposedly naff thing to do,' Dawn explained. 'But he finds it sad that the eighties have taught us to be sneering and he thinks it might be time to change things.' Although Dawn was the star of the show, she was backed by an impressive cast. Liz Smith, James Fleet, Gary Waldhorn, Roger Lloyd Pack and Trevor Peacock all had key roles in the show, and actress Emma Chambers was to prove a particular hit as Dawn's dippy verger Alice.

Appearing in a sitcom – something she'd sworn she wouldn't do until she was at least sixty – Dawn had to adjust to being part of a comedy ensemble. Although hers was the principal character, there were other actors to share the lines with and people were no longer relying on her to provide all the laughs. It was a situation that required a certain amount of getting used to. Dawn was by now accustomed to doing things her own way, and her natural inclination to hog the limelight led to a battle of wills between her and Richard Curtis.

'I quite often felt like the straight person,' she explains. 'All the instincts tell you that this is not the area where you'll get laughs but I had to be gracious, or at least pretend to be. Everything in me would say, "Hang on, I could do a great joke here where I show my bosoms . . ." I remember one rehearsal where Richard just sat there with his head in his hands saying, "Stop persecuting me", and it was there I thought, "I've pushed this too far". I was begging for jokes, and he'd just tell me to shut up. He's right, but I'm used to working in the kind of atmosphere where there's two of you and whoever speaks the loudest at the time gets the lines.' Curtis, it seemed, had anticipated that there might be problems. 'He wrote me a letter early on saying, "This is going to be a particularly strange journey, you won't find it easy or natural but please trust me",' she says. 'So I thought, "OK, I'll try it".'

The character of Geraldine was loosely based on real-life cleric Joy Carroll, the thirty-year-old vicar at the Church of Immanuel with St Andrew in Streatham, south-west London. The Reverend Carroll, who once went on her parish rounds wearing a short skirt and knee-high leather boots with her dog collar, is living proof that not all vicars are dusty old men. Richard Curtis met her on a research mission at the General Synod, and recruited her as an adviser to the show. He took Dawn along to meet Joy at her London vicarage, and Dawn quizzed her about her job over tea and chocolate cake. The two women later became friends, and Dawn and Lenny were guests at her wedding in 1997. The similarities between Geraldine Granger and Joy Carroll were striking, and the Reverend Carroll found herself the centre of attention in her parish. 'Friends who have seen the show have said, "Oh, my God, it's you",' she said. 'And when I sat down to watch the first show I just cringed with embarrassment when I saw myself coming back at me.'

The Vicar of Dibley was filmed in the picturesque Buckinghamshire hamlet of Turville, and some of the villagers appeared as extras in the show. Billie too was often on set. She loved going along to see her mum filming, and also went to watch Lenny record his new role in the BBC1 comedy *Chef*. As a result, the confused three-year-old was convinced her mother was a vicar and her father a chef.

'Nothing will persuade Billie otherwise,' Dawn laughed. 'She sees us on telly and it makes perfect sense to her.'

Dawn admitted that being a mother had had a big impact on her working life. 'I was always the strict, matronly one who insisted to Jennifer that we couldn't go home until we'd finished a sketch,' she explained. 'But now I have to leave to get home to Billie.' She was noticeably defensive when a journalist enquired how she juggled motherhood and work. 'I pick her up from playschool myself nearly every day,' she said irritably. 'What do people expect? Do they think she's whisked home in a private helicopter surrounded by armed guards?'

A new series of *French and Saunders* went out in 1995 and included the infamous *Baywatch* spoof where Dawn dressed up as Pamela Anderson. But the series ran into criticism from reviewers for being over-indulgent and relying too heavily on parodies of other TV shows and Hollywood films. For the first time in their careers, the golden girls of comedy found themselves at the end of a media backlash. Dawn mounted a stout defence. 'That's the joy of doing our show,' she insisted. 'We watch a film and go, "Hooray, I can't wait till we can have a go at this". When we see *Braveheart*, we think, "Great, we're going to get to go on horses". It was ripe for us. It's not great political satire.' But with their new-found power at the BBC, Dawn and Jennifer couldn't blame any of the criticism on other people. 'Nobody tells us what to put on the screen any more,' Dawn admitted. 'Any mistakes you see are totally down to us.'

For that year's Comic Relief in March, Dawn provided one of the most memorable moments in the show's history. Not only did she get to kiss heart-throb actor Hugh Grant, she also raised £1 million for charity in the process. The pair 'snogged' for almost a minute after the British public pledged the money. Dawn – wearing a safety-pin dress *à la* Hugh's girlfriend Elizabeth Hurley at the premiere of *Four Weddings and a Funeral* – made the most of her big moment, throwing her arms around the handsome actor and kissing him passionately. The money sent the total raised by Comic Relief since 1986 over the magical £100 million mark.

The charity remains enormously important to Dawn and Lenny, and to date they have helped raise more than £160 million. 'It's the most important fund-raising activity that goes on in our home,' she explains. 'I try never to say no to a Comic Relief request – and they come pretty thick and fast. It's so important because it's far-reaching and addresses problems both in this country and abroad, and it's very committed to long-term solutions.' But comedian Bernard Manning, the old enemy of the politically correct brigade, cruelly ridiculed her efforts. 'All them Ethiopian children needed was Lenny Henry and his big fat wife going over there, showing them what it looks like to eat ten meals a day,' he sneered.

An episode of *The Vicar of Dibley*, shown just before Christmas, made headlines when it inadvertently 'killed off' the veteran television presenter Hughie Green. The former *Opportunity Knocks* star protested after Dawn's character remarked: 'There hasn't been a bus through the village since Hughie Green died.' Despite a string of letters from Green, the BBC refused to broadcast a correction. 'Why Won't Hugh Tell The World I'm Not Dead?' pleaded the *Sun* on his behalf. His plight was even brought up in the House of Commons, and eventually the BBC caved in and put out a correction on *Points of View* and in the *Radio Times*. The family show also came under fire for its high content of smutty innuendoes. It was found guilty of breaching Broadcasting Standards Council pre-watershed guidelines on 'taste and decency' – particularly in the 1996 Easter special, which carried a saucy joke about Norma Major. 'Standards of taste in the BBC now seem to be in endemic decline,' fumed Tory MP Toby Jessel. 'There has to be an apology.' And Lady Olga Maitland said the show was 'lacking in taste and offensive'. 'What are they trying to prove by being gratuitously offensive?' she asked. The BBC defended the show, insisting that it was 'a bit of light-hearted fun' and had not intended to offend anyone.

Dawn had spent the three years since she returned to work flagrantly burning the candle at both ends. But early in 1996 she was struck down by a severe bout of the liver disease hepatitis A. The condition, caused by eating unhygienic food, inflames and enlarges the liver and in extreme cases can trigger liver failure. Dawn was ill for almost three months and suffered acute exhaustion, severe abdominal pains and vomiting. 'It's the worst thing I've ever had,' she later revealed. 'It zonked me out. I felt very sick, turned yellow and my body became a battleground. I just had to lie still while the war went on. It felled me like a tree. I felt incredibly tired and slept for long periods at a time. I was in bed for a month, and there was a good two weeks in the middle of it when I didn't know day from night. I got really frightened. I couldn't walk, I couldn't see and I was hallucinating.'

Dawn, who had almost never been sick before, believed her hectic schedule may have made her more susceptible to the illness. 'There comes a point when you can't push yourself any more,' she admitted. 'Your body says "absolutely not" and that's the time when, if there is a bug around, it can grab you. You are supposed to take three or four months afterwards to recover, so I'll be taking things easy for a while. My tendency is to say yes to everything because, like a lot of people in this business, I think it might all be over quite soon so I'd better take it while I can. But it has left me exhausted, and now the doctor says it has to stop.'

However, old habits die hard, and Dawn was soon every bit as busy as ever. She got up at 5.30 each morning to film a third series of *Murder Most Horrid*, frequently not returning home until late at night. But at the press launch two months later, she insisted that she was as fit as a fiddle. She was joined in six new tales of murder and mayhem by comedian Hugh Laurie and actress Minnie Driver, who is one of her closest friends. She also got to play a sex scene with dishy actor Nigel Havers. 'He turned out to be a lot more fun than I expected,' she says. 'He was very badly behaved and foul-mouthed, which was very refreshing.' Dawn's producer Sophie Clarke-Jervoise says that Dawn often draws on real people to come up with her telly characters. 'Off screen, Dawn's always very nosy about everyone's personal life,' she explains. 'She makes sure she knows everybody's name in the crew. She's very observational, and that comes across in her work. I watch her characters and I think, "Yes, I know that person".'

That summer, the Henry family rented a house by the sea in West Sussex for three months in order for Dawn to appear in the J. B. Priestley play, *When We are Married*. She was starring at the Chichester Theatre alongside *Rumpole* actor Leo McKern, and actresses Dora Bryan and Alison Steadman, and confessed she still found the theatre scary. 'It's terrifying, but that's why I do it,' she said. 'It's good to have things to be scared of. I've always enjoyed being in front of a live audience.' She also enjoyed working with new people and learning different approaches to her craft, but she certainly wasn't doing it for the money. Her fee was all but swallowed up by the cost of moving her family for the duration, but she was convinced the experience would be worth it. 'This will be great,' she said enthusiastically. 'It will be Billie's summer holiday, and I'll work at night while she's asleep and spend all day with her. I'm really looking forward to it. My heart hurts if I'm away from my daughter or my husband for too long.'

In the autumn, she joined up with Jennifer to record a *French and Saunders* Christmas special. It was becoming increasingly rare for the two women to work together, and Dawn revealed that they were constantly turning down commissions that involved working as a double act. 'Various television companies would have us writing and making comedy together every day,' she said. 'It's nice to work together, but I would rather be her friend when I die than have worked with her until that day. The important thing is the relationship. We're always happier if we've been apart. It's like you go off and have an affair with someone else for a little while, then you come back ready for your old partner. It just spices things up. You can get too insular and self-absorbed if you're working with the same person all the time. I don't know if we'll always work together. I think we want different things in the long run.'

The following year, Dawn was offered another solo project: the romantic lead in the Screen One drama *Sex and Chocolate*. As it was about her two favourite subjects, Dawn could have been forgiven for thinking that she had died and gone to heaven. During filming she had to swig champagne and munch chocolate, and the fridge in her trailer was well stocked with confectionery. 'It's in my contract,' she explained. 'It always is, whether or not the film is about chocolate.' Dawn starred as the wonderfully named Bev Bodger, a contented wife and mother of three who, completely out of character, debunks to Paris for an illicit weekend with an old flame. Her loving husband, played by Phil Daniels, dashes off to France in hot pursuit.

Dawn was delighted that the BBC had chosen to make a film with a large woman in the lead. 'It takes a lot for directors to cast a fat girl at the centre of a romantic sexual drama,' she conceded. She claimed not to be interested in what reviewers might think of the show. 'I don't care what the critics say,' she insisted. 'If I had listened to them, I would have stopped and would be teaching again by now. I wouldn't be sitting here with a fridge full of chocolate and kissing Phil Daniels!' But she proved she *did* care by continuing in the next breath: 'They've been so unkind. Why? Because we live in this country and we've had some success. I used to get hurt by the critics, but now the only ones I listen to are punters. Viewing figures tell you a programme is not crap.'

For that year's Comic Relief, Dawn and Jennifer impersonated the Spice Girls, with Dawn dressing up as a rather unlikely Victoria Adams, aka Posh Spice, and Jennifer as Geri 'Ginger Spice' Halliwell. They called themselves the Sugar Lumps and persuaded the Spice Girls to join them on stage for a hilarious skit. The all-girl band even released a single, 'Who Do You Think You Are?', especially for Comic Relief. It went on to become a number one hit.

She ended 1997 on a high, winning the title of 'Best Comedy Actress' at the British Comedy Awards. The accolade was in recognition of her role in *The Vicar of Dibley* 1996 Christmas special, which was one of the most-watched programmes over the festive period. The following year she was up for the same award, but lost out to Nicholas Lyndhurst. However, *The Vicar of Dibley* won 'Best Situation Comedy Drama' at the 1998 Royal Television Society Awards, and was nominated for the *Radio Times* People's Choice BAFTA award.

CHAPTER TWELVE

French with Tears

Family life is enormously important to Dawn, and her husband and daughter are the pivotal things around which everything else revolves. Coming from a small, close knit family, she has always believed that home life is sacred and that it should come before everything else. As a child, she had been extremely close to her parents and older brother Gary, and her father's death served only to strengthen that bond. To this day, her mother and brother remain key figures in her life, and she often returns to the West Country to visit them and the many relatives she has in Plymouth.

But for many years, the most important person in Dawn's life has been her husband Lenny Henry. The home they have built together with their daughter Billie means more to Dawn than anything else in the world. They have been together for the best part of two decades, and were long considered to have one of the strongest marriages in show business. Lenny was the one person Dawn never doubted, and she trusted him implicitly. When she was going through a bad spell after being at home with Billie, she consoled herself with the thought that even if she gave up her career, she would still have Lenny. As long as they were together, she knew that everything would always be all right.

Dawn never missed an opportunity to sing her husband's praises, and often told in interviews of how he and their daughter were the most precious things in her life. She movingly explained how her 'heart hurt' when she was away from them for too long, and declared that there was no point in having a family if you didn't put them first. The couple frequently boasted of their deep love for each other, with Lenny eulogising about how marrying Dawn was the best thing he ever did.

So when the bubble burst in May 1999, it was seemingly without warning. A string of lurid allegations about Lenny made front-page news, and in the space of a few hours the idyll of their happy home life collapsed like a house of cards. The *Sun* newspaper appeared to have caught Lenny red-handed having an affair with a pretty young blonde. The paper revealed how the star had spent the night in a hotel room with twenty-six-year-old receptionist Merri Cheyne. Lenny, who was in the middle of a nationwide tour of his one-man show, was exposed after the newspaper found out about his liaison at the Royal York Hotel. He had, it was claimed, gone to extraordinary lengths to ensure that no one spotted him with Australian Merri – embarking on a cloak-and-dagger operation to hide his antics from his road crew. But he didn't realise that a team of reporters from the *Sun* were at the hotel – and were watching his every move.

The journalists saw him carry out a 'furtive' reconnaissance of the hotel's stairs and lifts before sneaking Merri into his £175-a-night suite, and watched as a bottle of chilled champagne was delivered to the room. They later observed the pair take a midnight stroll in the hotel gardens, and saw the blonde leave Lenny's room at eleven o'clock the following morning. During his stage show, the comic had devoted most of his act to telling the audience about his happy home life with 'life partner' Dawn. After returning home to Berkshire the next day to spend the night with his family, an unwitting Lenny travelled to Newcastle to do another show – never dreaming that he was about to be turned over by the press. But the *Sun* followed him to Newcastle and watched as Merri Cheyne once again turned up at his hotel. However, this time there was no meeting. She hung around outside the hotel for two hours, but after a flurry of mobile-phone calls, left 'disconsolately' without seeing Lenny.

The story, when it appeared on the front page of the *Sun* on 24 May, caused a sensation. Everyone had truly believed Dawn and Lenny's marriage to be rock-solid, and the shock waves ricocheted through show-business circles. When news of his tryst emerged, Lenny hurried to be with Dawn, driving through the night from Truro, in Cornwall, where he had been performing on stage. He arrived home at 3.30 a.m. to face the music. A thoroughly shaken Lenny was forced to explain himself to his devastated wife, and warn her that their marriage was about to be held up to public scrutiny.

Upon hearing his news, Dawn's whole world threatened to collapse around her. It was her worst nightmare come true. She had placed absolute faith in her husband, but now he had betrayed that trust. During the many times that he had been working away from home, she had never dreamed for one minute that Lenny would cheat on her. She knew the perils of life on the road, and understood the temptations provided by the groupies and star-struck fans who are desperate to sleep with someone famous, but she never believed that Lenny would succumb to such attentions. However, it seemed that she had been wrong. The *Sun* revealed that Lenny had known Merri Cheyne for some time, having met her the year before when he toured Australia.

For the third time in her life, Dawn found herself bitterly let down by a man she loved. First, her beloved father had deserted her by taking his own life, then the fiancé she adored broke her heart by cheating on her with another woman. Now the husband she

loved and trusted so deeply had deceived her too. She felt humili-
ated and very, very angry. Not only had Lenny spent the night
alone in a hotel room with a young woman, he had also been stupid
enough to have been caught by the press. The situation would have
been hard enough for Dawn to deal with had she discovered her
husband's indiscretion for herself, but that it should be exposed in a
newspaper for the whole country to gossip about was intolerable.
Dawn would not have chosen for even her closest friends to know
something so private and personal, but as it was, she realised that
the whole sorry story would be played out in the full glare of
publicity.

Dawn had a commitment to be at the BBC the day the story
broke, where she and Jennifer were supposed to be filming their
new sitcom *Let Them Eat Cake*, and she decided to go into work as
planned. She had been up all night waiting for Lenny to arrive
home, and the couple had had an emotional and exhausting
heart-to-heart. But although she knew it would take a lot of courage
to walk into the BBC with everyone knowing what had happened,
she decided that it would be business as usual.

As she roared out of her drive in her Jaguar XK8 sports car,
grim-faced and hiding behind a pair of dark glasses, it seemed as
though the whole of Fleet Street was camped outside her house.
Dawn was made of sterner stuff than her husband, who cancelled
the remaining three dates of his tour and went into hiding. While
Dawn stoically carried on with her work, Lenny went to pieces. He
was fully aware that within a short space of time he had gone from
hero to zero in the eyes of the British public. Presented with the
CBE by the Queen for his Comic Relief work only two months
before, he now found himself cast in the role of adulterer. The
nation genuinely felt for Dawn, and Lenny was conscious of how
much he had let her down. He was under siege, and once again
called on the services of a minder to keep the press at bay. He
turned to the same man who had helped them when they were the

subject of media attention following Billie's adoption.

The ex-nightclub bouncer, who prefers not to give his name, has known Lenny for eight years. He says that when the star hired his services last May he was at pains to assure him that what had been written about him was not true. 'Lenny told me it had been made up by the press and that the girl was put up to it by the papers,' he says. The minder claims that during the whole time the press was camped at the end of the couple's drive, no one realised that Lenny was at home. 'Lenny was able to come in and out of the property without the press seeing him,' he says mysteriously. 'Sometimes he would even be driving the car. But the press didn't know Lenny was there. They didn't know where he was, but he was at home the whole time.'

As well as staking out Dawn and Lenny's home in Berkshire, the press also beat a path to Merri Cheyne's door in Hertfordshire. She was offered huge amounts of money to talk about her relationship with Lenny, and it was only a matter of time before the inevitable 'kiss-and-tell' story appeared. But anyone hoping to hear about lust-filled nights of passion between her and Lenny were to be disappointed. Merri Cheyne did sell her story to a newspaper, but instead of the juicy revelations that tabloid readers have come to expect from kiss-and-tells, she sensationally denied point-blank that anything had gone on between them.

Featuring over several pages of the *Mirror*, she admitted she had wanted something to happen but that nothing had. She said she had been hopeful, and had even bought herself a new matching set of cream lingerie to wear the night she saw Lenny, but she insisted that they never had sex. Instead of indulging in a torrid night of lust with her, she claimed the star spent the entire time talking about Dawn and Billie. 'He didn't so much as kiss me,' she told the *Mirror*. 'He was the most married man I've ever met. I might as well have had a crush on Jesus Christ. I admit I was willing. I was able. I had a huge crush on him and flirted all night, but he rejected me. The only time he touched me was to ruffle my hair like a father does to a daughter. All we did was talk all night.'

Merri, who was paid somewhere in the region of £12,000 for her non-disclosures, said she was only speaking out because she didn't want Lenny to lose his family. 'I couldn't bear to see Dawn leave him over something so innocent,' she said. 'It was obvious just how much she and Billie mean to him.' Merri claimed that her head had been full of romantic ideas about her and Lenny, and admitted that he had possibly thought the same thing. 'I don't know if maybe he fancied me and thought about straying,' she said. 'But when it came down to it he just couldn't do it. He asked me to leave, which shows how much respect he has for his marriage.'

She described how her friendship with the star had begun ten months previously when they met in a Melbourne nightclub. Back in Britain, she had bumped into him in a London street, and he later popped in to see her at the music company where she was working as a receptionist. She said he then telephoned her and invited her to go and see him in York. 'I have never had a fling with a married man before, but I went to York because I had built him up in my mind and I just hoped that something would happen between us,' she said. 'I was so excited my heart was fluttering. I thought he was asking me to go and see him, but now I think what he really meant was that he wanted me to go and see him in his show.' She explained how he telephoned her at her York bed and breakfast at 11.30 at night and asked her to come over to his hotel room. 'I mistook his friendliness and attention for something much more – something that just wasn't there,' she said. 'I feel so stupid. But I feel even worse for Lenny. He has done nothing wrong. I've ruined four lives – Lenny's, Dawn's, their little girl Billie's and mine.'

By newspaper standards, it was one of the most unusual kiss-and-tell stories ever. But it remained to be seen whether Merri Cheyne's well-intentioned attempt to put Lenny in the clear with his wife would be enough to save his marriage. All the things she and Lenny had said about each other in interviews down the years now came back to haunt Dawn. 'I think once you are married you should be faithful or there's no point,' Lenny had told the *Sun* in 1982.

The dust had barely started to settle on the Merri Cheyne story when the couple were dealt a fresh blow. Less than two weeks after the *Sun* exclusive, further tacky revelations surfaced about Lenny in the press. The *Sunday People* claimed that the star had embarked on a 'sleazy spree' while staying on the holiday island of Tenerife. 'Lust-Crazed Lenny Kept Pestering Me For Sex As I Danced Naked Before Him', screamed the headline. 'Shame Of A Comic Hero'. The paper alleged he had gone on a drunken twelve-hour 'bender' and harassed dancers at a strip club he visited. They said he had 'leered' at three lap-dancers who performed naked for him at a club, 'danced provocatively around their pole', made lewd suggestions to them and offered to pay for sexual 'extras'.

His night of shame allegedly occurred on the last night of a BBC film assignment in the popular resort of Playas de las Americas in November 1998. The dancers told the newspaper that the comedy star had ogled them and pestered them for sexual favours. 'I said we didn't do stuff like that and if he wanted that he would have to go to a brothel,' one of them said. The story also alleged that he had attended a sex and cocaine party on the island, but did not say that he had indulged in either.

The ribald revelations were the last thing Dawn and Lenny needed. Dawn made it clear to her husband that their marriage was in grave trouble. The thought of losing Dawn was more than Lenny could bear, and within days of the second story hitting the news-stands he cracked under the pressure. He checked into the exclusive Priory clinic, suffering from depression, and admitted through a friend that he'd had 'a bit of a breakdown'. The friend, obviously speaking with Lenny's permission, told newspapers he'd had an emotional collapse and that his marriage was under 'severe strain'. Lenny had apparently told the pal: 'This has been the worst two weeks of my life. I can't cope with this. I'm fighting for my life here.'

He checked into the world-famous Priory, in Roehampton, south-west London, as a last resort. The £3,000-a-week clinic specialises in treating addiction and depression, and is a favourite refuge of the rich and famous. 'Lenny desperately needs to sort himself out,' said the friend. 'He feels completely freaked out by it all. He knows his behaviour has been inappropriate and that he has let Dawn down badly. The stories have devastated her. Lenny also knows he has a battle on to save his marriage. He's been a fool. He's a broken man and wants to be left alone.'

Lenny maintained that he hadn't cheated on Dawn. 'He hasn't been unfaithful to her and that's what angers him most about these stories,' said the friend. 'They have all left people with the idea that he's some kind of sex maniac running around bedding bimbos. Nothing could be further from the truth. He's got drunk, watched a bit of lap-dancing, kissed a few fans when they asked him to and been silly enough to let one girl into his room. For that he has been crucified and it's hit him very hard. His reputation is in tatters, his marriage is on the rocks and he feels absolutely terrible. It's hit him like a nuclear bomb. It's a nightmare which he has no idea how to escape from. He hopes that by going into The Priory he can get his head together and sort things out. But he knows it isn't going to be easy. Lenny is facing the crisis of his life. He is acutely depressed and at rock-bottom. He'd like everyone to give him a break and let him come to terms privately with what has happened. He would like to appeal to the media to respect the fact that he desperately needs to sort himself out.'

But while Lenny fell apart, Dawn amazed everyone with her resilience. During what was an emotional and traumatic time for her, she remained the consummate professional and continued filming her new show. 'It has been a terrible two weeks, yet you wouldn't know it from the way she is handling the situation,' said one impressed colleague. 'Everyone thought that with all these problems she would be unable to work, but amazingly she has kept smiling and is wittier than ever. Inside she is probably having a tough time of it, but she's certainly not letting it show.'

But Dawn is nothing if not strong. As a young girl arriving at boarding school, she had quickly learned to stand on her own two feet. The early tragedy of her father's death, and the confidence he had imparted to her, also served to toughen her up and make her resilient. She had survived when David Smith broke her heart, and she was determined that she would survive now that Lenny had done the same. But whereas David had found someone else and no longer wanted her, Lenny *did* still want her. He also needed her, but she wasn't sure whether she needed him.

A friend of the couple says that Dawn's first inclination was to tell Lenny it was all over between them. But when she realised the extent of his torment she relented and agreed to give their marriage another try. Lenny's behaviour, and the amount of press coverage it received, affected many people. His seven-year-old daughter was confused by events she was not old enough to understand, and both his and Dawn's families were at a loss to comprehend what had happened. Their friends, too, were unsure of what to think. Everyone had been under the impression that their marriage was a solid one – a view which Dawn and Lenny had always gone out of their way to perpetuate – but in truth there had been strain in their relationship for some time.

After eighteen years together they had found, like many married couples before them, that it isn't always easy being in a monogamous relationship. Both Dawn and Lenny admit to having monster egos, and there have occasionally been battles of the will between the two big showbiz personalities. And although people were taken by surprise when their supposedly perfect marriage was revealed to have flaws, clues that the couple's relationship had not always been plain sailing were there to see. In 1991, Dawn hinted that living together was by no means easy. 'I'm conscious all the time that you've got to work very hard at marriage,' she said. 'I think everyone has to – I can't imagine how people survive otherwise.' And in August 1996, Lenny went so far as to say that having Billie had rescued their marriage. He explained in the *Mail On Sunday* that just before they adopted their daughter, he and Dawn were totally cut off from each other by their ever-increasing workload and accelerating careers.

'Before Billie came along our careers came first and, both being very ambitious, we worked very hard,' he said. 'We pushed ourselves to the brink. I'd come home at midnight and Dawn would arrive at three in the morning, which made things very difficult. We were ships passing in the night, and would go without a holiday together for nearly a year.' And he added, ominously: 'If you both do everything at the same time as each other, that way lies disaster. You learn from mistakes and discover that anyone working really hard and putting work first is in danger of ruining a relationship.'

Deciding that they would no longer work at the same time was not just so that one of them could take care of Billie; it also meant that Dawn and Lenny could see more of each other too. 'Since we adopted Billie things have got better because we decided never to work at the same time,' Lenny said. 'Nowadays Dawn books loads of holidays that I have to go on. I still put a lot of hours in. Sometimes family does suffer, and you have to realise that family must come first.' But the downside of their new childcare arrangements meant that when Lenny toured Australia in 1998, Dawn stayed at home to take care of their daughter. Faced with a long period away from home, it is perhaps unsurprising that Lenny lived the lifestyle of a bachelor in Australia, partying and going to nightclubs. It was on one such jaunt that he struck up the ill-fated friendship with Merri Cheyne.

And he was in Australia when he learned in August 1998 that his beloved mother had died after a long and painful battle against diabetes. Winifred Henry had been a major influence in her son's life, and losing her hit Lenny very hard. That he should learn the news while he was thousands of miles away from home – and in the absence of the other huge rock in his life, Dawn – was doubly unfortunate. Friends believe that his mother's death was responsible for bringing on a mid-life crisis in Lenny, as he brutally realised how tenuous life is. He admitted to Merri Cheyne that he was 'freaked out' about turning forty.

When he returned to Britain he embarked on a strict fitness regime, working out in the gym every day and losing two stone in weight. While hardly cast-iron proof that he was about to commit adultery, radical changes in lifestyle are often indicative of someone reassessing their life. His wife may be a staunch supporter of big is beautiful, but Lenny was determined to get himself into peak condition. Dropping in on an interview and photo shoot that Dawn was doing, Lenny enthusiastically told the journalist how good he was feeling about himself after his diet. But realising that he had strayed from the party line, he added hastily: 'It wasn't because I wanted to lose weight. It was because I wanted to get fit.'

In the Henry-French household, diet is a dirty word and Lenny's desire to talk about his weight loss provides a rare insight into what it is like to live with a forceful personality like Dawn. On occasion, he has given other glimpses into life as Mr Dawn French, and observers are left wondering if he's not just a little in awe of his wife. Lenny – who once admitted he would 'rather gnaw my own arm off than get into a confrontation' – does not share Dawn's devil-may-care attitude. 'I could never pose naked like she did,' he said. 'Dawn's got much more confidence than I have. She's totally unafraid. She just goes for it. I went to a secondary-modern school where nudity was something you ridiculed in the shower.'

But he hastily got back on-message by adding that he fully supported her. 'That's not to say I didn't back Dawn in her decision to pose naked,' he stressed. 'She looked beautiful. I'm her greatest fan when she's got no clothes on. If you feel good about yourself, then that's the main thing. For me, it is natural to be surrounded by big women as most of my female relatives are over a size 16. I can't understand what any man sees in skinny women.' Dawn too had often boasted how her husband didn't fancy skinny women. 'My husband's a Jamaican and comes from a family of big women,' she told *Tatler* magazine. 'For him it's the norm and thin women are a turn-off.'

And therein lay the crux of the matter.

Lenny had not been caught spending the night in a hotel room with a size 16-plus woman, but with that old cliché, a slim blonde. At most, Merri Cheyne was a shapely size 12, and some people would probably describe her as thin. Yet Lenny was sufficiently interested in her to invite her to visit him alone in his hotel room. It was ever thus. The dancers who Lenny had dallied with during the seaside summer seasons in his pre-Dawn days were a long way from being fat, yet he certainly didn't appear to find them a turn-off either. And, according to the *Sunday People*, Lenny had been very attracted to the slim lap-dancers who performed for him in Tenerife.

Having spent so much time loudly proclaiming how much her husband liked big women, and how turned off he was by thin ones, Dawn's embarrassment was compounded. In a way it was a double betrayal: how much less painful would it have been if Merri Cheyne had been a plump sixteen stone, instead of a slim young woman. But experienced people-watchers know that the chances of a rich and famous man being caught in a liaison with a fat girl are probably one in a million. When it comes down to it, the women are usually all the same: generally a great deal younger than the man's wife, often slimmer and almost always blonde. Dawn was painfully aware that those who had ridiculed her for her outspoken views in the past would no doubt be crowing exultantly now.

But her friends rallied round and her pain was shared by her many fans. Lenny too had a circle of people rooting for him – not least of whom was Dawn. Few spared a thought for the woman at the centre of the story. When the *Sun's* story appeared, Merri Cheyne found herself cut adrift by Lenny and was left to fend for herself in the dog-eat-dog world of tabloid journalism. A year on, she is older and a great deal wiser. Now living back home with her mother in Melbourne, she has had plenty of time to reflect on that peculiar time in her life, but has heard nothing from Lenny since the story broke about them. She explains how, alone in a foreign land and with no one to turn to for advice, she found herself sitting in the office of PR supremo Max Clifford, self-styled king of the kiss-and-tell.

'After the story appeared, I had no idea what to do or how to handle any of it,' she says. 'I had the press camped out on my doorstep, I had them outside work, and my very Christian landlord gave me twelve hours to get out of my house. My flatmate suggested I contact Max Clifford, so I rang him up and he asked me to go and see him at his offices in Bond Street. I was really distressed and upset, and explained that I had reporters everywhere and didn't know what to do. He asked me what I wanted out of it, and I said I wanted the reporters to go away and everything to go back to normal. He told me that for that to happen I would have to talk to a newspaper and put my side of the story. He told me that once that had happened I would probably be left alone. I didn't want to talk to the press, but he said it was the only way to kill the story.

'It's not exactly a fun thing to go through. I didn't speak to Lenny at all during the whole thing in case my phone was being tapped. The *Mirror* put me through a full interrogation. It was really intense – ten hours of interviews, going over and over every little point. I didn't want any money from it, so I paid my airfare home and gave some money to my mum. I gave the rest to charity.'

Merri still maintains that nothing happened between her and Lenny, but admits that even her own family is not sure whether to believe her. 'I still get members of my family asking which story was true, the one that they printed first or the other one,' she says. 'It's been weird to have to try to explain myself to friends and family. This whole thing has really unsettled me. It has been really traumatic, but I guess it's been worse for Dawn and Lenny.' Merri is still curious about how the press found out about her visit to York. She wonders if one of her friends or work colleagues tipped off the paper. 'If I could find out who gave the *Sun* their information I would be a lot better equipped to deal with the whole thing,' she says. 'I was casting an evil eye everywhere, thinking, "Was it you?" but no one knew that I knew Lenny. No one knew who I was going to see, or what was going on. 'It did cross my mind that the tip-off might have come from someone who knew him, but then I couldn't work out why anyone would do that.'

For Dawn, work proved to be her salvation during the troubled months that followed. Her new series *Let Them Eat Cake*, a comedy set in the court of Louis XVI of France, gave her the opportunity to take her mind off her marital problems. She threw herself into an intense work schedule, impressing those who were working with her. 'There was no way Dawn was pulling out,' says her co-star Alison Steadman. 'I don't think it even crossed her mind. She's an incredibly focused and strong person, and her work is very impor-tant to her. If something happens that's horrible in your life – and that was horrible – you go to work for a break and to get over it. She was amazing, and not for a second did it affect anything.'

Colleagues were keen to offer support, but talking about her problems was the last thing Dawn wanted to do. 'We didn't sit around discussing it with her, though she knew we were there if she wanted to,' says Steadman. 'We didn't say, "Ooh, you poor thing", and try to find out what was going on. We got on with work. That is what she wanted. But obviously I felt sorry for Dawn and Lenny because they were having a hard time.'

Let Them Eat Cake was filmed that summer and began transmission in September. Billed as 'murder, scandal and lots of rumpo', it was trumpeted as one of *the* highlights of the BBC's autumn schedule. It went out in a prime-time Thursday night slot on BBC1 and starred Jennifer Saunders as Colombine, Comtesse De Vache, and Dawn as her maid Lisette. But while the set was undeniably lavish, with beautiful costumes and furniture and impressive Marie-Antoinette-style wigs, the jokes quickly wore thin. Christopher Matthew from the *Mail On Sunday* said he had *wanted* to like it, and was a huge fan of Dawn and Jennifer's, but reluctantly pronounced it 'a right stinker'. 'On paper, it had everything going for it: cast-iron stars, classy support . . . terrific setting . . . yet, for all that, I was about as amused as a man in a tumbril on the way to the guillotine,' he said. 'There seemed to be an awful lot of floundering going on – not least by French and Saunders. Rarely have I seen two comedians working so desperately hard for their laughs.'

The show also gave the impression that Dawn and Jennifer, normally scrupulous in their preparation, could even have been making it up as they went along. The view shared by the majority of television critics was that *Let Them Eat Cake* was pretty dismal, although the *Express*'s reviewer thought it was marvellous and said he hoped a second series would follow soon. Dawn was disappointed by the reviews, but the show's poor reception did little to dampen her high standing at the BBC. Despite her troubled home life, her career had never been in better shape. In September, she and Jennifer signed new six-year contracts with the BBC, reportedly turning down big-money offers from commercial TV channels. They signed as a couple because they have their own production company, Saunders and French Productions, but – as before – their new contracts allowed for them to work independently of each other.

The BBC, faced with a string of big-name defections, including Des Lynam, Barry Norman and Frank Skinner, was delighted the pair were staying put. As was Dawn. 'We've had offers to move elsewhere, very generous offers that would quadruple our income,' she said. 'But we have decided we are well paid for what we do and are not tempted by massive wonga to work for other stations. If you write and perform, as we do, you have to be somewhere where you can do what you want. I can't see a single reason to go. The BBC lets us do whatever we feel the next project is, never knowing whether it is going to work or not – it's all about risk. We take risks, and they let us do it and the results have been good. I feel safer at the Beeb than I would anywhere else.'

As usual, Dawn packed an enormous amount of work into 1999. In February, she starred in a fourth series of *Murder Most Horrid*, and filmed a charity episode of *The Vicar of Dibley* for Comic Relief. Hollywood star Johnny Depp guest-starred in the two-part special, playing himself. She signed up to feature in *Bosom Pals*, an animated BBC series for the year 2000, based on the plump ladies created by artist Beryl Cook. Unsurprisingly, Dawn is a big fan of Cook's work, which she describes as 'a sort of visual Prozac'.

She also made her much-heralded movie debut in the British film *Milk*. A black comedy about a bachelor dairy farmer – played by Dawn's *Vicar of Dibley* co-star James Fleet – it also starred Francesca Annis, Joss Ackland, Phyllida Law and Richard Johnson. It was filmed the previous autumn and premiered at the London Film Festival in the summer of 1999. But disappointingly for Dawn, the movie – hailed as a *'Four Weddings and a Funeral* without the weddings' – did not go on general release, and was instead shown for the first time on Sky Premier in December. It wasn't immediately apparent why Dawn had chosen to be in *Milk*. She had a small role in the film, and few lines. But as her television career has grown, and her position as one of Britain's most popular actresses has become assured, Dawn has started to have serious aspirations to get into movies.

Like many big-name television stars, she is convinced she has what it takes to succeed in films too. 'When I was younger I wanted to be in movies because I'd heard about the large portions served up by film location caterers,' she says. 'Now it's because I'd quite like an Oscar on the sideboard.' Whether she is capable of making the difficult transition from TV to big screen, however, remains to be seen. 'She's desperate to get into movies,' says an associate. 'Years ago she told me that she and Jennifer were keen to get into films. They went to see a film director at the Hyde Park Hotel, the guy who made *Legends Of The Fall*, and they were both really excited. She is like many of these television types who would love to break into film. But she's a television comedy actress really – first and foremost.'

Dawn herself is under no illusion that, where Hollywood at least is concerned, her size lessens her chances of a successful movie career. While some large women have made it in Hollywood – notably Roseanne Barr and Kathy Bates – they are the exception. Dawn often refers to the ill-fated trip to Los Angeles in 1990 when Lenny was making *True Identity*, and is clearly still hurt by the way she was dismissed out of hand. 'Hollywood can't imagine a fat girl in the middle of a film,' she concedes. 'When they met me they seemed to feel terribly sorry for me. They looked at me as if to say, "What can you possibly think you have to offer to our glitzy world?" They couldn't understand why I thought I belonged there and it was patently obvious that I didn't. I actually found people were pitying me for being fat, which is something I'd never experienced before.'

She claims that in 1995 she was asked to audition for a Hollywood film, but says: 'Again they saw me as the sad, fat girl. I'm perfectly happy to play those roles, but only if there is a pay-off. In *French and Saunders* I will wear a swimming costume if I can have a joke about it. But I have to be in control of the joke. I'm not prepared to be a fat girl who is also the victim.' Despite having played the romantic lead in the BBC drama *Sex And Chocolate*, she still feels that she is discriminated against in Britain too. 'I am excluded from being the love interest in dramas because it's not done,' she says. 'To be a deliciously desirable woman is not open to me. If I was an actress who sat by the phone waiting for offers to come, I wouldn't get them.'

Her most successful role to date has been in the hugely popular *Vicar of Dibley*. The sitcom is one of the BBC's highest-rating shows, and has won Dawn a new army of fans. People who would never have dreamed of watching *French and Saunders* or the Comic Strip films have become ardent followers of the gentle comedy. While Jennifer Saunders's *Absolutely Fabulous* became a massive hit, its appeal was mostly limited to the under-forties. It was also very much of its time and quickly dated. *The Vicar of Dibley*, however, appeals across the board to all age groups and classes, and its timeless charm means that a long shelf-life is assured.

Dawn began filming a third series of the show in October 1999, and at Christmas the BBC appeared to be pinning all its hopes on her to pull in the highest ratings. Viewers tuning in over the holiday were served a five-course helping of the star. She appeared in a lavish production of *David Copperfield*, starred in a *French and Saunders* Christmas special, and featured in three episodes of *The Vicar of Dibley*. Twelve million people watched the Christmas Day edition, making it the most-watched programme after *Coronation Street*.

Both Dawn and the BBC were delighted with the result, but once again the show raised a few eyebrows for its lewd content. It was the third time it had made headlines for the wrong reasons. Having been found guilty of breaching Broadcasting Standards Commission pre-watershed guidelines in 1996, there were further complaints in January 1998 when viewers objected to comments about Cliff Richard's underpants, sex with poodles and the Pope's testicles. The Broadcasting Standards Commission upheld the complaints, saying that the language had gone beyond the bounds of what was acceptable in a show promoted as family viewing.

At Christmas 1999, the programme was again criticised for bad taste, this time by that most unlikely guardian of old-fashioned morals – the tabloid press. 'What grossly OTT "jokes" on *The Vicar of Dibley*,' blasted Garry Bushell in the *Sun*. 'A baby falling off a table, Geraldine's hands covered in faeces . . . does BBC1 really believe this junk was suitable for family viewing? TV has lost its taste meter.' And under the headline 'God Awful', the *Sunday People* indignantly wrote: 'Some of the jokes were so smutty, they'd have given Benny Hill pause for thought . . . Holy unfunny.' But the *Sunday Mirror*'s reviewer Ian Hyland voted the smut 'first-rate', and *Sunday People* columnist Carol Sarler applauded Dawn for managing to 'rescue, single-handedly, the entire television industry over an otherwise lamentable Christmas season'.

While *The Vicar of Dibley* was a ratings winner, the *French and Saunders* Christmas special was less successful. It was universally panned by the critics – yet again criticised for being too self-indulgent. Dawn and Jennifer's much-hyped *Star Wars* spoof, for which they had been coached by the team who worked on the Hollywood movie, proved to be the biggest let-down of all. '*French and Saunders* Christmas special was not very Christmassy and not in the least special,' concluded the *Sunday People*'s reviewer. 'Their *Star Wars* take-off never left the ground, and it looked as if they'd made up the script on the way to the studio. Two laughs in half an hour was hardly enough reward.'

The *Sunday Mirror*'s Ian Hyland agreed: 'The whole thing was cheap and shoddy,' he said. The sketch where Dawn impersonated soap-star-turned-singer Martine McCutcheon was praised, as was the one in which Jennifer pretended to be the teenage Mel C. from the Spice Girls. But Dawn's take-off of Diana Ross being searched by security guards at the airport came in for flak from the *Mirror*'s Charlie Catchpole. 'It might have worked better if Dawn had looked a bit more like Diana Ross and a bit less like Demis Roussos,' he bitched.

But whatever the poison pens may write, Dawn remains hugely

popular with television viewers. In December 1999, she was voted the twentieth century's funniest British woman in a poll commissioned by the Internet bank Smile. Hot on the heels of that accolade came a second poll by the same bank, which voted *The Vicar of Dibley* one of the most popular TV sitcoms ever. The show won third place behind *Men Behaving Badly* and the winner, *Only Fools and Horses*. *The Vicar of Dibley* is also shown in America.

Having worked so hard throughout 1999, and ending the year on a career high, Dawn felt she'd earned a rest. In January 2000, she and Lenny took a three-month break from work to concentrate on their marriage. After much soul-searching, Dawn had decided to forgive her husband his indiscretions and was determined to save their relationship. Two months after the Merri Cheyne story broke in the press, Ulster secretary Mo Mowlam emerged as an unlikely marriage counsellor to the pair. Mo, famed for her peacemaking efforts in Northern Ireland, appeared to have employed some top-level diplomacy to help Dawn and Lenny patch up their marriage. The couple travelled to Ireland to visit her at Hillsborough Castle, and after sharing a pub lunch, emerged smiling. They were photographed hand in hand, with a happy-looking Dawn gazing adoringly up at her husband. It was a picture that told the world they were back together and had never been happier.

But still the rumours persisted that all was not well within the Henry marriage. As Dawn and Lenny prepared to jet to the other side of the world for their extended vacation, a story went round Fleet Street that divorce papers had been filed at Reading County Court. The couple took the unprecedented step of faxing newspapers, denying they were getting divorced and assuring everyone that they were still 'very happy' together.

During their vacation with daughter Billie, the couple hired a camper van and toured New Zealand. They spent a month hidden away on the paradise island of Waiheke, a forty-minute ferry ride from Auckland, which Lenny had discovered when he toured New

Zealand in 1998. They rented a £1 million holiday villa and rarely ventured out, usually having their meals delivered from a nearby restaurant. They returned in the spring, and their friends are now hopeful that they have weathered the storm.

Show-business impresario Robert Luff has known Lenny for more than twenty years, and in the dark days following the Merri Cheyne affair the star turned to his former mentor for help. 'I've seen Lenny many times in the past year, all the way through the difficult patch, and he has coped very well indeed,' says Luff. 'He was very upset and asked my advice. It was a difficult time for them both, and Dawn is probably the one who has held them together. They had a little problem that some married couples get. Some people decide it's the end, but not in their case.'

TV comedy boss Andy Harries believes Dawn and Lenny's high-profile careers make it especially hard for them to enjoy a normal relationship. 'They have always been a very work-orientated couple,' he says. 'One of the difficulties of making a relationship like that work is that they get so caught up, so busy, and it inevitably brings a lot of pressure. Like any relationship, it's very complex but I would say it's definitely a marriage of equals. They are equally successful, equally famous and have gone through good-stroke-great career patches and then less good, and then good again. That's the nature of being a performer, particularly a comedy performer. Dawn is supportive of Lenny, but I think he's very supportive of her too. They have a strong relationship, otherwise they wouldn't have survived.'

Harries, controller of entertainment and comedy at Granada Television, reports that Lenny is now on 'jolly good form'. 'I'm sure it's true that Dawn can be formidable – she wouldn't be a huge success and be *The Vicar of Dibley* if she wasn't,' he says. 'She had to be seen to carry on during that period, and at the end of the day what choices do you have? You either hold it together and decide that you're going to work it through, or you say, "Fuck it, your

behaviour was unacceptable and that's the end of our relationship".
And she didn't feel – whatever the rights and wrongs, or whatever
did or didn't happen – that that was necessary. In the end, the
decision was to stay together.'

The couple keep counsel with a select band of friends. 'The
comedy scene is a small, fairly tight world and they have very close
friends,' explains Harries. But Dawn remains an enigma even to
some of her dearest friends. Photographer Trevor Leighton, whom
she met nearly twenty years ago when he photographed her, has
become one of her best friends. But he admits he sometimes feels he
doesn't know her at all. 'I have been best friends with Lenny for
eighteen years and Dawn is a very close friend of mine,' he says.
'But actually I don't really know her. I do and don't know her – it's
difficult to explain.'

Dawn's business partner Helen Teague attempts a better job of
describing her complex pal. 'People tend to associate Dawn with
her screen characters,' she says. 'I never did: I realised that she was
actually a serious person. Dawn has a sideways view on life. All her
friends are unusual, they have special qualities. She thinks I'm a bit
of a crank, but I look around me and think, "I'm in good company".
My theory is that Dawn actually likes to live dangerously, she has a
wild streak that she reins in. She's not really a risk-taker, and one of
her ways of living life on the edge is to cram in too much work.
People take advantage of her willingness and phenomenal generos-
ity. She is complex and there are dichotomies in her personality.
She is so wise, and then worries herself sick. In spite of her success
she is still a shy and very private person.'

Dawn values her partner's advice, particularly in affairs of the
heart, and often turns to her for reassurance. 'Helen possesses an
ancient wisdom, like a sage,' she says. 'I rely on her an awful lot
now, for her counsel – she is cheaper than a psychiatrist.' The two
women are part of a 'secret society' called The Lazy Sues. 'There
are five girls and one honorary, who take regular singles holidays

together,' Dawn explains. 'It's a rarefied atmosphere – we set out to have fun and we do. Quite a lot of nail-painting is involved.' Dawn finds that these jaunts away with her female chums help her cope with the pressure of life at the top. And when she is feeling especially stressed, she disappears on her own for a few days. 'I get grumpy and anxious under pressure,' she admits. 'My mum practises meditation and she constantly tells me it would help me, but each day is completely full. Every now and then I go away and have a couple of days to myself. I go to people's houses or lock myself away in a hotel for a couple of nights, just to calm down. A friend of mine has got a house in France and I've been there a couple of times.'

Her fans would no doubt be surprised to learn how shy and retiring Dawn can be, but it is not news to those who know her well. 'When you first meet Dawn you think she's very outgoing, very bright,' explains Jennifer Saunders. 'She seems gregarious and able to cope with social situations, but actually she hates those big dos.' As a result, Dawn generally shuns premieres and never goes to awards ceremonies because she thinks they are 'phoney'. 'I still get a thrill if someone asks me to a first night or a film premiere,' she says. 'But when you have to sit next to twits like some pop stars, and have your photo taken outside, I think I'd rather pay three quid and go and watch it at my local cinema. I particularly dislike awards ceremonies, and never go because the judging and the nominations are corrupt.

'Who can say if one programme is funnier than another, or one actor better than another? It's preposterous, and embarrassing that so many of us buy into it. If you want to give a prize you may as well be up front, treat it as a business and present a crate of champagne to the one who has the highest ratings. I'm told off for this attitude and have letters from authorities telling me I won't get my award if I don't turn up. Jennifer says it's only a bit of fun and not to be so silly. She's probably got a healthier attitude and can't be bothered to have the stress about it that I give myself.'

She even refused to attend the British Comedy Awards in 1993 when *French and Saunders* won the 'Top Female Comedy Performers' prize. Where most luvvies wouldn't have missed their moment of glory for all the world, Dawn stayed at home. And she was proved right when the evening descended into an embarrassing spectacle and Julian Clary caused outrage by making lewd remarks about Norman Lamont. 'Dawn French shone out as the one beaming ray of good taste and sense at the British Comedy Awards – because she'd chosen to stay at home,' wrote the *Daily Mirror* reviewer. 'She was dead right because it was the most boring, unfunny, long-winded excuse for a programme I've ever seen. With the exception, maybe, of last year's programme – which was worse.'

Apart from her lucrative contract with the BBC, Dawn is in constant demand for advertising work and can earn up to £50,000 a day for doing commercials. She has been the voice-over for everything from babies' nappies to cameras, although her most famous ads are the ones for Terry's Chocolate Orange. Her financial success has brought her an enviable lifestyle. Her daughter attends private school, and Dawn and Lenny dine regularly at the exclusive L'Ortolan restaurant in Berkshire – the inspiration for Lenny's television series *Chef*. She buys her food from Harrods and is in a position to be able to call on top designers to make her clothes. Many of their friends are rich and famous, and she and Lenny saw in the millennium at a star-studded party thrown by former Spice Girl Geri Halliwell. But the couple live quietly by show-business standards, and in 1996 revealed that they hadn't held a dinner party for eight years. 'We try to avoid being a celebrity couple as much as possible,' says Dawn. 'I can't think of anything more sick-making. Most nights I sit in with a chicken wing watching *EastEnders*.'

Their actor friend Clive Mantle reveals how they are more likely to spend their evenings watching TV than going out partying. Mantle describes how, when they watched him on screen in the hospital drama *Casualty*, Dawn and Lenny would play a macabre guessing game. 'At the beginning of each episode, they'd place bets on what would happen to each character and which ones would end up being horribly injured or killed,' he laughs. 'Then whoever was proved right cleaned up with the cash!'

Although the village in which they live is very small, the people of Shinfield don't see much of Dawn and Lenny. Grovelands, the garden centre opposite their house, is virtually the only place Dawn goes to in the village. 'They don't like opening fêtes and things,' says their 'minder'. 'They get pestered quite a lot. They get people going up their drive and knocking on their door asking them to do charity work – partly because of their connection with Comic Relief – but they don't want to do it.'

Dawn has an office at home and Jennifer Saunders occasionally makes the drive out to collaborate on projects. There is a full-time personal assistant based at the house – part of a team of paid helpers. As well as their sometime minder, the couple employ a garden landscape company to tend the grounds, and Billie is cared for by Cynthia, their Indonesian housekeeper and nanny. After more than eight years with the couple, Cynthia has become like another member of the family. 'She's like a surrogate mum to us and she provides the back-up,' says Dawn. 'She cooks fantastic Indonesian food, which is a bit of a rare treat for us. Usually, whoever gets home first cooks whatever's in the larder. If it's my turn, Lenny will be lucky if he gets a boiled egg.' She admits that she generally eats, while Lenny cooks. 'I can cook, but I am not a very good one,' she says. 'Lenny is more inventive than I am. He likes being in the kitchen, which I don't at all. It's better that he does the cooking than we all die of food poisoning!'

Despite being famous comedians, life at the Henry household is not one long wheeze. 'People have a funny idea of comedians being married to one another,' says Lenny. 'They seem to think that we wake up in the morning with Tommy Cooper hats on and tell each

other jokes and behave like comedians all day long. It's not like that. Jennifer is Dawn's partner, I'm just her personal partner.' But nonetheless, Dawn says she would never have married Lenny if he didn't have the ability to make her laugh. 'Lenny is an innately funny man, which is why I married him. I think a good sense of humour makes a lot of men very sexy. Women like being in bed with comedians because so many women have so little to laugh about in their lives. If you meet someone who can make you laugh, you couldn't have a better tonic. You can laugh before you make love and after, too. And during. Having a sense of humour is what makes someone attractive.'

Dawn believes her marriage is worth saving because it is built on such a solid foundation. 'Our marriage is pretty supportive,' she said a few years ago. 'If you don't start off with something good, what chance have you? Nothing is like the films. It's odd living with just one person. Marriage is odd, isn't it?'

As is often the case with those who become rich and famous, contacts made in the early days have not always been kept up. Don Ward, the man who gave Dawn her first break at the Comedy Store, is impressed by her success but feels sad that she no longer appears to acknowledge the role he played in her career. 'She's grown in great stature, and I think she does some fine work,' he says. 'She really is a good comedy actress now. When French and Saunders went off with the Comic Strip lot there were no bad feelings on my part. As an ex-artist I quite understood that you have to broaden your horizons. They didn't like being mixed up with the amateur stuff, they wanted to be slick and professional. But once The Comic Strip started making films, that was more or less it. I didn't see French and Saunders any more. They cut the line – absolutely. We never hear from them, we never see them. We send cards but we never get anything back. I think it's extraordinary.

'We invited them to our tenth anniversary in 1989 and alas, nobody showed. And when it was the twentieth anniversary the same thing happened. The Comedy Store was there as a vehicle to kick them off but there's no way any of them have ever come back and put something back in. I was the first step in their career, and maybe they don't want to be reminded of that first step. Some people want to leave the past behind when they become very successful. But then they never were that approachable. I have never had a social drink with them, which is unusual considering that I've had one with virtually every comic who's appeared here. It just never happened. They would do their act and then go home. It was very much a job for them, whereas other people would hang around and socialise a bit.'

At the time of writing, Dawn's career is in excellent shape. She is one of only a tiny handful of female stars deemed capable of carrying their own television series. She competes in a male-dominated industry alongside stars like David Jason, John Thaw and Robson Green, and is living proof that it doesn't have to be a man's world. Significantly, she has made it into the limelight without dieting or changing the way she looks. Even the government wants to know the secret of her success. In February 1998, Education Secretary David Blunkett asked her to join a think-tank to help schoolchildren become the stars of the future. She joined other high-profile achievers like Beatles producer Sir George Martin, TV presenter Melvyn Bragg and the chief executive of Marks & Spencer.

Dawn's own theory about what has made her successful is that it was simply 'dumb luck' – being in the right place at the right time, with the right partner. 'Everything that has happened to me has happened by chance,' she says. 'I'm not saying it's not hard work, but it's no harder than anyone else's job. I probably am ambitious, but if ambition means focusing on where you want to go in your career, I don't think I've ever done that.'

Her chief panic is still that she will stop working. This goes against all apparent reason as she continues to be in great demand

and, apart from when she was at home looking after Billie, she has never been out of work. Her enduring appeal seems assured. In October 2000, she and Jennifer hit the road for the first time in years with a *French and Saunders* live tour. They will perform in Manchester, Liverpool, Edinburgh, Bristol, Nottingham and London. She also features in the film *Maybe Baby* – written by Ben Elton – and has been tipped to play a Tory MP in a new BBC series called *Candida's Diary*.

She shows no sign of letting up her exhaustive workload and, crucially, still enjoys her work enormously. 'Being a comedian is a remarkably stupid way to earn a living,' she says cheerfully. 'I know it's absurd, but it's actually a job I like very much. What better job is there? Dressing up, showing off, being with all your friends *and* getting paid for it! All the things I do, I choose to do. It's totally enjoyable – I couldn't ask for more.'

✳ PICTURE CREDITS ✳

Section 1

Page 1: (top) Rex Features Ltd; (middle and bottom) Alison Bowyer

Page 2: (top and bottom) Ian Dobbie

Page 3: (top) Rex Features Ltd; (bottom) PA Photos

Page 4: (top and bottom) Rex Features Ltd

Page 5: (top and bottom) Retna Pictures Ltd

Page 6: (top left) Retna Pictures Ltd; (top right) Rex Features Ltd;
       (bottom) Special Photographers Library

Page 7: (top left) Capital Pictures Ltd; (top right) Retna Pictures Ltd

Page 8: Retna Pictures Ltd

Section 2

Page 1: (top and bottom) Rex Features Ltd

Page 2: (top and bottom) Scope Features

Page 3: (top and bottom) Scope Features

Page 4: (top) Rex Features Ltd; (bottom) Scope Features

Page 5: (top) Retna Pictures Ltd © Comic Relief; (middle) Rex
       Features Ltd; (bottom) Retna Pictures Ltd © Comic Relief

Page 6: (top and bottom) Rex Features Ltd

Page 7: (top) Scope Features; (bottom) Retna Pictures Ltd

Page 8: Retna Pictures Ltd

* INDEX *